Norman F. Dixon, Ph.D., D.Sc., M.B.E., is Professor in
Psychology at University College London, and a Fellow of
the British Psychological Society. He was awarded the
University of London Carpenter Medal in 1974 'for work
of exceptional distinction in Experimental Psychology'.

He is the author of *Subliminal Perception: The Nature of a
Controversy* and *Preconscious Processing,* as well as the
highly controversial *On the Psychology of Military Incompetence,* which was published by Futura in 1979.

Also by Norman F. Dixon and published by Futura
ON THE PSYCHOLOGY OF MILITARY INCOMPETENCE

OUR OWN WORST ENEMY

Norman F. Dixon

Futura

A Futura Book

Copyright © 1987 by Norman F. Dixon

First published in Great Britain in 1987 by
Jonathan Cape Ltd, London

This edition published in 1988 by Futura Publications,
a Division of Macdonald & Co (Publishers) Ltd
London & Sydney

ISBN 0 7088 4038 8

Printed and bound in Great Britain by
The Guernsey Press Co. Ltd, Guernsey, Channel Islands

Futura Publications
A Division of
Macdonald & Co (Publishers) Ltd
Greater London House
Hampstead Road
London NW1 7QX

A member of Maxwell Pergamon Publishing Corporation plc

For Jutta

Contents

We shall require a substantially new manner of thinking if mankind is to survive.

Albert Einstein

Preface

In 1983 I was honoured by the British Psychological Society in being invited to give the Annual Myers Lecture. Since the major contributions of Professor W. S. Myers had been to applied psychology, it was appropriate to choose a topic which concerned the application of general psychological principles to problems of everyday life. In developing this theme further, I have been particularly influenced by five books: *Psychological Aspects of Nuclear War* by James Thompson (British Psychological Society – March 1985), *Critical Path* by R. Buckminster Fuller (Hutchinson, 1981), *The Anatomy of Human Destructiveness* by Erich Fromm (Penguin Books, 1973), *The Fate of the Earth* by Jonathan Schell (Cape, 1982) and my own work, published several years earlier, *On the Psychology of Military Incompetence* (Cape, 1976).

Between them these books raised an interesting question: 'how could a species talented in so many ways be so incompetent when it came to ensuring its own survival?'

The original lecture, and now this book, suggest some highly speculative answers to this riddle. Doubtless, as with my book on military incompetence, many readers will consider it to be a collection of truisms, while others, with even greater vehemence, will regard the central thesis as far fetched and probably invalid. For some people the views expressed in this book may seem politically naïve because, instead of enlarging upon such factors as those of geography, climate, population growth, limited resources and national pride, all of which are playing a part in our present slide towards extinction, it dwells overmuch on politicians and political leaders – as if everything was *all their fault*!

In answer I would like to make three points. Of course it is these other factors that have produced a situation which threatens our survival. But the problems they pose demand political solutions. Hence politicians and heads of states should be gratified to know that they have become the most important people on earth, vital to our survival. It is because of this that the central theme of this book, i.e. that we are our own worst enemy, applies most particularly to them.

Whether or not these sentiments are acceptable, it is hoped that what follows will at least provoke those who enjoy life on earth into thinking about how it might be made possible for future generations.

London 1987   NFD

Acknowledgments

For permission to quote extracts, and use material, from works in which they hold copyright I am grateful to: Julian Jaynes (*The Origins of Consciousness in the Breakdown of the Bicameral Mind*, Boston: Houghton Mifflin, 1976), Brian Masters (*Killing for Company*, London: Jonathan Cape, 1985), the heirs of the late Stanley Milgram (*Obedience to Authority*, London: Tavistock Publications, 1974), and CBS Inc. (interview of a participant in the My Lai massacre, © 1969).

In addition I am grateful to the British Academy for a research grant towards collecting material, to the Civil Aviation Authority, and to the authors of those many books and papers which have provided much of the data on which this book draws, and in particular, David Beaty, J. Fox, Seymour Hersh, Alistair Horne, Lucille Iremonger, Hugh L'Etang, Lloyd de Mause, William Norris, Leo Rangell, the late L.T.C. Rolt, Jonathan Schell, and Peter Hill.

Finally I owe a great debt of gratitude to John Adams, Jutta Christian, Liz Cowen, Camilla Dixon, George Drew, Peter Fonagy, Adrian Furnham, Sue Henley, Jane Hill, David Oakley and John Sloboda for help they have given in various ways.

NFD

The gigantic catastrophes that threaten us are not elemental happenings of a physical or biological kind, but are psychic events . . . Instead of being exposed to wild beasts, tumbling rocks, and inundating waters, man is exposed to the elemental forces of his own psyche.

C. G. Jung

Conversation Piece

'How did this happen?'

'We had a disagreement.'

'About what?'

'Ideologies, freedom, fairness, human rights, values, life itself.'

'Wouldn't it have been better to have reached some sort of compromise?'

'Absolutely not.'

'Why?'

'One must be true to one's beliefs. Besides, compromises leave everyone dissatisfied.'

'So you decided to fight it out?'

'Yes.'

'Even though you knew that this would kill everyone?'

'Yes.'

'Then there would be no more disagreements?'

'Exactly.'

'Freedom, fairness, human rights, being true to one's values – all this would have been achieved?'

'Precisely.'

'But what about life itself?'

'You cannot have everything.'

'But isn't that irrational?'

'Of course! We *are* irrational.'

'You mean you *were* irrational.'

1

Our Own Worst Enemy

The only devils are those running round in our own heads.
Mahatma Gandhi

Few would dispute that, whether pleasant or unpleasant, living is difficult. It is really much easier to be dead. Survival of the individual and of the species is a task replete with problems. Its solution occurs in several ways – by chance, through fortunate mutations and natural selection, through instinct and through learning, through genetic evolution and through cultural evolution.

What *are* the problems?

As physical entities living creatures are complex constructions made from the environment in which they live. They are bits of the world put together in a particular way. The result has several indispensable characteristics. It resists falling apart and returning to the heap of ingredients from which it came. It grows and increases in complexity, and it reproduces itself. To achieve all this, it depends on the environment from which it came, of which it is a part, and to which it will ultimately return. It depends on it for food, water, air, warmth and all else which its organisation requires. It also has to resist all those things which threaten its existence – other organisms competing for the same resources, predators which like to eat it, extremes of heat and cold, bacterial invasion, and opportunities for falling from high places.

Various strategies are employed to bring all this about. Simple creatures such as sea anemones can sit around like guests in a well-run hotel, waiting for everything to be brought to them, but

1

many animals need to explore and discover all they can about their habitats.

If they strike lucky by finding, say, in the case of cockroaches, the warm, dark, dirty kitchen of a West End restaurant, their troubles are over. Having, perhaps, heaved a sigh of relief, they can settle down to a life of untramelled domesticity. However, the thing to notice about these so-called lower animals, whether land-based or sea-locked, is that they survive by adapting to, rather than seriously changing, their environment. Apart from such minor constructional activities as nest building, web spinning, or digging holes in the ground they seem content to leave this world much as they found it.

There are, however, a few animals which adopt a very different strategy for dealing with the problems of survival. The most conspicuous of these is ourselves, and the strategy that of cultural transmission culminating in civilisation and cultural progress.

For some people cultural progress probably means the arrival on this planet of such things as libraries, picture galleries, sewage farms, birth control clinics and the British Council. For others, it might include the Women's Institute, Beethoven's Fifth, British Rail, false teeth, the Royal Family and bank holidays.

Then there are the people themselves. We think of these consequences of cultural evolution – 'civilised people' – as law abiding, well behaved, decent and polite. They use plenty of soap and there are quite a few things which they wouldn't dream of doing in public.

But there are other less attractive products of cultural evolution – prisons, the Mafia, electric chairs, VAT, other people's politics and, in a class of their own, nuclear weapons. The thousands of nuclear missiles now stockpiled by the purportedly more civilised countries of the world are in a class of their own because (at the time of writing) they and they alone can put the clock right back to the beginning. Not only can they destroy the culture which begat them but everything else besides. They can probably do it in about twenty minutes and, just in case there is a hitch, there are enough of them to do the job several times over.[1] And this is where this book really begins, for it is the existence and ultimate use of nuclear weapons which best illustrates the fact that we are, beyond any shadow of a doubt, our own worst enemy.

Our own worst enemy?

Certainly only the most blinkered optimist could deny that the present outlook for humanity is bleak, and growing bleaker, and it is entirely our fault. The trouble is that people dislike being told this. Prophets of doom are notoriously unpopular. From earliest childhood, from the first time we heard mother saying 'If you're naughty Father Christmas won't come', or 'I'm warning you, if I catch you doing that once more I'll tell your father', there is little pleasure to be found in pessimistic or threatening predictions. References to the future of others, as implied by such ominous snatches of overheard conversations as 'I've been told he's riddled with it . . .', or 'It seems they're going to lose every penny', or 'She's had everything taken away down below . . .', may of course be accepted with equanimity, if not a mild *frisson* of pleasure. But when it is about oneself, even such helpful warnings as 'Did you know you've left your lights on?' instead of eliciting an immediate flood of gratitude probably evoke the thought 'What a damn silly question: of course I didn't bloody well know!'

No wonder then that, when it concerns all of us, gloomy forecasts receive a cool reception.

Over the years a number of writers have pointed out that unless we control population growth,[2] conserve our resources[3] and discard nuclear weapons[4] we will soon become extinct. For all the effect they've had they might just as well have saved their breath. Their books have not slowed down the birth rate or the arms race. They are not hailed as potential saviours of the planet. If what they say is true, and there is no reason to doubt that it is, people evidently don't want to know, let alone do anything about forestalling the catastrophe which lies ahead.

Why should this be? Why are we content to go on living on the brink of extinction? Why do we go on electing reactionary governments which pile up armaments and seem hell-bent on doing everything in their power to increase world tension? And why do so many of us denounce with venom 'peaceniks', prophets of doom, advocates of disarmament, the CND, the women of Greenham Common, Bruce Kent and anyone else who in one way or another tries to extend the life of the world? (And why, as a subsidiary question, should 'peaceniks' be thought of as wet and effeminate sissies, while the advocates of bigger and better weapons of destruction see themselves as tough, virile he-men, when it is really they who are the more frightened of the two?)

Such stock answers to these questions as 'Since they feel helpless to do anything about it most people would rather not know', or, It's better to be dead than Red', or 'Since it is unthinkable it must be undoable', or 'The last forty years of peace prove that nuclear weapons are our best safeguard against war', range from half-truths to sheer rubbish. People do know. They are not helpless. It *is* thinkable and even were it not it's certainly *doable*. Because we've spent forty years living on the edge of a precipice does not mean we won't eventually fall over it. You can push your luck too far.

So could there perhaps be another reason why some politicians and large sections of the general public turn their faces so resolutely against warnings, let alone attempts at prevention of the forthcoming holocaust?

Maybe the 'better dead' argument comes nearest to the truth. Could it be that at some deep, or maybe not so deep, level many people want or are at least prepared to accept the possibility of an end to life on earth? Absurd? But if they don't, how else do we explain the calm acceptance of such ludicrous concepts as a limited nuclear war? What other interpretation can we put on the fact that when some of the best brains in the world forecast a nuclear winter, which nothing or nobody will survive, instead of adopting the failsafe position of acting on the basis that the forecasters just might be right, every effort is made to discredit the idea on the basis of nit-picking objections to the theory?

For those who don't share this philosophy, the short-sighted pacifists who want to keep the world much as it is, the alarming thing is that the 'lemmings' have in fact a very strong case.

By presenting the contents of this book in the context of a thesis entitled 'It's better to be dead' maybe there would be more chance of getting people to read it. So let's consider the case for this shocking but seductive suggestion.

Although, under even the most adverse circumstances, most people cling to life, they are in this respect merely the victims of a biological pressure which evolved as a mechanism for survival and not to prolong happiness. When one considers the fearful suffering of the living – the millions who have died and still are dying slowly of starvation, the billions who contract hideous and painful diseases, the vast multitudes who spend their day in the degrading squalor of prisons and concentration camps, one might well conclude that for many it would be better to be dead. When one thinks of the beaten, the tortured, the oppressed, the deprived, the bereaved, the lonely and the cold; when one contemplates the prolonged misery of the pathologically depressed, the perpetually terrified, and the self-mutilating victims of neurosis and schizophrenia; when one considers those born to spasticity or AIDS; and when one remembers all those who say, 'I wish I were dead', and mean it, then surely the notion that all this suffering could be terminated once and for all has a certain appeal?*

Being dead may be awful. We simply do not know. But being alive, for many people much of the time *is* awful. Many people do not believe in any sort of survival after death, and if they do it is presumably because they believe it would be enjoyable rather than unpleasant. Most people probably regard death as a merciful escape from the vicissitudes of life into a state of non-existence. As for the so-called joys of living they are so transient, so ephemeral, and so often paid for (with interest) later, that they are hardly worth the candle. If there *is* life after death it could only be a change for the better. As to whether people really hold these beliefs, it is perhaps noteworthy that those pronounced clinically dead on the operating table or after a road accident and are then miraculously brought back to life report their period of being dead as extraordinarily happy,[5] so much so that they sometimes felt rather dismayed at being brought back to life. Whether or not they were actually dead and then brought back is immaterial to the present argument. Dead or alive, they evidently *believed* it's nice to be deceased. We can continue in this vein. If there is no life beyond the grave then, by definition, the dead won't know what they're missing. Nobody (to my knowledge) worries about all the jolly things they missed out on during the billions of years before they were born, so why should they care about all those missed out on after they're dead?

But what about theological arguments against having a holocaust, i.e. that it would undo, perhaps literally in a flash, the whole miracle of creation? Instead of this extraordinarily complex interlocking

---

*For some a disagreeable feature of being dead is envy of those one leaves behind – like being forced to leave an ongoing party. The beauty of a holocaust is that the party would be over for everyone.

system of animals, plants, soil, sunshine, water and politicians, there would be nothing but a lifeless cinder whirling endlessly (but now of course peacefully) through space. For those who believe in the existence of God the idea of a holocaust brings the added shame, the ultimate blasphemy, of having destroyed at one fell swoop what He so lovingly put together.

At first sight this seems a powerful argument against the notion that anyone could risk, let alone want, a final cataclysm. But even here those who seem bent on destroying the world may have a point. If there is a God who created the world, then it is He who created the wherewithal (i.e. ourselves and atomic physics) for its destruction, so why waste time trying to interfere with His plans? Instead of trying to baulk His intentions (which because they are His are, by definition, ultimately unbaulkable) we should be glad to do His work.

If, on the other hand, there isn't a God, if the world came about by accident, then to others the only argument for keeping it in being is for the pleasure it gives to those who experience it. But we have already seen that this pleasure is, to say the least, very mixed. For many, if not most, people the costs of being alive far outweigh the benefits.

According to this argument, since the beauties of nature exist only in the minds of those whose brains are responding to patterns of energy radiating from the environment, there is absolutely no point in worrying about preserving the physical sources of these aesthetic experiences once the brains which make them seem enjoyable have ceased to exist. A retrospective view of this planet supports this contention. Before the arrival of mankind there was no doubt much which would have delighted the then non-existent senses of beings yet to come – vast tracts of lushest green, sparkling streams, shining seas, huge lumbering beasts, exotic birds, shimmering sands and, between times, dazzling fields of virgin snow; and before that, long before that, a magnificent incandescent orb spinning through an azure sky; and before that, for *aficionados* of firework displays, breathtaking exhibitions of stellar explosions and other pyrotechnic marvels. What a waste that there was no one here to see it! Such a waste that it would really not have mattered one jot if it had never been. Since we are so unconcerned about all the events of the Universe which passed unwitnessed, why should we care about those which lie beyond the next great series of explosions – those of our own making?

Before leaving this philosophical digression, there is one final argument in favour of a holocaust – the possibility, as implied by investigations[6] of children who appear to recall events from a previous life, of reincarnation. Whether or not reincarnation occurs we simply do not know, but if it does then, for this writer anyway, the prospects are horrific. On statistical grounds alone, if you are born again into the world the chances are you will be an insect or maybe something smaller, living, probably, inside the intestines of someone else. If we come back as people, then the chances are we will be poor, hungry, diseased and living in some awful place without running water and decent sanitation. The chances of coming back as a well-fed professor living in an affluent democracy are so infinitesimally small as to be hardly worth considering. And even if one did end up as a well-fed professor how frightful it would be to endure prep school all over again.

But if there is a really efficient holocaust, any danger of reincarnation is ruled out, for there'll be nothing to come back to. For which we should be profoundly grateful.

Now, whether or not these various arguments occur to those who are either actively assisting or at least condoning the present accelerating slide towards extinction is, to say the least, debatable. They should however, draw heart from the fact that a case *can* be made for their self-destructive philosophy. Far from being defensive about the subject matter of this book, they can now take comfort from the evidence outlined that unless we radically alter the ways we think, feel and act (which is highly unlikely) they will soon have their wishes granted and be dead. The same holds true for the thousands of people who every year take their own lives, the hundreds of thousands who would like to but dare not, the millions who are finding a way out through alcohol and heroin, and, to name one quite specific group, those referred to in the following excerpt from Verdoorn:

In 1977 more than 300 billion dollars were spent on world armament. And in the same year four hundred thousand scientists – that is about 25 percent of all the scientists in the whole world – were engaged, in some way or other, with the production of modern armaments. Among these scientists were also a considerable number of *physicians and medical specialists* [italics mine] who were employed in this armament business, trying to invent new and more perfect techniques and methods and to investigate their effect in war. This medical contribution to the production of armaments had the obvious, exclusive purpose of destroying human life.[7]

Anyway, whatever one's philosophy about the worthiness of continuing to risk and probably bring about the end of the world, there remains the interesting question as to why we should have become the most self-destructive animals ever to stalk this earth.

Between 1820 and 1945 according to a conservative estimate[8] murderous quarrels and wars accounted for fifty-nine million human deaths. In the six years between 1939 and 1945 the actions of just one so-called civilised country terminated the lives of over thirty million people.

Every year all over the world some hundreds of thousands of people are killed in road, rail and air disasters. Although this planet is quite capable of producing enough food for everyone, millions die of starvation; millions perish through preventable man-made diseases, through poisoning by toxic wastes, through improper use and distribution of the world's water supplies, and millions take their own lives either deliberately or through self-destructive patterns of behaviour.

No less extraordinary is man's reaction (or rather lack of reaction) to such great natural threats to survival as earthquake, fire and flood. As one tiny example of this latter phenomenon, take the curious case of what has sometimes been called 'hazard city'.[9]

If one knew that a certain location was particularly liable to earthquakes, landslides, tidal waves, bush fires, drought and floods, one would surely be justified in regarding it as the exact opposite of what estate agents call 'a desirable residential area'. Los Angeles has them all. And yet so many people flock to live there that they have not only substantially increased the incidence of at least four of the above hazards, but have introduced a new one entirely of their own making – photochemical smog. Now one doesn't wish to be unkind, but the most frequently given reason for living in Los Angeles is its many hours of sunshine. Yet it is this same solar benefit combining with the exhaust hydrocarbons from the eight million gallons of petrol burnt each day by four million vehicles that not only damages the eyes and destroys the lungs of those beneath the yellow blanket, but in fact blots out the very thing that brought them there in the first place.

To someone who doesn't have these territorial preferences, those who do may well seem bizarre if not actually psychotic. But Los Angeles is only one very small example of what appears to be self-destructive irrationality. There are many other far more dramatic cases of the same type.

How can we explain such strange phenomena? A clue came from considering another field rich in human irrationality – that of military behaviour.[10] It started with the belated (because counter-intuitive) conclusion from peering down the long corridor of martial lunacy that more often than not the presence of an enemy *reduces* rather than *increases* military incompetence. From Balaclava to Dunkirk, from what has been called 'the imbecilic' Walcheren campaign of 1809 to the equally imbecilic French stand at Dien Bien Phu in 1954, invariably it was events *before* contact with the enemy which spelt ultimate disaster. The lack of preparation for wintering in the Crimea, for resisting the Japanese invasion of Singapore, or for stemming the German *Blitzkrieg* of 1940 have as their common denominator the simple fact that, when not busy with the foe, maundering and baseless optimism seemed to be the order of the day. Once locked in combat, however, some signs of competence were evident (relatively speaking). Was this then the beginning of a possible explanation for other wider and ultimately more devastating cases of irrationality – that we are, in fact, suffering from a lack of enemies? That we need enemies to keep us functioning properly? Certainly this is true for all those political leaders who depend upon 'enemies' to divert attention from their own shortcomings. It also applies to those for whom peace of mind seems to depend upon some evil/hostile outgroup on to which they can project their less agreeable traits. Needless to say many of those in the first group also fall into the second.

Finally, there are those like the armed forces, the police, rat-catchers and even undertakers, whose *raison d'être* depends upon some sort of external foe. But relatively speaking their numbers are small. As for the rest of us, it could be argued that not only do enemies play a useful role in natural selection, but they may also reduce that scourge of civilisation – boredom. Few people seem able to withstand long outbreaks of peace. Even such enterprises as the

Falklands campaign and the bombing of Libya are hailed in some quarters with wild enthusiasm.

Could this need for enemies be likened to the necessity for a track in one of those tracking tasks which psychologists use to test perceptual motor skills? Without a track the pen can wander anywhere. Without it we'd be lost. Or is there something more than this? Could it be that the greatest threats to our survival are those aspects of ourselves which evolved to deal with threats which are now largely non-existent?

Let us examine this possibility in a little more detail: for millions of years, mechanisms, talents and patterns of behaviour evolved (or were acquired) to deal with external threats to survival, in which respect and until recently they have been remarkably successful. People in the richer and more advanced countries (the same people who now have it in their power to extinguish all life on this planet) no longer die of cholera or plague, famine or drought, while the number eaten by hungry carnivores is a tiny percentage of those who enjoy teasing the lions and tigers in some ducal park.

This is all to the good, but inevitably a price is paid. The reasons are embodied in two general truths. The first of these might be described as the 'laws of side effects', one of which is that anything added to a system to improve, enhance or protect its main effect inevitably produces a counter-productive side effect. Thus it is the adding of congeners to alcohol, to improve the latter's flavour, which produces the worst hangovers. More lethal (and less fun) were the consequences of adding increasing amounts of electronic equipment to the German Star Fighter. Such gear may have improved the fitting qualities of this deadly little plane, but at a sad and self-defeating price. For under their added payload these aircraft became dangerously unstable, resulting in the deaths of many pilots. Rightly were they renamed 'widow makers'.

No less serious (or trivial) are the outcomes of adding something to a system to reduce its own unwanted side-effects. Thus it is that preservatives spoil the flavour of jam, silencers diminish the efficiency of petrol engines and militarism (that conglomerate of rules, regulations, rituals, and bullshit without which armies and navies seem incapable of functioning) reduces fighting ability.

The other general truth of particular relevance to this book is that nature seems to abhor relinquishing what was once useful but is now no longer needed. As a result we are left with tiresome devices like wisdom teeth, which, with nothing better to do, now threaten the health of the body they were once designed to serve. Could it be that it is these general truths which lie at the heart of the matter? That it is through them that we have now become our own worst enemy? Are the now redundant side-effects of our own evolutionary history not only inappropriate but actually lethal? Is it that the once good servant has now turned against his master and will in time destroy him?

These suppositions are not entirely novel. An important aspect of the thesis was referred to by Tinbergen[11] when he drew attention to the fact that as a consequence of cultural evolution achieving greater changes in a hundred years than genetic evolution had in millions of years we have created an environment with which our biological make-up is inadequate to deal. As for the ultimately lethal consequences, these have been spelt out by Higgins.[12] According to his thesis there are six interrelated threats to survival of the human race – over-population, increasing scarcity of resources, degradation of the environment, nuclear abuse, the food crisis and galloping technology. Together these threats are converging at an ever-increasing rate towards the ultimate catastrophe. Only one thing (says Higgins) could halt this slide towards the brink – ourselves. But far from helping to do so, we seem to be set on giving the whole process an extra push in the wrong direction. Hence the title of his book *The Seventh Enemy*. We ourselves are the greatest, the seventh enemy. How and why this should be so, and what could be done about it, are discussed in the chapters which follow.

Before embarking on this thesis, there are, however, one or two general points worth bearing in mind. All the characteristics discussed have two common denominators. It is hypothesised that they were acquired (whether through learning or genetic evolution) out of necessity; without them we would not be here. But now, each, in its way, is hastening our demise.

A second point is that though this book may seem to take a somewhat jaundiced view of some political leaders and their governments, they and their shortcomings are only symptoms of the underlying discrepancy between what we are and what we need to be in order to survive. As for political differences, neither the extreme right nor the far left need feel affronted. This book takes no sides.

Third, this book is not intended to be a political polemic for unilateral or even multi-lateral nuclear disarmament. The contemporary cliché that we cannot disinvent nuclear weapons is also a truism. We can no more 'disinvent' or guarantee the total riddance of nuclear weapons than we could 'disinvent' or rid the world of nerve gases, cyanide or botulism, any one of which could, with a little ingenuity, be used to exterminate mankind. Ultimately, it is not the weapons themselves which demand attention, but the attitudes, motives and behaviour of those who are responsible for their production, deployment and possible use. This book is not about whether we should, but why we might, and probably will, destroy ourselves.

One final point. A bias throughout this book towards using terms like 'man' and 'mankind' and male rather than female pronouns when either might seem appropriate should not be taken amiss by those with strong views about sexual equality. The bias is deliberate for one simple and obvious reason. This book is mostly about destructiveness and this is largely the province of the male. For whatever reason, men tend to be more aggressive and destructive than women. Most crimes of violence are committed by men. The history of ruthless tyrants, warmongers, mass-murderers, and trigger-happy politicians is largely the history of males. With few exceptions, decisions and the machinery to destroy all life on this planet are in the hands of men. If the human race is brought to an untimely end it will be by men. Need one say more in defence of favouring the pronoun *he*?

Part One

The Limited Capacity of Conscious Experience

2

Accidents Are Rarely Accidental

He heard it, but he heeded not – his eyes were with his heart, and
that was far away.

Byron, *Childe Harold*, cxli

Imagine an extremely large university department. With its million
students and hundred thousand members of staff, it provides what
has come to be accepted as the normal staff/student ratio. Imagine
too that this vast department is controlled from two small, adjoining
offices. The outer one is inhabited by a woman with a manner
as forbidding as the north face of the Eiger. She is efficient, strong-
willed and neurotically possessive. She is the department secretary.
And in the inner office sits the focus of her protective instincts
– the department chairman. He is an ageing, introverted professor.
He much prefers thinking about his research, his orchids and the
Vice-Chancellor's very young wife (but not necessarily in that order)
than the day-to-day running of the department. Together these two
manage the department. How do they do it?

The short answer is by delegation and defence. He delegates all
the routine tasks to his academic staff and senior students. She, the
dragon at the gate, defends him against all those who might otherwise
disturb the calm of the inner office. In this capacity, she acts as an
almost impenetrable barrier to bad news.

So much for a caricature of how to run a large university department with minimum disturbance for the chairman. To the perceptive

reader it will have become clear that there are striking similarities between this way of doing things and relationships between mind (i.e. consciousness) and brain.

Nobody knows at what stage of evolution brains began to provide the wherewithal for subjective mental life. We assume that other people have conscious experiences – thoughts, feelings, sensations and percepts. We are prepared to allow that apes, cats and dogs, possibly even pigs, sheep and birds, enjoy a private, subjective mental life, maybe even fish and reptiles, but it is hard (and not entirely enjoyable) envisaging the consciousness of dung beetles, and almost unimaginable that slugs, worms and bacteria have feelings. How, when and where consciousness started we simply do not know. But one thing is certain: whatever its origins, a capacity for conscious representation of the external world evidently had survival value for organisms so blessed. It enabled registration, in a relatively unambiguous form, of the end-products of extensive preconscious cerebral activity. It provided a means for the establishment of priorities and plans for action, and it enabled those 'feelings' which signal the necessity for adaptive behaviour. But to achieve its multiple, time-saving purposes, conscious experience had of necessity to be of very limited capacity and it is for this that a price is paid. First, undue importance may be attached to what is, as opposed to what is not, *consciously* experienced, with consequent neglect of intuitive processes and peripheral events. Second, there is the relegation to brain processes of habitual responses that run off without conscious control. Third, there is the denial or prevention of aversive feelings. Each of these side effects contributes to self-destructive behaviour; together they may well terminate survival once and for all.

Returning to the analogy, because consciousness is limited, the brain (like university department chairmen) delegates habitual routines to its unconscious processes, and somewhere inside our heads, to defend us against disturbing information, lurks something suspiciously like the dragon secretary. But there are also of course big differences. Consciousness is to unconsciousness not in the ratio of one to a million, but, in terms of the amount of information which they each contain, something nearer to one to a billion. Conscious awareness is but the tiny tip of an immense iceberg – a diminutive, flawed, barred window on the great tide of information which flows unceasingly into, around, and out of the four hundred thousand million neurones and hundred billion synapses which comprise the human nervous system. And the consequences of being aware of only a fragment of what is going on can be immeasurably worse than anything that ever happens in even the most mismanaged university department. What is worse is that, for obvious reasons, they are most likely to occur during what might have seemed the safest of activities. Purely by way of illustration, consider what was described, in the following example, as 'the recklessness of Driver Robins'.[1] The periodic changing of animals at coaching inns was standard practice on long-distance journeys by horse-drawn vehicles. With the coming of railways a comparable ritual was maintained. So it was that, on the night of June 30th, 1906, the boat express from Plymouth to Waterloo pulled into Templecombe to change its 'horse', or to be more precise its locomotive, No. 288, for the four-coupled bogie express engine No. 421. While they were awaiting their train, the crew of 421, Driver Robins and Fireman Gadd, exchanged words with Richard Furze, the Templecombe night inspector, and a shunter, Walter Millet. Standing on the platform at Templecombe on that warm summer night neither of these men knew that this would be the last conversation they or anyone else would ever have with Robins and his fireman, that within a very few hours both would be part of the mangled wreckage of a major rail disaster. Subsequently, Millet remembered commenting, 'The boat train's running well to time', and Robins's reply, 'Yes, but I shan't get into Waterloo before time, else I shall have to go up and see the governor'.[2]

Robins and Gadd backed No. 421 onto their train and within a few minutes, after some violent slipping of the driving wheels on the slippery track, were under way. The Plymouth to Waterloo express was soon averaging 70 m.p.h.

Robins knew that he could maintain this speed until approaching Salisbury, where because of sharp curves at each end of the station, there was a permanent speed restriction of 30 m.p.h. The night was fine and clear. There was no reason why a driver so familiar with the route should have been ignorant of his whereabouts. And yet, as he approached Salisbury, Robins did not slow down. To the consternation of the signalman in the West Salisbury box, the express, steaming hard, its whistle shrieking, stormed into the station. Somehow, swaying wildly, it clung to the rails at the west end of the station but, on the ten chain reverse curve at the east end of the platform, it became completely derailed to collide with a milk train which by ill luck was trundling through in the opposite direction.

It has been estimated that Robins was travelling at more than twice his permitted speed. The destruction that occurred supports this conclusion. As a result of the express locomotive overturning across the down line, three first-class carriages and five vans of the milk train were completely demolished. A light engine that had been standing on an adjacent line was so badly damaged that its fireman died and its driver suffered terrible scalding from escaping steam. Forty yards of the down line were destroyed, leaving a trench three and a half feet deep. The accident killed twenty-eight people including half the passengers on the express, Driver Robins, his fireman and the guard of the milk train. Seven other passengers were seriously injured.

Why did it happen? The regulator of the express was closed, but the vacuum brake, which was in perfect order, had not been applied. There were no grounds for the rumour that passengers had tipped the driver to make a fast run or that the Great Western Railway company encouraged record breaking. Besides which, Robins had been heard to say that he would be reprimanded if he reached Waterloo before the stated arrival time. Under the circumstances it is not surprising that the official report on the accident concluded 'the recklessness of Driver Robins is inexplicable'.[3]

If the Salisbury derailment was a unique event we could perhaps dismiss it as a freak occurrence brought about by the one in a billion chance of two men, sober and sane one minute, showing such an aberration the next, that they not only commit suicide, but take twenty-six other people with them. But it was not a unique occurrence.

1906 was not a felicitous year for British railways. Within three months of the Salisbury accident the night mail from King's Cross to Edinburgh was involved in a very similar disaster, if anything even more mysterious than its predecessor.

As on previous occasions, Driver Fleetwood and Fireman Talbot, riding the footplate of a nearly new Atlantic Class locomotive, were due to stop at Grantham. But this time, to the bewilderment of the night inspector and several postal workers waiting on the down platform, they failed to do so.

'It's a run through,'[4] exclaimed one of the postmen as the mail roared past them through the station. To the north of the station the mainline signals, which protect the Nottingham junction, were set to danger – their red lights glowing brightly on this dark clear night. Without reducing speed, the train passed beneath them, its tail light disappearing into the blackness beyond. Moments later they heard what sounded like an explosion. Within seconds the northern sky was lit by flames. The men on the platform ran, stumbling across the network of rails and points to give what help they could.

This derailment which killed fourteen people including the driver and his fireman, which destroyed sixty-five yards of a bridge parapet, which demolished six carriages and sent three others toppling over an embankment, left the locomotive so badly damaged that it was impossible to tell the position of the regulator or whether the brakes had been applied.

Railway workers at Peterborough who had spoken to Fleetwood and Talbot before the accident testified that the two men were sober, healthy and not fatigued. The only person who had seen them immediately before the accident was the Grantham South Box signalman. He described them as standing motionless on either side of the footplate, each staring ahead through his cab spectacle glass. This, and the fact that they did not follow the usual practice of sounding the whistle as they approached Grantham, suggested that they had mistaken their whereabouts. But even this seemed highly unlikely. Both knew the route well and had in fact worked the same shift the previous day. According to a number of footplate men who gave evidence at the inquiry, the approach to Grantham was quite unmistakable *under any conditions* – and on the night of the accident visibility was good. By all accounts the disaster was baffling. As one expert has put it, 'What precisely took place on the "Ivatt" Atlantic No. 276 on that September night sixty years ago is a question that Sherlock Holmes himself could not answer. It remains the railway equivalent of the *Marie Celeste*.'[5]

But on October 15th of the following year there was another equivalent of the *Marie Celeste* – an almost identical accident which seemed equally inexplicable. The driver of a train bound from London to the West Country appeared to 'forget' that because of very tight curves on the approach to Shrewsbury station speed was restricted to 10 m.p.h. on this section of the line. He also failed to notice that as a cautionary measure the down signals were set to danger. Drivers were requested to stop and make contact with the signalman before entering the station. On this occasion, however, to the dismay of the signalman, the train from London tore past his box without reducing speed. He knew that disaster was inevitable.

When the engine left the rails it carried on for seventy-five yards before crashing over on to its side. The carriages of the train piled up against it. The accident took eighteen lives and tore up 140 yards of track.

How did it happen? The night was fine and clear. The driver was an experienced man who knew the route well. Had he perhaps dozed off? But, even if he had, it is scarcely credible that the fireman had failed to notice the warning signals and not realised they were heading for disaster.

Clearly this succession of disasters, involving apparently normal, conscientious and experienced professionals, cannot be dismissed as one-off freak occurrences. Moreover, as we shall see, events like these are not confined to the early history of British railways. They continue to occur. It is also worth considering their implications in a nuclear age. Suppose Driver Robins or his modern equivalent had been conveying nuclear waste through a populated urban area. Imagine what might happen if the apparent 'recklessness' of these footplate men was displayed by those who run nuclear power stations or who fly bombers loaded with hydrogen bombs. For those who harbour the comforting and totally unwarranted illusion that comparable catastrophes could never happen on a nuclear scale (for the simple reason that it would be so unimaginably disastrous if they did) such questions would probably elicit the reply, 'Yes but these things are peculiar to railways.' This is not so. Though there is indeed something about railways which might encourage this sort of disaster, the feature of train-driving which results in this type of human error is also, unfortunately, a common denominator of other, far more dangerous, kinds of human enterprise, including those involving the control of nuclear weapons. So why do they happen? What are the biological origins of this particular brand of self-destructive behaviour?

Since the beginning of time the survival of living organisms depended upon their successful interactions with their environment, getting what's required for bodily needs and avoiding what is harmful. To achieve these ends knowledge of the environment was obviously of paramount importance, without it there could be no survival. So, there evolved ever more sensitive and elaborate receptor systems for obtaining information.

For every sort of signal – chemical, light, pressure, magnetic, gravitational and even electrical – which the environment 'gives off', species overall have developed remarkable sensitivity. In the remorseless competition for limited resources, the smaller the signal which could be registered, the greater the distance at which it could be detected, and the finer the detail that could be discriminated, the greater the advantage that the animal in question would have over his competitors. Little wonder then that even long before the advent of man (let alone railways) the amount of information about their habitats which animals could respond to was staggering.

But all this information and the thousands of millions of nerve cells upon which its reception and analysis depended, were only means to an end. Without the capacity to respond appropriately to this mass of available knowledge animals might just as well be dead. Herein lay a problem. The sheer time taken to sort out the essential from the inessential and, having done this, to 'decide' what to do about it became itself a major hazard to continued survival. The problem was compounded by another – memory. Hardly less valuable than the capacity to perceive the external world is that of being able to profit from this experience on some subsequent occasion. Animals that could remember from one day to the next that the inside of coconuts are good to eat, that red berries with yellow spots result in stomach aches and that mother was killed by something long, thin and wriggly with a forked tongue, had an advantage over those without a capacity for storing yesterday's knowledge. Hence, over millions of years memory storage systems grew apace, brains became bigger and connections and interconnections between nerve cells more numerous. Animals became less dependent upon the fixed, 'wired-up from birth' behaviour patterns of reflex and instinct and pushed ahead with their wonderful new trick of being able to modify behaviour in the light of past experience. Apart from the constraints imposed by such restrictions as those of weight, vascular plumbing, gravity and skull size, there seemed no limit to what living organisms could store inside their heads. By the time evolution had got as far as Driver Robins with his 400,000 million neurons and their billions of interconnections, brains had a capacity, so it has been claimed, to store more items of information than there are particles in the Universe.[6]

All this was quite a breakthrough on the survival front, but unfortunately the advent of storage capacity only increased the afore-mentioned snag. For with all this explosion of biological technology one thing had not changed appreciably – speed of transmission. Admittedly, the faster conducting fibres of myelinated nerve appeared on the scene, but this was still only nibbling at the problem. From a communication standpoint the business of transmitting information into, within and out of brains has remained painfully slow. Imagine a telephone system in which all wires were replaced by slow-burning fuses which had to fizz and splutter from A to B every time one made a call, or a library of say a thousand million books staffed by someone with bad eyesight and a limp, and one can begin to appreciate the immensity of the problem. Survival often depends upon deciding rather quickly what to do. With these brakes on rapid information handling, decisions threatened to become either so protracted or so inaccurate as to be hardly worth the effort.

But then nature in her wisdom (or, if you prefer, a combination of mutations and natural selection) produced two excellent practical solutions to this problem of neural sloth – parallel processing and conscious representation. In a sense, evolution of the first – a neural capacity for doing things in parallel, of doing lots of things at once – necessitated advent of the second, the representation, in a psychological domain of a very limited capacity, of no more than the bare end-products of all the extensive pre-conscious processing which had gone on before. But this raised another problem. For if these administrative arrangements were to function in a way which would be helpful to their owner, what were to be the criteria for conscious representation? Of all the millions of stimuli raining on the animal, which should have priority for conscious representation, and of all the billions of items of information lodged in its memory banks, which should be readiest to hand for conscious scrutiny?

The obvious answer is those events of greatest relevance for the animal's ongoing needs – food if he's hungry, water if he's thirsty, and a nubile companion if he feels like making love. As for an animal's other big need, that of avoiding trouble, this could be (and is) catered for by the simple expedient of making him sensitive to novelty and change. Since sudden changes in the external world – the unexpected shadow falling across his path, an unaccustomed smell, the crack of a twig which leaves ripples of suspense in the hot still air, the creak of a board at dead of night – are all potential threats of approaching danger, there is and always has been survival value in noticing the unexpected (to be technical – events of high selective information content).

But what has all this to do with the untimely death of Driver Robins?

If our very limited capacity for conscious attention means that it must be reserved for signals of especial interest, there must be a huge remainder of unsurprising things which don't qualify for entry into awareness and, even more important, from Robins's point of view, there will be a large repertoire of things we do which have become so habitual that they don't require conscious attention for their efficient execution. It is these simple truths which killed poor cock Robin.

What we are talking about is so-called 'absent-minded' behaviour, the lovable eccentricity of doing the right thing at the wrong time or place, of, for example, saying thank you to a vending machine or, as in the following instance contributed by Professor Reason, doing the right thing with the wrong object:

> My Friend Will Honeycomb is one of the Sort of Men who are very often absent in Conversation, and what the French call a *reveur* and a *distrait*. A little before our Club-time last Night, we were walking together in Somerset Garden, where Will had picked up a small Pebble of so odd a make, that he said he would present it to a Friend of his. After we had walked some time, I made a full stop with my Face towards West, which Will knowing to be my usual method of asking what's a Clock, in an Afternoon, immediately pulled out his Watch, and told me we had seven Minutes good. We took a turn or two more, when, to my great Surprise, I saw him squirr (fling) away his Watch a considerable way into the Thames, and with a great Sedateness in his Looks put up the Pebble, he had before found, in his Fob. As I have naturally an Aversion to much Speaking, and do not love to be the messenger of ill News, especially when it comes too late to be useful, I left him to be convinced of his Mistake in due time, and continued my Walk . . .[7]

All this is good harmless fun. Surely, when doing something as important and potentially dangerous as driving a train, natural caution would preclude such errors. Or would it?

Do these railway catastrophes fit the theory of absent-mindedness? So violently destructive are high-speed railway accidents that, unhappily, not one of the footplate men who were responsible lived to tell the tale.

There are common denominators in all these catastrophes which support that euphemism for absent-minded behaviour, 'misapplied competence'.[8] First, there is no evidence to suggest that the people involved were anything other than sober, healthy and not overly fatigued. Second, these drivers and firemen were professionals with extensive experience of what they should have been about. Third, all were doing a job which, by its very nature, had become habitual. Unlike cars, trains don't have to be steered. The task does not call for continuous adjustments to changes in the external world. Behaviour is largely determined by expectations based on past experience.

But there is a fourth common denominator which appears to pose something of a paradox. Engine drivers, like airline pilots, are in one very important respect, on a continuum with those world leaders who have it in their power to unleash a nuclear holocaust. Like world leaders they are responsible for the control of immensely destructive forces with the capacity for annihilating not only themselves but also large numbers of people ostensibly under their care. Do we then have to entertain the alarming possibility that there may be situations in which grinding responsibility actually makes people *more*, rather than less, absent-minded. Is being absent-minded in some way motivated? Does the individual have to 'absent' himself from what is really going on?

In a moment we shall consider some rather different sorts of evidence for this conclusion. But now, in case credulity for these speculations is being overstretched, let's return to the more mundane cases of people who literally, as well as metaphorically, go off the rails.

They illustrate another apparent paradox which needs to be resolved. If animals evolved to respond to the unexpected – this being one of the criteria for an event achieving conscious attention – then, in theory anyway, the sometimes serious outcomes of absent-minded behaviour could be prevented by novel warning signals. Unfortunately, judging from the following examples this seems not to be the case. Rolt sets the scene:

Owing to engineering works in the Watford tunnel, expresses from Crewe to Euston on the 30th September 1945 were being diverted at Bourne End, Berkhamsted from the fast to the slow line. For a safe crossing from one track to the other speed was restricted to 20 m.p.h. Three signals gave prior warning – one a mile and a quarter before the crossover, another a mile further on, and finally, after another 440 yards, a pair of 'splitting' semaphores to indicate the diversion.[9]

For the 8.20 p.m. Perth–Euston sleeping-car express this series of signals might just as well not have existed. Without reducing speed it entered the crossover at 50 m.p.h. The engine, a 'Royal Scot', left the rails to overturn in a field nine feet below the line. Piled up against it were the shattered remains of the six leading coaches. The accident blocked four lines and took the lives of thirty-eight people, including those of the driver and his fireman. Five more people died later. Sixty-four others were seriously injured. According to Rolt, 'the driver, an experienced man, knew of the diversion and his lapse could not be explained'.[10]

Seven years later, on October 8th, another Perth–Euston sleeping-car express, having passed three signals at danger on the approach to Harrow and Wealdstone station, was still travelling at 60 m.p.h. when it struck the rear of a stationary local commuter train packed with 800 passengers. So violent was the impact that the last three carriages of the local were reduced into the length of one. As if this were not enough, within seconds of this first collision a northbound express, travelling at speed, burst upon the scene to pile upon the wreckage which lay across its path. The remains of three trains and their passengers, of whom 122 died, were now compressed into a heap of wreckage 45 yards long, 18 yards wide and 30 feet deep.

Of this, the second worst accident in the history of British railways, Rolt remarked, 'We know how Harrow happened, but not why, even now.' Perhaps he was being unduly pessimistic. For a start, unlike the mystery of the *Marie Celeste* to which it too was likened, this sort of disaster is not unique, but has continued to occur up to the present day.

At Lewisham on December 4th, 1957 the London–Ramsgate express not only ran into the rear of a local train, but in so doing brought down a 350 ton girder bridge on to the already damaged carriages.

Crushed by this enormous weight, 90 people lost their lives and 109 were seriously injured. Apparently neither the driver nor his fireman had 'seen' the relevant warning signal.

On January 23rd, 1955 the driver of the York to Bristol express was warned, because of engineering works, to proceed through Sutton Coldfield station at no more than 30 m.p.h. His train in fact entered the station at between 50 and 60 m.p.h. Seven coaches overturned, killing or injuring 52 people. On May 7th, 1969 a sleeping-car express approached Morpeth (between Newcastle and Berwick) at 80 m.p.h. instead of the 40 m.p.h. required by the sharp curve in Morpeth station. There were 127 casualties.

And so on, and so on. It is not the purpose of this book to catalogue disasters on British railways or to deter the reader from ever travelling again by train. Notwithstanding the foregoing accounts of carnage, travelling by train remains one of the safest of occupations, or, as someone once remarked, 'There are few safer places on earth than a passenger compartment on a English train'.

The intended lesson of this chapter is not that railways are potential deathtraps, but rather that, *even* in such a safe environment, one of the self-destructive products of human evolution may, despite the very best of intentions and every brilliant built-in safeguard, result in minor holocausts of death and destruction.

Fortified by these encouraging thoughts, we can return to consider one last issue of some practical importance. An odd feature of the accidents so far considered is that in every case they occurred even though there were two people, the driver and his fireman, on the footplate of each engine which came to grief. Three non-mutually exclusive conclusions might be drawn. First, since it is inherently unlikely that two people could be equally absent-minded at one and the same time, the accidents must have occurred for some other reason. Second, that through diffusion of responsibility (i.e. each thinks the other is watching out for signals) neither of the crew was sufficiently vigilant – from which it follows that two heads are by no means necessarily better than one. Then again, perhaps the errors made were due to one man being distracted by the other. Perhaps on his own and left to his own devices, no engine driver, considering the immensity of his responsibilities, would be so absent-minded?

There is probably some truth in all these possibilities. But for the moment let's consider the last. There are two pieces of evidence, again from our safest form of travel – railways – which support the view that, even on his own, undistracted by any companion, and even when the consequences of error would be horrendous, the absent-minded slip may still occur.

On the evening of May 4th, 1971, having deposited its passengers, on the termination of its run, at Tooting Broadway, a Northern Line Underground train accelerated into a siding off the running line. Though this railway cul-de-sac was distinguished by yellow lights along the wall and a red stop light, the train crashed through the buffers and the sand drag to hit the end wall of the tunnel at between 20 and 30 m.p.h. The three leading coaches were reduced in length by thirty feet and the driver killed. He was alone, but it was thought he had been reading a book!

Four years later on February 28th there occurred a comparable, but in terms of lives lost, far worse accident on that independent section of the Northern Line which terminates at Moorgate. Reason's analysis of this disaster leaves little doubt that it too was a case of absent-minded behaviour.[11]

At 8.46 a.m. a heavily loaded train entered Moorgate station, but, unlike all other trains which over seventy-one years had trundled peacefully into Moorgate, this one failed to stop. To the surprise of people waiting on the platform, instead of slowing down, it ploughed through the sand drag just behind the red stop light and began disappearing into the twenty yards of over-run tunnel beyond the platform end. Seconds later they heard a muffled crash as the three leading carriages, having struck the end wall, crushed themselves into a compact mass of wreckage thirty feet shorter than their original length.

In this accident, the worst ever on London's Underground, many people died. Why did it happen? What, if anything, was wrong with Driver Newsome?

It took four days to reach his body. Since his hands were still resting on the controls it may be assumed that he did not show the startle pattern reflex which normally occurs just before a collision. From this it may be concluded that he did not anticipate a collision. Driver Newsome had not been drinking, neither was there any reason to believe he might have been suicidal. Reason's conclusion, with which I see no reason to disagree, is that the most likely cause of the accident was absent-mindedness – that the driver was behaving in place A as if he was in place B. Place A was the half-mile between Old Street and Moorgate stations. Place B was the two mile stretch from Essex Road to Old Street. Between the latter two places trains usually reach a speed of 35 m.p.h. – a fatal speed at which to enter Moorgate.

But why, after years of experience on this short run, should he have confused A with B? One possibility could be that he may have been thinking of something else. Researches[12] have shown that internally generated thought, so-called stimulus independent thought, effectively blocks the simultaneous uptake of information from the external world.

This chapter has concentrated on the hazards of absent-mindedness in the context of railway accidents. There is every reason to believe that they constitute a risk to survival in every other field of human activity where the successful running off of well-worn habits has lulled the mind into a false sense of security and encouraged that prime antidote to the boredom of repetitive tasks – stimulus independent thought.

Since sheer weight of responsibility appears to be no safeguard against the possibility of absent-mindedness, it would surely be wise to consider the implications of this chapter for all those who have the job of operating the nuclear armaments of this world. We know that for them the tasks they perform are dull, repetitive, and therefore likely to be productive of various unsafe patterns of behaviour including stimulus independent thought. An absent-minded error on the part of just one of them could make Driver Robins's little lapse seem hardly worth a mention.

But maybe this is being unduly pessimistic. Just because the responsibility of an engine driver's job doesn't protect *him* from the hazards of absent-mindedness, this hardly justifies the view that the much greater onus of controlling nuclear armaments wouldn't prevent comparable slips and errors of judgment. After all, railways *are* very safe, so safe that they could easily lull one into a false sense of security. But everyone knows this is far from true of nuclear weapons. Surely the much greater risk and infinitely worse consequence of a nuclear disaster provide a more than adequate safeguard against the possibility of an absent-minded slip?

Let us hope that this is so, but there remains (like Chernobyl) the uneasy suspicion, as intimated earlier, that the greater the responsibility and the worse the risk, the more imperative it becomes to preserve peace of mind by detaching oneself from the full implications of what one is about. Is there perhaps some quirk of the mind, some mechanism of the brain, which like the protective secretary to the harassed Professor tends to trade safety and survival for tranquillity of mind?

3

The Need for
Peace of Mind

Alas, regardless of their doom,
The little victims play!
No sense have they of ills to come
Nor care beyond to-day.

Thomas Gray

Survival depends on knowledge of the environment. But knowledge by itself has no survival value. To succeed the animal must not only acquire information but also know what he needs to know, what he needs to have, and what he needs to do. Species which never felt hungry, thirsty or sexy would quickly become extinct.*

Nature came up with two elegant solutions to these problems. The first was that of selective attention and the second that of the affective signalling system. Working together, they are essential for survival, but together or apart they may also have lethal consequences for the future of mankind.

Through selective attention, external events which are novel, important for the satisfaction of bodily needs, or threatening, have priority when it comes to being noticed. This is obviously a good thing. It is useful, to say the least, to detect signs of water when you are dying of thirst, and nubile ladies or virile men when you feel like

---

* We cannot know in any strict sense that so-called lower animals have 'feelings', but this Chapter assumes that they do. Whether or not this is true makes no difference to the general argument so far as man is concerned.

adding to your family. As for the affective signalling system, a rough outline of how this works is shown in Figure 3.1.

When a need occurs, say for food, this gives rise to an affect. The individual *feels* hungry. As the need and therefore the hunger increases so it becomes motivated to do something about it. As nature intended, extremes of hunger, like thirst, sexual frustration and fear, are unpleasant and demand speedy termination. Goaded into behaviour, he or she procures food and then, if there's nothing better to do, falls asleep. Peace returns to the jungle.

This apparently simple negative feedback system is, however, more complex than it sounds. First, small amounts of most affects are enjoyable. In small doses it's nice to feel hungry, thirsty or sexy. This could serve two purposes. Some toleration of a frustrated need may be essential in the particular situation in which a creature finds itself. In the interest of survival there may be other more important things to do first. Second, the pleasant feelings associated with most needs motivate the organism towards seeking out those situations which will whet the appetite, and these are most likely to be those involving what he requires. People go to strip shows because it's nice to feel sexually aroused. Even fear and anxiety, usually regarded as wholly unpleasant, are enjoyable under certain circumstances – horror movies, roller coasters and mountaineering. As to why natural selection should have favoured animals which enjoyed these so-called negative emotions, one can only suppose that it has to do with the ultimate benefits for survival of having to explore dangerous places and situations.

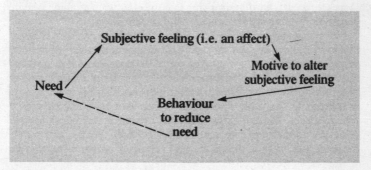

Figure 3.1

The affective signalling system confers other benefits. If it is working properly it not only motivates but also directs. The animal 'knows' it is hungry and not thirsty. Attention is directed towards that which is needed. For humans anyway, hunger makes the individual notice, recall and, if he falls asleep, dream about food. A comparable train of mental experiences attends the other needs as and when they arise.

However, there *are* complications. A major problem for behaviour which satisfies needs is knowing when to stop. Overeating, for example, besides interfering with the satisfaction of other needs (not only are the very fat sexually unattractive but also less athletic in bed) is also ultimately a killer. Here again the Affective Signalling System (or ASS to use an appropriate abbreviation) comes to the rescue. After a need has been satisfied the feeling by which it was signalled is normally supplanted by its opposite. Once the meal is over any mention, sight or smell of food may be positively repellent. One of the horrors of washing up is having to do it *after* one has just eaten.

There are yet other complications. If gratification of a need is too long delayed the feeling by which it was signalled may diminish. Finally, as intimated earlier, needs may interfere with each other. Not only is it extremely difficult, if not impossible, to run away from danger, eat a meal and make love all at the same time, but one unrequited desire may obliterate another. On the other hand, needs may combine to produce behaviour, like oral sex, which may be pleasurable, but has no survival value (for the female spider which devours her lover immediately after copulation, this particular sort of oral sex is literally the kiss of death for *his* survival). Given the complexities, it is hardly surprising that the affective signalling system can go terribly wrong in a variety of different ways.

The symptoms of affective disorders range from excesses of rage, misery, jealousy, depression out of all proportion to the apparently precipitating cause, to a total absence of the capacity to feel anything about anything – so-called flattened affect, a state of affairs found at its most extreme in the disease of schizophrenia. But it is as motivators in relation to the basic drives that affects may have the most dire consequences. Incapacitating phobias, excessive and inappropriate fears of closed or open spaces, of spiders, mice, snakes and public conveniences, may so dominate and restrict a person's life that he or she loses freedom of movement. Inappropriate feelings towards food may lead to anorexia or bulimia (eating too much). Too much or too little capacity for sexual feelings may result in comparable problems. In other words, not only quality and appropriateness, but also quantity may go awry.

Since the whole purpose of feelings is to activate behaviour, such anomalies may have dire consequences. In terms of such destructive (and self-destructive) acts as murder, rape and suicide the ASS has much to answer for. But the biggest hazard comes from our attempts to control our feelings. We do it in two ways – chemically and psychologically. The first, which might involve taking anything from aspirin to alcohol to heroin, acts directly on how we feel – either by blotting out the unwanted signal, or by substituting a nice feeling for a nasty one. Clearly these products of our culture threaten human survival. Not only do we cut ourselves off from information which may be essential to survival, but even worse the particular route to oblivion chosen may well terminate our need for information once and for all.

Whereas the consequences of chemicals range from reducing anxiety to producing messianic delusions of grandeur, the *psychological* devices whereby people try to get the better of their feelings are primarily suppressive – denial, repression, rationalisation, projection and isolation – the so-called mechanisms of defence. In one way or another all serve to insulate the mind from unpalatable truths.

All in all then, thanks to the products and sophistication of his culture, modern man can short-circuit the need → affect → motivation → behaviour cycle which we considered earlier. Instead of, for example, acting in such a way as to remove the external causes of anxiety he can now, like the kings of old who chopped off the heads of messengers who brought bad news, attack the noxious signal with flat denial or a double whisky. But in so doing he is trading survival for peace of mind. Take the case of people threatened with the possibility of having a malignant disease.

Any theory which maintains that we act to ensure our physical survival would predict that the merest suspicion of having a potentially fatal illness would give rise to checking this out and, if necessary, seeking treatment. But, in a study of breast cancer,[1] it was found that those patients who coped by using the defence of denial and rationalisation (the single most commonly employed form of defence) had delayed longest in reporting their symptoms, thus significantly reducing their chances of successful medical treatment.

According to a survival theory such women would immediately seek medical help for two reasons: first, because they know that they have the symptoms of what could be a potentially lethal disease; and, second, to reduce the unpleasant feelings evoked by the knowledge. That they don't implies either that they don't know or that they don't care, or that knowing *and* caring, they find the emotional consequences of this knowledge too painful to bear. In the latter case, of 'It's folly to be wise when ignorance is bliss', the only option left is the defence of denial. Needless to say, such a strategy brings its own, if short-lived, reinforcement. By postponing medical help they prolong the illusion that they are not ill. They also avoid the risk of receiving confirmation of their worst fears from an authoritative source. Evidence in favour of this hypothesis has come from a computer analysis of words used by women who because of positive smear tests were considered at risk from cervical cancer.[2] Whereas those patients ultimately found to have cancer used significantly more words connoting hopelessness and fewer words connoting hope than did those for whom biopsies proved negative, these findings were stronger for concerned than defended patients. Moreover, while the 'cancer' group used the word 'death' significantly more often than did the other group, their usage of the word tended to be metaphorical (e.g. 'I was tickled to death') rather than literal. Such results suggest that people may go to extraordinary lengths to conceal from themselves even (perhaps especially) such information as is crucial to their own survival. They are also consistent with the finding that cancer patients rate high on repression and low on depression, so much so that predictions, made on the basis of psychiatric interviews at the Heidelberg surgical clinic[3] as to whether suspicious lumps in the breast would prove to be malignant, were found to be correct in 95 per cent of cases.

Repression, denial, rationalisation, isolation and projection are well-documented mechanisms of defence, but there is another more wide-spread, insidious and probably more dangerous device for preserving peace of mind – optimism and its close cousin, positive thinking. In the light of such horrific tribulations as bubonic plague, which in four years killed seventy-five million people (one in three of the population), it is hardly surprising that people developed the habit of looking on the bright side of things and counting their blessings, however few and far between these may have been. Unfortunately, this agreeable strategy has a darker side due to an alarming relationship that has been found between affective and cognitive processes, namely that positive feelings activate positive memories and vice versa.[4] The trouble is that if, as Bower has shown, the induction of a happy state of mind brings back happy memories and evokes positive expectations of future events, then it is fair to assume that these enjoyable thoughts would quite naturally increase feelings of happiness, which would in turn evoke even more pleasurable memories and so on – a runaway system. This potentially catastrophic positive feedback is probably encouraged by the fact that a particular mood not only reactivates consonant memories but changes the way in which what may have been quite indifferent events are recalled – possibly one of the factors responsible for that most deceptive of emotions, nostalgia. As might be expected, it works both ways, so that while happy people become happier, sad ones become sadder. However, of the two positive feedbacks, that leading to a state of unquenchable cheerfulness and that which spirals downwards to depression, the first is probably the more common. There are three reasons for so thinking. Happiness is self-reinforcing – it is nice to feel jolly and there are plenty of artificial aids, from drink to TV comedies, to assist what may be a flight from reality. Secondly, the culture reinforces a happy mien. Gloom is unattractive. Finally, there is a greater readiness to label depression as a psychiatric disorder even when the depression is justified, than there is to accord the same label to euphoria (however unjustified). Very few people get hospitalised for cheerfulness! But if positive feedbacks are ultimately self-destructive, how can we claim optimism as a side effect of what was once an evolutionarily useful device? Perhaps the answer lies in a 'selfish gene' hypothesis that optimistic organisms – e.g. the male who dashes across a busy street to meet up with (or mate up with) a nubile female on the other side – maximise their chances of achieving good selective breeding. If he gets run over by a bus on the way across, this could be a useful incident in natural selection. If he is struck down on the way back it doesn't really matter, his work is done.

Obviously, though tragic in their consequences, none of the examples so far cited could be in any way regarded as catastrophic for the species. But this is simply because the self-destructive behaviour of the individuals concerned affected only themselves and a handful of others.

More to the point are cases where the trading of survival for peace of mind had the effect of killing thousands, maybe millions, of fellow human beings. For such instances we must lift (or rather lower) our gaze from engine drivers and cancer patients to people who have it in their power to destroy mankind on a massive scale – military leaders and politicians.

And then we have to ask, would such individuals just to preserve their own peace of mind, and perhaps quite unwittingly, bring about the wholesale slaughter of their fellow men? Or would the immensity of their responsibilities save them from dangerously irrational behaviour? Can they, so to speak, rise above their neurotic defensiveness? Unfortunately, as Chapter 4 shows, the former eventuality seems more often to be the case.

4

The Fall of France, 1940

Our war up to the very end, was a war of old men . . . it was saturated by the smell of decay rising from the Staff College, the offices of a peacetime general staff, and the barrack square.

Marc Bloch

Far from reducing ostrich-like behaviour, power and responsibility may have quite the opposite effect. A prime example is the fall of France in 1940, which, at a conservative estimate, accounted indirectly for at least thirty million human deaths.

In the late spring of 1940 General Maurice Gamelin, chief of the General Staff of National Defence and Supreme Commander of all French land forces, confided to the Italian military attaché in Paris that he would be happy to give Germany a billion francs if only this would induce her to attack France without delay.[1] On May 10th, without having to resort to bribery, his wish was granted. Hitler launched his attach on the West. By June 22nd it was all over. France capitulated and an armistice was signed.

How did it happen? How, in so short a time, could the heirs of Napoleon I come to suffer a defeat, so total and humiliating, at the hands of an enemy whose tanks were no better, and number of soldiers no greater, than their own? Several reasons have been given for this apparent paradox. Economic, political, even geographical and technological factors certainly played their part. However, while in no way diminishing the importance of these other causes, the plain fact remains that the fall of France illustrates how military disasters flow from the need to keep the mind free from tiresome worries and painful thoughts. Stupidity is not the answer. Gamelin, who had passed first out of St Cyr in 1891, and his successor, General Weygand, were neither stupid nor uncultivated. There is no reason to suppose that their subordinate Generals, however tearful, defeatist, and 'deliquescent'[2] they became, were not just as intellectually gifted (and in some instances probably more so) than many other, far more competent and successful commanders. And yet, between them, these members of the French military élite offered hardly more resistance to the German onslaught than would shreds of paper to a hurricane.

How could this happen? Certainly it was not those dimensions of commanders considered so important in some military circles, their size and appearance, which hastened military defeat. When Air-Chief-Marshal Sir Arthur Barratt described Gamelin as 'a button-eyed, button-booted, pot-bellied little grocer',[3] his words probably tell us more about his own character and prejudices than they do about the Frenchman's likely value as a military commander. After all, Gamelin's subordinate, General Billotte, was over six feet tall, massively built[4] and a stranger to the grocery trade, and yet, as a commander of armies, fared little better than his boss.

An alternative and more likely possibility is that the fall of France in 1940 began with her ignominious defeat by Germany seventy years earlier. It can be argued that this traumatic, pride-wounding experience set in motion a chronic conflict between two of the possible responses to threat – fear and aggression, and that it was this conflict working itself out in the minds of her military leaders which, at both a practical and emotional level, led to her eclipse.

Following the Prussian victory of 1870 fear was in the ascendant. France adopted a defensive posture – a line of forts along her frontier with Germany. Then came a resurgence of military pride and a thirst for revenge. Fear gave way to aggression. Attack was *in* and defensive positions were *out*. But hardly had the forts been stripped, their armaments dismantled, than France found herself committed to the ten-month battle of Verdun. With this battle came the belated realisation that it might have been wiser to leave the forts intact.

However, with the arrival of one of the world's worst military commanders, General Nivelle, mobility and attack were once again reinstated as the preferred mode of response. But not for long. At Chemin-des-Dames, with more self-confidence than foresight, Nivelle over-played his hand. In sorrow and in anger French military thinkers turned their attention (and taxpayers' money) to the construction of a heavily defended line of fortification – the Maginot Line. For several years French peace of mind was achieved through this vast fortified wall. Within the magic of its expensive girdle Gallic fears (and progressive military thinking) were laid to rest.

But the magic girdle was never quite completed and when German armies arrived on French soil they did so, inconsiderately, via places where there *was* no Maginot Line.

Instead of German aggression, the only thing deterred by the Maginot Line was French cerebration. The absence of imagination shown by French Chiefs-of-Staff, their blindness to the outside world, their failure to progress beyond a 1914-18 mentality, their subservience to their own politicians and incuriousness towards their enemies, suggest minds so long protected by concrete that they had begun to take upon themselves the properties of this rigidifying commodity.

By 1939 France had, in the words of one historian,[5] 'an army and air force trained for defeat'. It looked as if the prolonged conflict between fear and aggression had eventuated in such less active responses to threat as submission and denial. Many of the generals whom France fielded for the Second World War were afflicted in this way, but none more so than General Gamelin, her top man at the outbreak of hostilities.

One of the youngest and most competent of French divisional commanders in the First World War, Gamelin nevertheless displayed many of those personality traits which seem to make for disaster at the highest levels of command.

Though apparently self-confident he gave the impression of one whose quest for power and status must be carefully disguised. Subservient to authority, never pressing a point, forever anxious to please, he threaded his way through life with what appeared to be the suave assurance of an intelligent if obstinate head waiter. By the time he had 'taken over the hotel' as Commander-in-Chief, a lifetime of avoiding trouble, with all the suppression of aggression which this entails, left him ill-fitted for the supreme job. Though apparently underestimating the enemy's strength and intentions, his own over-cautious nature prevented him from launching an attack upon Germany during that opportune period when her attention was still occupied with Poland.

Thenceforth, up to and after May 10th, in accordance with his *penchant* for avoiding trouble, Gamelin studiously ignored evidence of the holocaust to come. From April 20th information accumulated that the Germans, judging from their assemblage of pontoons, would attack across the Meuse. On May 7th, 8th and 9th further warnings of an impending attack were received from intelligence services and other military sources. Returning from a flight over the Saar, a French air force Colonel reported a sixty-mile column of enemy tanks moving through the Ardennes towards the Meuse. According to advice from 'benevolent sources', the German offensive would start between May 8th and 10th, so they forecast correctly, 'the attack will begin tomorrow'.

When it was suggested, to Gamelin's Chief-of-Staff, that officers and men (in all some tens of thousands, including several Generals) should be recalled from leave, he replied, 'Recall men on leave? Whatever would be the point, it won't be tomorrow they will have to fight'. It has been suggested this optimism was based on the Chief-of-Staff's belief that Germany was in a state of disintegration. As for the idea that the main German attack would be *south* of the Belgian Meuse, in the region of Sedan, this had seemed so unlikely for so long that information supporting the notion tended to be discarded. As Bond has remarked, 'The accumulated weight of evidence ignored by Gamelin remains formidable'.[6]

Now one, though by no means the only, reason for a lofty ignoring of military intelligence might well be an excess of confidence, however misplaced, in the superiority of one's own army to that of the other side. In Gamelin's case, before May 10th, he had expressed great confidence in the morale and fighting efficiency of the French forces.

There is, however, another quite opposite reason for closing the mind to information – *lack* of confidence. In this case the lower the confidence and the larger the real threat the more necessary would it be to avoid unpleasant facts that might shatter peace of mind. This seems the more likely explanation for Gamelin's behaviour.

That anxiety lurked beneath the complacent façade of the Commander-in-Chief is suggested by the moves he made to divest himself of ultimate responsibility if things went wrong. One of these was to dissipate his authority between three widely separated headquarters. Thirty-five miles lay between him and General Georges, Commander-in-Chief of Allied forces on the north-eastern front, and neither he nor Georges was nearer than seventeen miles to GQG (Grand Quartier General). Provided they possessed a teletype system, or even adequate telephones, sheer distance between the nerve centres of the French High Command need not have resulted in an almost total lack of communication between them. But they did not enjoy these amenities. Even those modest purveyors of information, carrier pigeons, had not been pressed into the service of their country. Any exchange of news or ideas depended upon time-consuming personal visits or upon despatch-riders. Unfortunately, many of the latter were killed before delivering the messages with which they had been entrusted.

Gamelin's second move which suggests a degree of anxiety was to bury himself in his own headquarters, where he lay immersed 'like a submarine without a periscope'[7] in paper work and intellectual discussion. When he 'surfaced' it was to implement his dubious Plan D. According to this plan Allied forces would defend a position on the River Dyle. Few, except Gamelin (and ultimately the Germans), were enamoured of this scheme. Pushing up into Belgium looked daring but was ill-advised. An attack elsewhere, as predicted by intelligence reports, could leave the armies encircled and cut off. Though they had grave doubts regarding the wisdom of Plan D, and subsequently blamed it for the disasters which followed, the British High Command kept their reservations to themselves. Surprisingly, neither they nor Gamelin had any knowledge of Dutch war aims.

The adoption of and clinging to Plan D was based on the supposition that the main German attack would come from the north. Not only was this what the enemy had done in 1914, but the belief received spurious confirmation from one of those incidents which mercifully come along to relieve the tedium of military history – the Mechelen affair. On January 10th, 1940 a German aircraft bearing a staff officer crash-landed near Mechelen-sur-Meuse in Belgium. By happy chance the officer was carrying *the complete operational plans for Germany's attack on the West.* He tried to burn the plans but failed to complete this task before he was captured.

In this way a somewhat charred, but still legible account of German intentions became available for allied perusal. Hitler's response to this *faux pas* was to adopt a new and, as it turned out, far better plan, which involved shifting the main weight of his attack southwards to the Ardennes. For his part in thus helping the German war effort the staff officer who lost the old plan should, by rights, have reaped generous rewards. Beyond a reprimand, he received nothing. Such are the fortunes of war.

Despite overwhelming evidence that the Mechelen incident was not a *ruse de guerre*, designed to mislead the Allies, and that therefore Hitler might well adopt a new plan, Gamelin's strategy remained unchanged. Though influenced by political factors, his failure to develop a more flexible approach during those fateful days, notwithstanding respectful suggestions from his subordinates, appeared to be based upon an underestimation of the enemy's capacity for doing something unexpected. It is possible that he imputed to the foe his own abject lack of imaginative leadership. On the grounds that important decisions, made in the face of strong contrary evidence, are sometimes the overdetermined consequences of unconscious motivation, it is tempting to speculate regarding Gamelin's deeper reasons for Plan D. For an inherently cautious man who is nevertheless anxious to shine as an apparently aggressive commander, Plan D offered a compromise solution. It *was* daring and aggressive to push far forward, but at the same time kept the conflict removed from his own country and doorstep.

With the stage already set for disaster, matters were made worse by several other factors. The first was hostility and mistrust between the so-called Allies. One outcome of these negative attitudes was their (the Allies) penchant for sitting on information rather than passing it on to their brothers in arms. Anglo-Belgian-French relations did not bode well for a united effort against the common foe.

A second factor was that jealousy between services which militates against co-operation for a common cause. Though made supreme Allied commander, Gamelin had absolutely no influence (nor did he seek to have it) upon either the air force or the navy. He entered the fight like a purblind eagle whose claws, wings and beak are controlled by three unconnected nervous systems.

A third and final factor was really a side effect of the general human tendency to avoid receiving information associated with threatening events. Not only was France's First Army vague about the enemy, but frequently did not even know the whereabouts of its own corps and, on one important occasion, was actually ignorant of the position occupied by Lord Gort's headquarters.[8] The French were not unique in this respect.

Lord Gort's act of removing himself to a command post many miles from his own GHQ has been described as 'an administrative disaster'. No less unfortunate was what Field-Marshal Montgomery called Gort's 'amazing decision' to transfer his Director of Military Intelligence and another senior intelligence officer, from their staff duties, to command a scratch field force. According to Montgomery, the British and French control of the forces arraigned against the German invasion was 'a complete dog's breakfast'.[9]

At this point an already deteriorating situation was helped on its way by General Georges. Apparently overwhelmed by his responsibilities, particularly at having to command not only two French armies, but also the British Expeditionary Force and the Belgian army, Georges engineered the appointment of the already over-committed and hopelessly unsuitable General Billotte. This shelving of responsibility by Georges was deplored by Gamelin, but he in turn shelved the responsibility for doing anything about it.

Though no doubt unique in other ways, Billotte had characteristics in common with his unsuccessful colleague. Beneath his large exterior and genial, courteous manner lurked those handmaidens of defeatism – fear and indecision. Though channelling his anxiety into an obsession with paperwork, Billotte proved incapable of inspiring confidence or of seriously influencing the flow of events. When his whole Army Group was in danger of encirclement it took him two days of gnawing indecision before he could make up his mind to extricate his forces.

Faced with this dangerous hiatus, created by his anxious subordinates, Gamelin should have intervened. Unfortunately, his will, not strong at the best of times, became almost totally paralysed. This was too much for Billotte, who, having spread out his map, took to a slow counting – 'Un panzer, deux panzers, trois panzers . . .' and so on up to 'huit panzers' adding – 'et contre ceux-la je ne peux rien faire'.[10]

As the end drew near, the expedient was tried of replacing Gamelin by someone older (though not unfortunately more experienced), the 73-year-old General Weygand. Though no doubt hurt by this change of fortune, Gamelin left the military stage apparently well pleased with his first and last order of the campaign – a vague instruction to carry out a counter-attack.

There are probably many Generals who believe, like Viscount Montgomery, in the importance of a good night's sleep. Unfortunately, for some people a penchant for getting the head down may also provide an easy escape from the nasty realities of waking life. Such a one was Marshal Bazaine in the Franco-Prussian War of 1870. It is possible that Joffre also had inclinations this way. But now it was Weygand's turn. Having examined Gamelin's parting 'order', the new Commander-in-Chief went on record with the encouraging remark, 'There's not a moment to lose'. The vibrancy of this call to arms was, however, somewhat muted by his immediately stated intention 'to get a good night's sleep'.

Contrary to the old belief that a change is as good as a rest, the appointment of Weygand did little for the Allied cause.

While he did not, like General Georges, dissolve into tears when things went wrong, and had about him a deceptive sprightliness, the new Commander-in-Chief's handling of the battle lacked distinction. Having toyed, until it was too late, with Gamelin's suggestion of a rapid pincer movement to cut off the German panzer divisions from their supporting troops, he instituted his own plan for a counter-attack.

Though it sounded impressive, the plan was vacuous, a wish-fulfilling fantasy based upon 'facts' about the enemy and Allied forces that bore no relation to reality. His first operation order, which laid down that German forces should be prevented from reaching the sea, overlooked the fact that enemy troops had already broken through to the coast two days earlier, while his promises regarding available Allied forces for the planned attack lacked substance. There *were* no available Allied forces.

Weygand, who had never commanded troops in the field, who has been described as a sort of 'human jack-in-the-box, a very ancient toy, whose vivacity still startled, though he had but one trick to play',[11] had not kept up with the times. Like Gamelin, his mind, still dominated by memories of the previous war, was unable to absorb the realities of this one. Unlike Gamelin, however, who tried to conceal his incapacity by divesting himself of responsibility, Weygand resorted to the more dangerous, because more misleading, ruse of pontification and hollow rhetoric.

As noted by one observer, the situation under Weygand produced 'the utmost confusion of crossed lines, misinformation, and absence of information, of contradiction, of leaping to conclusions without verification, followed by suspicion, distrust and accusation'.[12]

Reeling under the impact of a new type of warfare, Weygand became increasingly defeatist. Ignoring the fact that armies are but means to ends, the paid servants of the country they are supposed to defend, his last act was to sacrifice his country for the honour of his army. When the military situation was irretrievably hopeless, the Prime Minister demanded that the army should surrender in the field. By so doing it would enable France to continue the war from Africa. But Weygand refused. To preserve the honour of the army, he insisted that the government should ask for an armistice – and this they did.

The events recounted in this sorry tale which, by allowing Germany to continue the war for another five years, cost upwards of thirty million lives, typify many of the points made elsewhere in this book. But running through the entire range of idiotic happenings is one central theme – the tendency to shut out, deny, repel, suppress, misinterpret or ignore those realities of a situation which, were they consciously experienced, would endanger peace of mind.

The implications of this chapter and its predecessor for those worried about modern holocausts should be fairly obvious. Every sane person (including even politicians) who reads or watches television must surely know by now that our survival as a species is threatened by the presence of enough nuclear warheads to wipe us all off the face of the earth several times over. Every sane person who has thought about it at all must know that the risk, through accident, miscalculation, incompetence or psychotic design, of these weapons being used is growing exponentially. And every sane person must know that the only safe way to remove this threat is to remove the weapons. And yet this essential step towards survival is never taken. This is perhaps hardly surprising when we consider that even *after* a major nuclear disaster peace of mind regarding the future is quickly restored:

At the Vienna conference, government and industry delegates had to
face up to the accident [at Chernobyl] and come to terms with it. They
took only the length of the conference. Within five days, August 25-29,
the mood of the delegates underwent a remarkable metamorphosis. On
the Monday they were grim, gloomy and tense. By Friday they exuded
bonhomie and *esprit de Corps*, a global nuclear community that had
pulled itself together and convinced itself that it had little to worry about
after all.[13]

Part Two

Motives in Conflict

5

The Dark Cellar

What profits now to understand
The merits of a spotless shirt –
A dapper boot – a little hand –
If half the little soul is dirt?
Tennyson, *The new Timon and the Poets*

One does not have to be a dedicated Freudian to accept that for most people the psyche comprises three sorts of motive which pull in opposite directions.

In this respect, to paraphrase Bannister, man is a battle field, a dark cellar in which a well-bred spinster is locked in combat with a sex-crazed monkey, their struggle being refereed by a nervous bank clerk.[1] For those less worried about sex than aggression, there is an alternative formulation: man is a shoal of piranhas, directed by a computer which has been programmed by an archbishop.

More prosaically, having been born with a set of biological drives, we gradually learn to gratify these with minimum risk by acquiring two new sets of motives, the first pragmatic, the second strictly moral. Together they achieve an uneasy compromise between what we want to do, what we ought to do, and what we can get away with.

However one likes to describe it, the end result of this tripartism is a creature so apparently well rounded as to earn (if not deserve) the sobriquet 'Civilised Man'. Unfortunately, this well roundedness is only skin deep. Though every stage in the evolution of our tripartism contributed to biological survival in a basically hostile natural environment, their end results now threaten our destruction.

49

Part Two is about how and why these end results pose such a threat. To discuss this, however, necessitates using a nomenclature with which to label the three sets of motive that are causing all the trouble. That adopted here is from psychoanalytic theory. Though 'a rose by any other name would smell as sweet', id, ego, and superego are of course Freudian concepts. But herein lies a difficulty. Some people become enraged by the use of psychoanalytic labels (presumably they touch a raw spot in their psychopathology).

So, before we go any further, a few words in defence of this irritating practice.

1   It is surely a matter of common observation, not to mention personal introspection, that people are born with and thereafter continue to possess biological drives for sex and aggression. If they weren't and didn't they wouldn't be here. Nor should it occasion surprise that people are prone to aggressive or libidinal wishes and desires. As a label for all this, id is surely as good as any other and has the added advantage of being short and memorable.

2   It is also evident that most people learn to conceal or moderate their more socially unacceptable wishes. They also use their cognitive abilities to achieve the best possible compromise between what they want to do and what society will let them get away with. These are functions of the ego.

3   Most people claim to experience the voice of conscience and feelings of guilt if they transgress society's moral code. These are manifestations of the superego.

4   A rationale for distinguishing between id, ego and superego is also to some extent supported by anatomical, physiological and pharmaceutical discoveries. For example, subjective ego experiences which involve learning, thinking, language, memory and perception rely upon the cortex; and manifestations of the superego appear to decline with severance of the frontal lobes. Nor should we forget that the superego has long, and correctly, been thought of as that part of the mind which is soluble in alcohol! If something can be made to come and go so easily and relatively inexpensively, then surely it deserves a label.

All in all, on heuristic grounds alone, there seems to be a good case for using Freudian concepts in the present context.

For a species to survive it has to obtain food, water, warmth and suitable mates, but in so doing must compete with others for limited resources. Hence, successful competitors in the struggle for survival were those who evolved in such a way as to give them an advantage: either physically in terms of such assets as strength, speed and protective armour; or mentally in terms of learning and problem-solving capacities.

Of these two general strategies, we are the final product of the second. It is an ironic feature of our preoccupation with physical prowess in athletics that many lower species can run faster, jump higher and display greater strength than even the finest gold medallist. When considered alongside the anti-intellectualism of many civilised societies, it is as if, at some level, man with his soft-vulnerable body, teetering along on spindly legs, is regretting that natural selection favoured cerebral rather than muscular talents for dealing with the outside world. For many people (the author included), from the beginning to the end of their schooldays, learning and thinking were not popular as pastimes. For some they were positively painful. Indeed, so aversive are the feelings produced by cerebral activity, that many go to the end of their days without ever realising the enormous potential of even the most ordinary human brain – and theirs may be by no means ordinary.

But this is by the way. More to the point is that being relatively weak in body but strong in brain, we are, more than any other species, driven towards two sub-strategies. The first is co-operation, and the second, made possible by the first, technology. The common denominator of both is that they aim to compensate for our natural physical inadequacies. From the pyramids of ancient Egypt to the advent of space travel, from the first use of rollers and levers to the latest development in robots, from the gigantic effigies of stone raised upon the slopes of Easter Island to the controlled delivery of a hydrogen bomb, we have proved that we can now think faster, fly higher, move more quickly, and dispense greater force than any of our erstwhile competitors. All in all, this gargantuan exercise in prosthetics (extensions of or substitutes for parts of the human body) is a magnificent achievement – the fruits (if not the joys) of progress. But, as with the advent of consciousness, a price is paid. There are three main reasons. First, co-operation meant subordinating self-interest to the common goal. Second, it meant abiding by ever more complex sets of rules and regulations, and third, it meant being dependent upon the goodwill of others. All this sounds fairly innocuous, if not actually cosy. But the processes of socialisation, for this is what we are talking about, have potentially lethal consequences. The first has to do with individual differences in the degree to which people are socialised, the second with the emergence and eventual dominance of so-called ego motives, and the third, undoubtedly the nastiest of the three, with collusions between morality and aggression.

In so-called civilised societies people vary along a continuum from totally unsocialised at one end to over-socialised at the other, with most individuals being semi-socialised, a few remaining fairly unsocialised, and a few over-socialised.

The business of becoming socialised does of course take time. We all start as babies – hedonistic, pleasure principled, noisy, messy, aggressive, demanding and intolerant of frustration – in Freudian terms, unrestrained ids. This is fine for a month or two, possibly a year or two, but from repeated experiences of being frustrated which, judging from the noise babies make, is unpleasant if not down-right painful, it eventually dawns on the infant mind that living by the pleasure principle is far from pleasurable.

They begin to learn the hard way that even worse than being hungry or thirsty is experiencing their own frustration. They learn that they are the helpless victims of one or two large, ungovernable creatures who are not only intolerant of noise and mess but may, if crossed, become positively dangerous.

Since few, if any, can remember what they thought about (if they thought at all) before the age of three, and despite the ingenious researches and theorising of those who study babies, we cannot be sure what really goes on in the minds of those who are enjoying or enduring this first stage in the long slow process of what for some parents amounts to' creating little ladies and gentlemen out of tiny primates'.[2] But the end results are usually some signs of obedience, the burgeoning of conformity, some indications of dependency upon the approval of others and some patterns of behaviour which are directed towards achieving what they can get away with. In Freudian parlance, the ego, that part of the mind which mediates between the id and the environment – essentially selfish, innocently pragmatic, transparently crafty and surprisingly realistic, has arrived on the scene. Some people, for reasons that are not entirely clear, never get beyond this early stage of socialisation. They have been described as psychopaths or possessed of psychopathic tendencies. They are strangers to shame, unrestrained by guilt, living by their wits and sometimes ruthlessly aggressive. They may lie and cheat their way through life. If sufficiently clever, sufficiently attractive (until one knows them better) and sufficiently aggressive, they may acquire enormous wealth or power and end up as dictators, presidents, or chairmen of huge multi-national companies. They may also end up in jail or the electric chair or as a charred corpse outside a Berlin bunker. Their importance in the context of this book is that they are often highly destructive and self-destructive.

Two other facts about aggressive psychopaths make them particularly dangerous. Because they behave quite shamelessly, in ways that others would love to emulate but are afraid to imitate, even their most ruthless and flamboyant acts may become objects of envy and admiration. One has only to consider the soft spot which some people had for the villains who successfully pulled off the Great Train Robbery to realise that there is a tendency in society to enjoy vicariously, if not actually condone, even their most ruthless and dishonest antics. Finally, because they are notoriously bad at foreseeing the consequences of their actions, they may take enormous risks which (unlike those taken by the Train Robbers) may not come off.

There is, unfortunately, no shortage of psychopaths, but when it comes to creating mayhem for the rest of society some are more talented than others. One such was Hermann Goering, Hitler's most popular henchman. Firstly, he possessed certain characteristics which earned him a powerful position in the Nazi hierarchy. He had shown himself to be a courageous and impetuous fighter pilot. He was big, hearty, rumbustious, hail-fellow-well-met; superficially, at least, the sort of genial and humorous individual one might welcome as a drinking partner. And if he did seem rather too flamboyant, too swaggering and exhibitionistic, one could perhaps forgive him! After all, he did on occasions dispense the most lavish hospitality, and he did have another asset on his side – his looks. In comparison with the other top Nazis who (with the exception of Speer) were far from easy on the eye, he had a not unpleasing face, a sort of cross between Harry Secombe and John Wayne – if you like that sort of thing.

All in all, there was much about the gross self-indulgent Reichsmarshal which struck a sympathetic chord in many fellow Germans. He represented what, at a deeper level of man's animal nature, many would like to be and like to do. There was much about 'Our

Hermann' which made others tolerate the fact that, for example, 'He laughed uproariously when his pet lion urinated on a lady's dress'[3] or that his idea of entertaining an assembly of guests was to have a cow and bull copulate in front of them. No doubt some deplored the coarseness of his humour. But for others, such vicarious and guilt-free gratification of their own aggressive and libidinous wishes made him a winner. And for them there were, because of this, no limits to what he could get away with. For, once the contortion of seeing evil as good has been successfully accomplished, almost any transgression of ordinary morality can be countenanced; and so Goering's unbounded cynicism, self-interest and ruthless sadism, his re-introduction of capital punishment, his self-confessed urge to destroy and extermi- nate, his planning and execution of the Reichstag fire and subsequent blood purge, and his introduction of concentration camps could be conveniently overlooked, if not actually applauded.

The incidence of psychopathy is not confined to the white races. Much that has been said of Goering applies well to another monstrous tyrant – Idi Amin; and this even down to the military background where, like the fat Reichsmarshal, he too earned a reputation for genial, loudmouthed masculinity. Like his predecessor, Idi Amin was flamboyant and exhibitionistic. Not only did he dress in the uniform of a Field-Marshal, but he had a miniature version of the same outfit made for his small son. And he too had some rather disagreeable habits, not the least unpleasant being his practice of cutting off the penises of his enemies.

It would be nice to have a world devoid of psychopathic leaders. For two reasons this is unlikely ever to come about. First, throughout history the possession of psychopathic traits has proved a useful passport to high office. Men or women who are unfettered by moral scruples, who are prepared to lie or cheat their way to the top, who will make promises they know they cannot keep and may, in extreme cases, think nothing of assassinating their rivals, have a huge advan- tage over those held back by notions of fair play. A second reason for finding that top jobs in politics, as indeed in many other walks of life, are successfully held on to by people with psychopathic traits is that such characters are (though they may not know it) fulfilling Ashby's Law of Requisite Variety.[4] According to this law the successful control of any system depends upon the latter's complexity being matched by that of its controller. In other words, the control system must be capable of adopting the same number of states as the system it is trying to control. By these lights the possession of psychopathic traits is advantageous to a leader. They give him more degrees of freedom in his control and manipulation of those under him and most particularly in his dealings with potential enemies.

It can be argued that many 'strong' leaders like Stalin or Marcos of the Philippines, or the Duvaliers of Haiti, held on to power notwithstanding their various shortcomings because of, rather than despite, their psychopathic make-up. Looked at purely from the standpoint of requisite variety psychopathy would seem an admirable trait for world leaders. Since, through survival of the fittest, potential leaders have an above average chance of being psychopathic (because this is helpful if you want to come out on top) all this would be good news were it not for the fact that psychopaths are, on the one hand, notoriously bad at anticipating the final outcome of their actions (like 'Watergate') and on the other, that they may be much more determined by their own selfish needs than by those of the society they are trying to control.

The two sides of this problem are well exemplified by the sad case of ex-President Richard Milhouse Nixon. In the game of international politics (arguably the most important activity of a super power leader) Nixon must surely be counted as one of the ablest of American Presidents – head and shoulders above his successors – and yet, in terms of psychopathology so fatally flawed that it eventually cost him his job.

Of him, the American psychoanalyst Leo Rangell wrote, 'Nixon was sick in the realm of integrity – pathognomic of the Nixon syndrome was his predictable preference, whenever a life situation presented the necessity to choose, for the alternative which led him to self-advancement at the expense of truth',[5] which is a roundabout way of saying that whenever it suited him he lied. Many people lie to further their own ends. Many politicians are, to say the least, 'economical with the truth'. But Nixon, according to his biographer, was in a class of his own. He lied as a matter of course. He had, it seems, learnt that it pays to be circumspect, that manipulation, persuasion, and most of all lying, offer bigger rewards than sheer coercion. Rather than resorting to overt aggression, gentle but deadly character assassination of his potential rivals became his special forte. But even unscrupulous politicians have to operate in the context of a particular reality, and the reality for Nixon involved two constraints – the voting behaviour of a democracy and his physical appearance. The first ruled out naked force and the second any easy winning of American hearts by his physiognomy. He does not, like Carter, exude bonhomie with a wide and toothy grin, or display an honest, open countenance. Rangell has noted the contrast too with Reagan:

> Reagan's trademark has always been a look, the stamp of the good guy, the sheriff's tough but likeable face. This visual image may be used to convey an opinion of rough idealism, or a call for violent action. Reagan's look may be consonant with or at complete variance with what he says. His acting face has, first by training and now in a realistic role, the look of being sincere. It is the look which Nixon always tried to achieve but at which Reagan is better . . . Reagan's face is the opposite of the face with which Nixon was endowed. What looked put-on with Nixon seems the real thing with Reagan. Perhaps this is the basis of the charisma which is so much a part of Reagan and which Nixon always lacked.'[6]

All this makes good sense and is indeed a matter of common observation. But there is another aspect of a person's appearance which needs to be considered – its relationship to self-esteem. Research[7] has shown that a person's self-esteem is very much tied up with what he or she looks like. Hardly surprising! But this is no simple matter of an individual's *actual* physical appearance but rather of how he *thinks* others see him. There are, for example, plenty of people with no illusions about the fact that they would never get short-listed for a beauty contest, yet who enjoy apparently, tank-like egos. Moreover, as far as we know, they are respected, even loved, despite their looks.

Yet a further complication, with far-reaching consequences, results from how a person *reacts* to how he thinks he is perceived by others. How he does so probably also has its origins in early childhood. It is a sad fact that some mothers (probably for reasons which go back to *their* childhood) are cold and unloving towards their offspring. Feeling unloved, the child draws the conclusion that he is unlovable. With his self-esteem now damaged, possibly beyond repair, he may well begin acting in one of two equally disastrous ways. Either, like Shakespeare's Richard III who announces, 'And therefore, since I cannot prove a lover . . . I am determined to prove a villain', he sets about confirming his unlovableness by behaving in an unlovable way, or he might adopt a lifestyle of over-compensations for his real or imagined shortcomings. Since such typical compensations as being affected, bombastic and domineering are themselves fairly repellent, his underlying belief of being unlovable gets its confirmation, albeit by a rather more circuitous route.

There are other neurotic spirals. Unloving mothers may show their lack of affection by what they say or what they do, or what they don't say or do. High on the list of these dos and don'ts are an absence of kissing and cuddling, *and under or over-feeding* (the former a function of sheer indifference, the latter to deal with guilt about this indifference). A possible consequence of these early patterns may be a lifetime of anomalous eating behaviour, a chronic tendency to under- or over-eat. If exacerbated by later stresses, this dealing with bad feelings by oral behaviour may (subject to such other variables as embarking on a slimming diet or being over-exposed to quantities of tempting food) eventuate in anorexia or gross obesity. In either case, the individual is achieving not only what he or she craved (attention in the case of anorexia and both attention *and* oral gratification in the case of obesity) but is also once again confirming the original hypothesis of being, as mother had intimated long ago, physically unlovable.

Although eating disorders are far from rare, they do not exhaust the strategies used by people with problems over self-esteem. For a more bizarre instance, there is the case of an attractive young woman who believed people didn't like her because she smelled. To mask the imaginary smell, she took to using perfume in such large quantities that wherever she went people sniffed. This of course confirmed her delusion, which led to more perfume and therefore more sniffing.

But to get back to Nixon it is reasonable to assume that his self-esteem may well have been reduced by doubts about his appearance. But this raises a puzzling question. How, in the circumstances, could he eventually succeed to the highest office in the land?

Truman, as forthright as Nixon was devious, expressed the paradox in no uncertain terms:

> All the time I've been in politics, there's only two people I've hated and he's one. Not only doesn't he give a damn about the people, he doesn't know how to tell the truth. I don't think the son-of-a-bitch knows the difference between telling the truth and lying . . . Nixon is a shifty-eyed

goddam liar and people know it. I can't figure out how he came so close to getting elected President in 1960 . . . he's one of the few men in the history of this country to run for office talking out of both sides of his mouth at the same time and lying out of both sides.[8]

In posing the question, Truman in fact provides us with an answer. It was just *because* he didn't give a damn about the people that, unhindered by conscience yet driven to repair his damaged self-esteem, he could lie without what Rangell has called the 'friction of guilt', and so the populace believed in him.

But Nixon is only one example of the price that might be paid for our tripartism when it comes to the making of co-operative efforts towards group goals. To restate the problem: because physically weak, man has to operate in groups. For a group of individuals to co-operate towards a common goal necessitates that its members abide by certain rules. For society to work the majority of its members must be prepared to sacrifice some personal freedom for the common good. In a word they must be socialised.

But groups, however socialised, need leaders to direct and orientate their efforts. Through leadership, the art or technique of so influencing others that they can and will do what the leader wants them to do, groups can achieve goals which would be impossible if they had been left to their own devices. Unfortunately, however, it only needs a concatenation of three factors to bring about a relationship between the leader and his group which may eventually destroy them both. If the leader is a psychopath and unconcerned about the welfare of others, he will exploit them to gratify *his* wishes, not theirs. He achieves this by implanting the belief that if they accept his leadership, they will be able to gratify their hitherto repressed desires without guilt. He frees them from the constraints of morality. As someone who emerges from childhood without the burden of these constraints, he is an object of envy and delight. He represents the promise of aggression without retribution. He can, by example, display the promised land of unalloyed hedonism wherein destructive impulses can be acted out with impunity. His id speaks to theirs, and because he can lie with such disarming ease even his most barefaced deceptions are accepted as the truth.

People find it hard to see through lies which they so urgently wish to believe. From small lies the leader can move on to bigger ones.

Like an astute drug pusher, he can feed his addicts with yet larger helpings of what they not only expect but have come to demand. For them, to believe big lies becomes progressively easier. There are two reasons for this. To question a big lie is to question the veracity of the liar, which means having doubts about all the lesser lies which they had previously swallowed, which means having to admit they might have been wrong, which is intolerable. So, with increasing abandon, they have to continue throwing good money (or rather sense) after bad. In a word, they're hooked.

The second thing about big lies is that their very size confuses. In everyday experience, lies as big as that, which appear to contradict so many facts, just don't occur. Therefore, they can't be lies, they're so breathtakingly large they must be true. Were it necessary, the hook is even more firmly embedded.

There are three final points. The likelihood of all this happening could be much greater in a democracy than in a totalitarian regime because, in the former there are two sources of dissonance. Besides the decision to believe in the liar there was also the prior decision to elect him in the first place. Second, if the purpose of the leader is aggression, he will have prevailed upon the electorate to provide the technological wherewithal for gratifying his purpose. And so we have another dissonant situation, as in the present arms race, with more good money going after bad, until eventually the final product of what might have started in the mind of one man with a chip on his shoulder does for them all.

The last point is simply this. The psychological factors which can turn co-operation into catastrophe have as much to do with the ego as the id. Or (for those with a distaste for psychoanalytic jargon) there comes about a reciprocal relationship between biological drives and the learned talents of the maturing brain. Like a terrorist who has discovered how to make bombs, the id uses the talents of ego to further its ends. But the converse also occurs and the consequences may be even more catastrophic, particularly when the political leader has such a 'frank open countenance' that it induces a level of trust far beyond his deserts. Mixing metaphors with abandon – it is sugar-coated 'pills', like wolves in sheep's clothing, that are the best dressed to kill.

6

The Exorbitant Ego

I am the batsman and the bat,
I am the bowler and the ball,
The umpire, the pavilion cat,
The roller, pitch, and stumps and all.
                Andrew Lang, *Brahma*

The recognition of oneself as an entity, of 'I'ness has considerable survival value. The animal which has a sense of ownership, not only of its body but also of its feelings and thoughts, which recognises that the hunger, thirst, pain or fear belongs to it, has a great advantage over those which lack such insights.

So essential are feelings of personal identity that their loss is experienced as extremely unpleasant. Rattray Taylor[1] cites the case of a young army officer who reported sick with what he claimed to be the following recurring symptom. When addressing his troops he would suddenly feel he was talking like an automaton, everything felt unreal, flat and lifeless, even his hands and feet felt detached as if they did not belong to him, his senses of taste and pain, even of the fullness of his bladder, seemed muffled and far away.

In some ways less extreme, but perhaps equally unpleasant, were the experiences of another sufferer from this curious malaise – 'I feel as though I'm not here at all. My mind appears to be here, but the rest of me seems to have gone. I have to touch things to make sure I'm still here'.[2]

Milder forms of depersonalisation are far from rare. Of those who, following a lecture on depersonalisation, were asked if they

60

had ever experienced the sensation, nearly half reported that they had.

Finally, as the same writer points out, the fact that after a murder many false confessions are made indicates the desperateness of the desire to achieve an identity – to be an object of attention. To feel one is a 'non-entity' – a featureless cog – is for most people extremely disagreeable.*

An integral part of personal identity is an individual's self concept – the way he regards himself, his attainments, his position in society, his appearance. Is he in his own eyes a worthwhile person? The consequences of discrepancies between how a person sees himself and how he would like to see himself range from enormous achievements at one end to despair, depression and suicide at the other. Attempts to close the gap may result in all sorts of behaviour motivated by what, for want of a better label, can be termed ego needs.

Whether one subscribes to the notion of a hierarchy of human motives from simple biological drives at the bottom to such lofty urges of the spirit as the need for self-understanding at the top,[3] or entertains the belief that everything we do is driven from below by one single overriding 'purpose', that of passing on one's genes,[4] the plain fact remains that so impervious are so-called ego needs to the requirements for physical survival that people in whom they are over strong may be highly self-destructive. If, as Dawkins has suggested, we are mere 'survival-vehicles' for our genes, then our ego needs appear to have missed the message. Indeed there are grounds for the cynical observation that the ego seems bent on dealing with biological needs by slow destruction of the body from which the latter spring. By working too hard, drinking too much, driving too fast, and striving towards a lifestyle beyond that which he can afford or that which is good for him, many an individual manages to trade physical survival (including his particular set of genes) for short-lived ego trips. No less devastating in their effects are the multitudinous worries and anxieties of the ego. They are of two sorts. Worries about 'what other people will think' and worries that the Joneses (who in terms of sheer human misery have a lot to answer for) are creeping ahead.

* Within hours of writing this paragraph an American policeman who had defused a bomb in a busload of Turkish athletes was arrested for having planted the device himself, in order, he said, to draw the attention of his superiors to himself.

Though emanating from that region of the psyche which is regarded as the conscious, rational, cognitive mediator between the demands of the id and the restraints of society, ego needs are not only physically destructive but often irrationally, ridiculously, self-defeating. For example, trying to impress others by name dropping, displaying invitation cards, hanging up pictures of your own house, attempting to socialise with the rich and highly born, boasting about your car, your yacht, your children and your dog; referring to the famous by Christian name (as if you were on such intimate terms with them), and forever speaking of 'my lawyers', 'my bankers', 'my stockbrokers', and 'my chap in Harley Street' (as if not only were these professionals wholly dependent on your custom but actually owned by you), may well have an effect quite opposite from that which you intended.

Particularly is this so when the people you most want to impress will also tend to be the most sophisticated, the most discerning, the most cynical and the most amused of all those treated to manifestations of your ego needs. Instead of thinking what a great person you are they may well snigger and, what is worse, come away with the thought that, since you evidently crave their approval more than they do yours, they are even more superior to you than they might have thought in the first place.

It is probable that many people don't actually think this through but, even if they did, it is also probable that it wouldn't stop them. Something drives them on to make asses of themselves.

Though embarrassing to contemplate, such relatively harmless affectations are unlikely to threaten survival of the species. There are, however, other consequences of the same underlying motivation which are not so innocuous. Plenty of examples are to be found in the long history of military disasters – those seemingly inevitable consequences of trying to professionalise aggression. But now, by way of a change, let us contemplate a number of peacetime tragedies. All of them concern another basic need of living creatures, that of having to move about, and the troubles which ensue when this requirement is affected by the ego needs for approval and the desire to please.

In April 1912 the largest passenger liner then existing sailed from Southampton to New York on her maiden voyage. It must have been a proud moment for her Captain, Edward Smith. Professional, enormously experienced, he had been chosen to demonstrate to his passengers, the White Star Company and the general public that his was the greatest, safest liner in the world. It is not entirely fanciful to suppose that so involved was his ego in the 'unsinkable' *Titanic* that he may have identified himself with the ship – strong, famous and indestructible.

During the calm but very cold night of April 14th the *Titanic*'s telegraphists received warnings by Marconi radio of icebergs on the route ahead. Undeterred, Smith allowed his ship to proceed at twenty-two knots. For a vessel of 46,000 tons travelling at that speed, plenty of time and distance is needed to avoid collision with an obstacle in its path. By the time a look-out saw the huge shape of an iceberg dead ahead the *Titanic* was too close to avoid it. When the liner struck there was no violent shock of impact, just a prolonged jarring as the ice slit open the underwater hull.

Through a 300-foot gash the sea poured in.* Two and a half hours later, with her lights still blazing, the *Titanic* slid, bows first, beneath the surface, taking with her Captain Smith and 1,403 of the passengers he had tried so hard to please.

For a more complex case of the same genre, there is that of one-time Secretary of State for Air, Lord Thompson. Against the advice and better judgment of those who knew its imperfections, Thompson demanded that, on October 4th, 1930, the largely untested R101 should leave for India with him on board. His insistence on this suicidal act ignored the fact that the airship lacked sufficient buoyancy and that its gas bags, made, so it has been claimed, from the intestines of a million oxen,[5] leaked hydrogen continuously. He overlooked the fact that the four diesel engines were not only unreliable, but far too heavy for what was supposed to be a lighter than air machine and he closed his mind to the fact that weather conditions were totally unsuitable for the October departure. What were the motives for this behaviour? He wished to arrive in India aboard 'his' airship by a certain date because this would improve his chances of becoming the new Viceroy. And why did he want to become Viceroy? One reason was so that he could then lay the viceregal crown at the feet of a European princess for

---

* Recent exploration of the wreck has indicated that it was the riveting of the hull which failed.

whom he had formed a romantic attachment. Any doubts about the vanity, selfishness, and social-climbing arrogance of this egomaniac are dispelled by considering his personal effects. Since success of the venture depended on the R101 weighing less than the air which it displaced, the crew were limited in their personal luggage to little more than a toothbrush and a change of socks. But Thompson brought on board cabin trunks (one of which contained a silver slipper* belonging to the aforementioned princess) with a combined weight equal to that of twenty-four extra people. He also took 600 feet of heavy Axminster carpet (as a gift to *please* the King of Egypt) and an abundance of silver tableware, cases of champagne, etc., etc. Finally, because it would inconvenience him and his guests if the airship was refuelled *en route*, he decreed they should carry enough fuel for the entire voyage – a quite unnecessary extra weight.

The sequel was tragically brief. In appalling weather and only after discharging several tons of its ballast water (partly on to the heads of those waving goodbye) the R101 gained enough buoyancy to leave its mooring mast, passed slowly over London and crossed the channel barely fifty feet above the waves. Early the next morning it struck the low hills of Beauvais. In the resulting holocaust Thompson and all but seven of the crew (i.e. forty-six people) were killed.

Maybe society has now outgrown such acts of suicidal irrationality as those displayed by Smith and Thompson. It seems not, however.

In 1956 two aircraft flying north from Los Angeles, on different routes and at different altitudes, failed to reach their respective destinations. Their wreckage and the 128 bodies of those on board were eventually located in the area of the Grand Canyon. Both the pilots involved in this mid-air collision had over 16,000 hours' flying time and knew their routes well. Yet, when they collided, neither aircraft was where it should have been. The subsequent Board of Inquiry concluded that the pilots had not seen each other in time, presumably because absorbed in giving their passengers a good view of the scenic beauties below.

Any residual doubt that the pressure to please may override not only the dictates of professional experience and safety regulations, but also any instinct for self-preservation, should be dispelled by the case of a Boeing 707 *en route* from Tokyo to Hong Kong.

---

* Subsequently recovered from the ashes of the burnt-out hulk.

To many people the main hazard of volcanoes is that, from time to time, they erupt with unpleasant consequences for anyone living nearby. Hence, one might be forgiven for believing that the old proverb 'When the sky is blue Fuji is angry' originated as a sort of rule of thumb about warning of imminent activity by the Japanese volcano. There is, however, another more scientific basis for the saying, which has less to do with eruptions than with the wind.[6] Whatever else it may portend, a blue sky over Fuji's 12,395-foot-high crater signifies the presence there of hurricane-force winds, which, having risen high above the summit, come cascading down the leeside of the mountain. This mountain wave effect must certainly have been known to the Captain of the 707 which on March 5th, 1966 left Honeda Airport, Tokyo, for Hong Kong.

On the day in question the pilot of this aircraft, a man with 12,000 hours' flying time behind him, having visited the meteorological office would have seen the high-level weather charts with their many tailed arrows denoting high winds from the north-west blowing at 60-70 knots across the Japanese Alps. But from his seat in the nose of the 707 he must also have seen, 70 miles to the north, Fuji's snow-covered cone rising majestically in lonely isolation against a clear blue sky. Conditions were perfect for photography, if not for the unfortunate amateur photographers sitting behind him with their cameras.

We cannot know for certain what was going on in the Captain's mind, but having filed a flight plan for a route well to the south of Fuji, he then abandoned this to steer his aircraft towards the mountain's summit, thus emulating a very small moth moving towards a very large candle.

When it was 20 kilometres from the volcano, eye witnesses on the ground saw the 707 break up – first the starboard wing, then the forward fuselage. The 124 people with their cameras began falling towards the ground. There were no survivors, apart that is from a reel of 8mm ciné film taken by one of the passengers. It shows Fuji getting nearer and nearer, followed by vague shots of passenger seats, and the cabin carpet. These were the last pictures the camera's owner ever took.

This disaster was not unique. Six years earlier a Constellation struck the icy slopes of Mount Gilbert, Alaska, killing all on board. Lacking any other explanation, the Board of Inquiry concluded that the pilot had deviated from his correct course to let his passengers see a famous glacier.

One year later a disaster, very similar to that at Fuji, occurred over another volcanic mountain, Mount Ruapehu in New Zealand. As at Fuji the wreckage of a mid-air disintegration yielded up a ciné film depicting the last minutes before disaster struck.

With this history of catastrophes behind them, one might have expected that every pilot of a civil airliner would have learnt to distrust the less rational promptings of his ego. Such expectations have not been borne out. One reason is that there are occasions when other pressures begin acting in unison with the simple wish to please. When this occurs, as in the following example, lessons from the past may be easily forgotten.

A Boeing 747, one of the world's largest, safest, most successful airliners, has a wingspan of 195 feet, an overall length of 231 feet, and a tailplane higher than a seven-storey building. Driving such a vehicle is not a matter to be taken lightly. But, on Sunday March 27th, 1977 at Santa Cruz Airport on the island of Tenerife when two such aircraft demolished each other and killed 582 of their occupants, it evidently was!

Several factors contributed to this worst-ever air disaster. Through swirling sea fog, visibility on the runway was already down to 500 yards and becoming worse every minute. Of the Airport's three radio frequencies two were out of action, which meant that the pilots of the eleven waiting aircraft could only communicate with the control tower over the babble of the one remaining frequency, and, because Las Palmas Airport happened to be closed on that particular day the three controllers at Santa Cruz were having to deal with an unusually large number of air traffic movements.

Given these conditions, there was a special onus on Captain Jaap van Lanten piloting the KLM 747, flight no. 4805, and Captain Victor Grubbs at the controls of the Pan Am 747, flight no. 1736, to exercise particular caution. They did not do so. Because of congestion on the perimeter tracks the two jets, with the KLM leading, were told to taxi up the main runway. The Captain of the Dutch plane was ordered to go to the start line and prepare for take-off. Captain Grubbs's instructions were to leave the runway at the third turning to the left. He did not do so. Presumably because Slipway 3 necessitated having to manoeuvre his aircraft through 130 degrees he elected to remain on the runway until reaching the easier access to Slipway 4.

Meanwhile the KLM Captain, having reached the end of the two-mile turnway, turned his aircraft at the start line. His co-pilot informed the control tower, 'KLM 4805 is now ready for take-off. We are waiting for clearance'. To which the reply came, 'OK. Stand by for take-off. I will call you'.[7]

The controllers then turned their attention to the Pan Am jet still groping its way towards Slipway 4. Captain Grubbs was asked to report immediately his aircraft was clear of the runway. He was never in a position to do so. For then the unbelievable happened - the other plane began to roll.

When through the fog he saw the lights of the Dutch 747 bearing down on him Captain Grubbs did his best to swerve off the runway. But he was too late.

Captain Van Lanten's sighting of the American plane also came too late. He too tried to avert disaster at the eleventh hour. From the deep furrow gouged out of the runway by the KLM's tailplane it was evident that he had attempted to leap his plane over the huge obstacle which suddenly loomed before him.

When a mass weighing 240 tons and travelling at 160 m.p.h. meets another of identical proportions the results are cataclysmic. Scythed down by the KLM's giant engine pods 300 passengers on the American plane died instantly. Sixty others were seriously injured. From the Dutch airliner, which disintegrated into pieces of flaming wreckage spread far and wide across the airfield, there was not a single survivor.

And so it goes on. Time after time the need to please combined, in the latter case, with that of impatience and jealous preservation of self-esteem which comes with power and seniority, results in otherwise competent, conscientious and experienced professionals killing themselves and those for whose safety they are responsible. Well might it be said that for airline pilots the ego is a deathtrap.

However, provided it is confined to those who drive ships and planes, the threat of such behaviour to survival of the species is not excessive.

But suppose that, instead of people who operate the world's transportation systems, we were to consider the case of political leaders, could we be so sanguine? Airline pilots, like train drivers, may well be responsible for many lives and have at their disposal the wherewithal for destruction on a fairly massive scale. But their responsibilities and the forces under their command are slight compared with those of national leaders.

This would not, of course, matter too much if politicians and Heads of State did not have the sort of ego needs which prove so hazardous in those who pilot airliners. The reverse, as we have already seen with Nixon, is probably the case, and, let's face it, there are far worse instances than that of Watergate. Why should this be so? Let's return to airline pilots.

The primary aim of these people is to be good at flying planes. This is *their* ego involvement, the skill for which they have been trained and of which, no doubt, they are duly proud. They *may* wish to please people, to have a glamorous image, and to prove their virility, but these are (fortunately) quite secondary motives. As for accidents, the immediate risks to their reputations and their lives are so great as to warrant extreme caution.

With political leaders *their* primary aim is to acquire power, and one of the easiest ways of achieving this is by pleasing people on the way up. This is their special skill, their ego involvement – winning friends and influencing people. So it seems reasonable to assume that the ego needs of political leaders are probably greater rather than less than those of people who sometimes drive their aeroplanes into mountains or each other. A further point to bear in mind is that, relative to airline pilots, political leaders have more to gain and less to lose when risking the lives of their fellow men. It is extremely rare for a pilot to escape death in a major air disaster. The opposite holds true of political leaders. In a Third World War it is highly probable that the American, British and Russian leaders would be the last to perish as a consequence of the politics they pursue or the risks they take.

Absolved from guilt by the rationalisation that their continued existence is essential for the good of their country, it is highly likely that they would provide themselves with the deepest shelters and largest stocks of food to get them through a nuclear winter. Heads of State like the birds of the air have a great capacity for staying far away from the firing line. To date, the number of such people killed in war by enemy action is zero.

But how would the ego motives of politicians constitute a threat?

The short answer is by allowing any of the following needs to play a part in major political decisions:

The need to please one's allies/electorate/party/marital partner/anyone else.
The need to appear 'macho'.
The need to appear younger than one is.
The need to capture the attention of the world.
The need to boost one's self-esteem.
The need to prove to oneself that one is brave, decisive, confident and powerful.
The need to avoid feelings of shame, weakness or cowardice.
The need to go down in history as a great leader.

The sorts of political decision wherein the influence of any of the above needs would be not just irrelevant but downright dangerous include:

To humiliate another country or its representatives.
To escalate a war of words.
To escalate an arms race.
To interfere, with or without the giving of military aid, in the affairs of another country.
To infiltrate, attack, or invade another country.
To start a nuclear war.

It should be noted that not one of the above decisions is necessarily right or wrong, but all are of the sort crucial to human survival. For this reason alone they should be based on purely rational considerations. To the extent that they are biased by the ego needs of the decision-maker, to that extent they are irrational and this the world cannot afford.

At the risk of seeming repetitive, there are already at least six situations wherein ego needs of an individual have played a part.

First, there is the case of the man (or woman) who indirectly gains approval by fomenting aggression against other nations. What they are really doing is to distract the attention of their fellow countrymen from trouble at home. Galtieri's invasion of the Falklands falls into this category.

Second, there is the case of political leaders who, when their nation is threatened (or apparently threatened) by another power, feel that they will lose face if they fail to react belligerently.

Third, there have been those who seek popularity at home by endorsing policies which aid the military-industrial complex.

Fourth, there have been and still are those who, again for ego reasons, attempt to model themselves, however inappropriately, upon past war leaders. Eden's hysterical reaction to Nasser, which culminated in the ridiculous Suez *débâcle*, is a case in point. A female politician who modelled herself on a cross between Boadicea and Genghis Khan would fall into the same category.

Fifth, there is the inherently insecure individual who, in order not to appear weak in the eyes of his hawkish aides and colleagues, lets himself be persuaded towards actions which may well run counter to his own better judgments. Typical was Kennedy's role in the Bay of Pigs fiasco.

Finally, there are those who, from a deep sense of personal hurt coupled with infinite reserves of murderous hostility, seek reduction of the former and expression of the latter by using talents of the ego. Because their behaviour is powered by two motives, reduction of shame *plus* need to destroy, those who fall into this category are perhaps the most to be feared.

As mentioned earlier, one feature of ego motives is that they are largely concerned with closing the gap between what one would like to be and what one is. Failure to close this gap is experienced as shame. The experience of shame will be obviously greatest in people who, on the one hand, are overly narcissistic and grandiose, but, on the other, have experienced a lifetime of failure. If to their history of not making the grade are added serious doubts about their appearance, physique and masculinity (or femininity), the outcome may be catastrophic, not only for the person concerned but for the rest of society as well. For an extreme example, there is none better than Adolf Hitler. According to Bromberg and Small,[8] the origins of Hitler's part in the rise and fall of Nazi Germany can be traced back to a combination of three factors – his physique, his parents and, possibly, the after-effects of encephalitis. Physically he was a poor specimen, puny and monorchid. Parentwise he suffered from an authoritarian, cold, often absent father and an over-indulgent, over-protective mother. As might be expected, his performance at school was abysmal.

Even without the possible after-effects of encephalitis, this concatenation of factors did not augur well for the future Führer's character, or for that of the German nation. By the time he left home for a poverty-stricken existence as a painter of third-rate postcards in the doss houses of Vienna, he had developed some rather unlovable characteristics – paranoid, hostile, suspicious and imbued with a deep sense of shame. According to his biographers, his sense of shame was chronic and intense. He was ashamed of his failure at school which culminated in the scholastic finale of using his leaving certificate as toilet paper. He was ashamed of repeated failures to gain admission to the Vienna Academy of Art. And 'he was ashamed of having allowed himself to deteriorate to the level of the dregs of society in Vienna and having to peddle "artistic" productions which he himself despised.'[9]

Hitler was also ashamed of his physical deficiencies and sexual abnormalities, of being monorchid and of enjoying such perversions as having young women urinate and defecate upon his naked body. Plagued by incestuous wishes and intense castration anxiety, he had much to hide, much which conflicted with the grandiose fantasies which, in his narcissism, he entertained about himself.

All of this had two far-reaching consequences for the way he conducted his life. Thus, he lived in constant fear of his deficiencies becoming known. He was ever anxious lest he make a *faux pas*, seem ridiculous, inferior, betray weakness or ineptitude, or suffer defeat or humiliation, and he would never submit to a full physical examination.[10] Second, because of the underlying fear of losing his followers, who were, after all, the primary source of confirmation that he was a worthwhile person, Hitler demanded total loyalty, admiration and subservience from his entourage – a state of affairs which, to a similar (though admittedly lesser) extent in the case of Nixon, resulted in a circle of aides and advisers that for defects of character and/or intellect has rarely been surpassed.

Finally, any situation, word or action which threatened to diminish his self-esteem brought down upon the heads of those who had offended the full force of his murderous hostility. Thus it was that in 1944 he ordered that piano wire be used for slow strangulation of those implicated in the July 20th plot.* And thus it was that, in the

---

* On July 20th, 1944, an abortive attempt was made on Hitler's life by von Stauffenberg and fellow army officers.

end, for failing to fulfil his dreams of grandeur and omnipotence, he turned his fury on the German people themselves.

In the context of this book, there are several questions still to be answered. How is it that someone so repellent and, judging from his table talk, so excruciatingly boring could ever achieve the power to bring a great nation to its knees? After all, the more usual fate for sadistic perverts and mass murderers is the electric chair or an asylum for the criminally insane. And the proper fate for bores is that they are avoided. The short answer is that, like other successful leaders at other times in history, he told the people what they wanted to hear, suggested a scapegoat for their present miseries and extended the promise of better things to come. In all respects the symptoms of his own disordered psyche played a decisive role in the downfall of Germany.

As touched on earlier, a seemingly inevitable consequence of the feuding factions which make up tripartite man are those various mental strategies whereby unpalatable truths are prevented from entering, let alone disturbing, the conscious mind. Hitler, so poorly endowed in some ways, made up for these deficiencies by being a master of such strategies, the so-called mechanisms of defence. He could deny the undeniable, forget the unforgettable and rationalise the irrational so easily that others, because it suited them, found no difficulty at all in swallowing his words and following his example. But his primary defence was 'projection' – imputing to others those things about himself which he most secretly deplored. The 'others' were gipsies, Slavs, blacks, defectives and primarily, and most important, Jews. For him Jews did not, as one might have expected, fit the usual negative stereotype – old, grasping, beady-eyed, hook-nosed, etc., but were epitomised by 'The *black*-haired Jewish youth [who] lurks in wait for the unsuspecting girl whom he defiles with his blood'. He talks (in *Mein Kampf*) about 'their *unclean* dress and their generally *unheroic appearance*, their revolting *sexual ways* and . . . the fact that nine-tenths of all literary filth, *artistic trash*, and *theatrical idiocy* can be set to [their] account'.[11] As Bromberg and Small point out, it hardly needs a great stretch of the imagination to accept that these images are really of himself. Since the German people not only went along with his anti-Semitism but, in their turn, used comparable defences to insulate themselves from the fact that millions of Jews were dying in pain and misery through the machinations of their master, the real horror of this tale is not the nature of one man's diseased personality but the fearful infection which it spread.

But even if we accept the exorbitant demands which the ego might make on any given individual, how could a whole society fall victim to such a pestilence?

One reason is that they are deceived through that predilection for covert behaviour which seems to afflict the egos of political leaders.

Since they are designed to deceive, covert political actions are a form of lying. Yet even the most sanctimonious leaders of purportedly free and open societies, who should be setting examples of democratic morality to the rest of the world, are not above such behaviour.

As the following *Guardian* editorial points out, their resultant dishonesties are not only irrational but also hypocritical and ultimately self-destructive.

Why on earth do they do it? A question for Eisenhower (over Gary Powers and the U2); for Kennedy (over the Bay of Pigs); for Nixon (over Watergate); for Carter (over the Iranian rescue); and for Lyndon Johnson most of the time. A question, indeed, which – with parallel force – might currently be addressed to Mrs Thatcher . . . and a shadowy cast of characters as they sink ever deeper into the Aussie mire.* Why do they do it? What is it about secrecy, and covert action, which exerts such strange fascination for the leaders of the West's biggest democracies? Ronald Reagan is not the first President of modern times to land face down and flailing in the mud of deception. To the contrary, every President through the last thirty years has had terrible problems in exactly the same bog. Some (like Eisenhower) have struggled free; usually by making a clean breast of things and openly admitting error. Others (like Nixon) have ended their careers in shame and exposure. Set a statistical analyst to work in America – or France, or Germany, or Britain – and the bottom line of his findings would be

* This was an attempt by the British government to prevent publication in Australia by ex-MI5 agent, Peter Wright. On March 12th, 1987 Mr Justice Powell found against the British government. Costs were awarded to Mr Wright (at the expense of the British taxpayer). What was particularly farcical about this episode (which assumed almost psychotic proportions) was that, as in the subsequent Zircon satellite affair; the 'secret' information had already been published elsewhere.

utterly clear; the best possible advice to any incoming leader. Don't get involved in covert action. Don't listen to the covert professionals you inherit with the keys of office. Act legally and openly, keeping the major officials (and congressmen, and MPs) who need to know in the picture. If Congress turns you down (on Contra funding, for instance) bow to that voice of democracy. If your secret service (the CIA or MI5) is out of control, then make sure it is brought to heel. Sack publicly; talk about it; explain and prescribe . . .

Don't do it, Mr President (or Madame Prime Minister). The secret, illegal way isn't the easy fix. It is the way that – on hard statistics – will bring you to dust. It is a game demonstrably not worth the candle, or the unravelling humiliation. The odds on exposure are formidable. Why do they do it? And why do they never seem to learn?[12]

As to the question, 'Why do they do it?', one reason is explored in Chapter 7.

7

'Secret Agent'

. . . for they know not what they do.
St Luke 23:34

Few if any take kindly to the suggestion that they are unaware of why they are behaving in a particular way. There are at least three reasons for this cool response. It is extremely irritating when someone claims to know more about you than you do yourself. You may not want to know what lies behind your behaviour. And of course they could be wrong. But why should we be driven by unconscious motives, and what makes their revelation so unpalatable?

The short answer to both questions is that thanks to a curious relationship between brain and mind, what we ought to know and what we want to know are by no means synonymous.

One of the troubles arising from our tripartite nature is that communications between the three domains appears poor to non-existent. This is of course an illusion arising from the fact that our capacity for conscious representation of the internal and external environment is not only extremely limited, but hedged around with defences – those mechanisms of the mind/brain relationship which seem guaranteed to ensure that the right hand (metaphorically speaking) never knows what the left hand is doing. In fact, the evidence from such diverse fields as those of hypnotic phenomena,[1] psychogenic blindness (and deafness), perceptual defence, and the history of such well-intentioned acts as, for example 'liberating' corrupt regimes from the threat of their own revolutionaries, suggest that unconscious communication between the various component systems is extensive, continuous, devious and subtle.

75

With its 400,000 million neurons and their billions of interconnections, the brain has a prodigious capacity for storing information. According to one recent estimate (referred to earlier, see page 21) we could, if pressed, carry around in our heads more facts than there are particles in the Universe. Even if not approaching such astronomical and tiring proportions, it is theoretically possible that not a single one of life's experiences is ever totally forgotten. Somehow, somewhere in the brain, its trace may be retained. Given such a wealth of potential knowledge and the consequent length of time it would take to retrieve any particular memory, evolutionary processes have resulted in special priority being given to those events which were of extreme emotional importance to the animal in question. Thus, at the human level, it is the best moments, the greatest joys, the most fulfilling relationships, that are the most memorable. It is the most exciting parties, the best restaurants, pubs, books, plays, concerts and sexual experiences which remain most clearly indexed, for future reference. This is an excellent arrangement. It helps people to recall, and then repeat, those activities which most closely met their needs.

But survival also depended on remembering what to avoid – that which was most frightening, infuriating, frustrating or painful.

Animals which could remember, for example, what not to eat had an advantage over those less able to profit from past experience. This too is a splendid idea, but for one thing. Under certain circumstances, the emotion evoked by these negative experiences may be so profound and so unpleasant, as to change the individual, adversely and for ever. Two fairly mild examples, both related to eating, should make the matter plain.

The first involved a lady who, during the First World War, was a nurse in a famous London hospital. As a general rule, her appetite sharpened by the chronic food shortage of the time, she looked forward to supper in the nurses' dining-room. But this was to change. One evening the first course, of pale sausages half-submerged in soggy batter, passed off without incident. Next came prunes and custard – predictable (because it was Friday) and unexciting. But then she was pleasantly surprised to see that one of the prunes was distinctly fatter, smoother, blacker and generally more youthful than its companions. In the belief that this would make up for the rest of the meal, she saved it for the last mouthful. Recounting what happened next she said, 'I suppose my first suspicion that it was not what it seemed was the distinct crunch and sort of crackly sound as I bit into it. After all, prunes don't usually make a noise when you eat them.' She paused. 'Nor do they have little legs on their lower side.'

There are just two points to make about this. First, if you are expecting to eat a cockroach (and there may well be parts of the world where they are regarded as a delicacy) then, whether or not you like the flavour, there is no violent shock. But this woman was not expecting a cockroach, she was expecting a prune, and so was quite deeply shocked. Second, never again could she face a dish of prunes. Just one traumatic experience, albeit of a very minor kind, had changed for ever her attitude towards one of nature's humbler puddings.

My second example may well strike a chord in anyone who has had the misfortune of spending what could have been their best years in an English preparatory school for boys. To say that the children in one such establishment suffered from what has been described, euphemistically, as 'menu fatigue' would be an understatement. In its quality, quantity and deadly predictability, the cuisine would have started a riot in one of H.M.'s prisons. But for connoisseurs of bad cooking it was the porridge which commanded especial respect. Even at its best, porridge is not one of the world's great dishes. Rather is it a vehicle for such pleasant things as brown sugar and cream. But the porridge at this school was of a different calibre. If it was a vehicle, it was one which had broken down.

By what strange alchemy the cook could transmute harmless ingredients like oatmeal, milk and water into a grey, glistening, impermeable mass, half-way between lava and Superglue, remains a problem for the higher reaches of organic chemistry. From a purely architectural standpoint, one of the most startling features of this daily miracle was its lumps. They were no ordinary lumps but steep-sided mounds, of various shapes and sizes, which appeared to have been heaved up by mysterious forces operating far beneath the surface. Imagine a circular patch of grey slime, flecked here and there with brown blotches of carboniferous origin, from which are erupting two or three mole-like constructions, and one has a fair idea of the scene with which the boys were confronted.

Ordinarily, through acclimatisation, they accepted their porridge without comment, but one morning, and here at last we are coming to the point of this tale, the child who was seated opposite me had something in his bowl which claimed the attention of even the most blasé gastronome. For there, rising like Everest from the Salt Lake flats of Utah, was a lump of such monstrous proportions that it made the onlookers gasp with admiration, not untinged with envy. Here was no ordinary lump. Here was an excrescence that cried out for entry in the *Guinness Book of Records*. It wasn't just its size. Closer inspection showed it to have a very interesting shape – a pair of humps, on larger than the other, joined by a 'saddle' terminating in what mountaineers might describe as a steep north face.

After some tentative prodding, the owner of this awesome thing tried cutting into it with his spoon. The lump gave a little, spongily, but refused to fall apart. There was something inside which resisted his intrusion. He began scraping. There *was* something inside it – a complete, beautifully preserved and very peaceful mouse. Though glazed in death, its sad little eyes still peered out reproachfully from beneath their fringe of porridge.

Now all this happened a very long time ago, yet to this day I cannot eat porridge, even of the finest quality, without subsequently suffering what can only be described as 'gnawing pains'.

While these two examples illustrate the lasting effects of *mildly* traumatic experiences, there are others so emotionally unpleasant as to activate those powerful defence mechanisms whereby the conscious mind maintains its equanimity. The original incident is 'forgotten', but the consequences may be far more serious.

Take the case of accident-prone pilots. There is evidence to suggest that being accident-prone may result from unconscious motivation and that, in at least one group of people, the consequences of this are invariably fatal. Every year, throughout the air forces of the world, a great many young men kill themselves during training. Most of these accidents are caused by pilot error. And much of the 'error' can be laid at the door of two unconscious motives – firstly, to undertake a peculiarly hazardous and difficult task; secondly, to defend oneself against anxiety engendered by this task.

The antecedents of this tragic waste of life are rooted in the fact that progress in the technology of modern weapons has not been matched by comparable progress in the minds of those who operate them. On the contrary, the impact of the very high information loads demanded by modern weapons on the neurotic complexes of those who use them has brought about a potential for disaster far greater and more expensive than anything seen in days gone by.

Nowhere is this truer than in the case of aerial warfare. In the First World War military aircraft were comparatively simple affairs of wood and piano wire from which adversaries shot at each other with revolvers. Accidents were more likely to occur through bad weather or mechanical defect than through pilot error. But all this has changed.

Not only has the increasing complexity of modern aircraft made them far more costly to produce, but also, as sources of information overload, considerably more stressful than anything seen hitherto, which brings us back to the problem of unconscious motives and complexes in self-destructive pilots.

Over the years, Sweden, like most other countries which boast an air force, suffered a loss of lives and aircraft which, with modern aeroplanes costing upwards of eleven million pounds each and the price of training replacement pilots over two million pounds a time, the country could ill afford.

On the assumption that some young men entering the air force were more accident-prone than others, it was decided to try and weed out these susceptible individuals before they killed themselves. To this end Professor Kragh of the University of Lund developed what has turned out to be one of the greatest benefits that experimental psychology has ever conferred upon suffering humanity – the Defence Mechanism Test (DMT).[2]

The test involves drawing, and describing in words, the briefly exposed picture of a young boy, the 'hero' figure, who is holding in his hand what the Swedes refer to as an 'attribute'. The latter may be a violin, a gun or a toy car.

The test may not sound too difficult and may seem of little relevance to the job of piloting a faster-than-sound aircraft. But there is more to it than meets the eye, or rather the mind. Unbeknown to the candidate the briefly exposed picture also contains in its upper corner the dim outlines of another countenance – an ugly, threatening male face.

Upon some aspirants for flying duties in the Royal Swedish Air Force this 'threat' stimulus seems to have the effect of seriously interfering with their drawing and description of the rather insipid-looking 'hero' figure. They might, for example, see him and draw him as a girl or as a rigid lifeless doll. And sometimes, without knowing why, they draw a line across the page as if to shield the 'hero' from the unseen threat.

For fifteen years the Swedish authorities, under the direction of Dr Thomas Neuman of the Institute of Aviation Medicine, set about validating the test. Every candidate for the air force took the DMT before starting his training and his career was then followed up.

By the time the fifteen years was over one thing was clear. The test results *did* predict ultimate disaster. Those young men who failed to reproduce the 'hero' without some characteristic distortion, were the very ones who subsequently showed an above-average chance of crashing their aircraft or being invalided out of the service with some crippling psychosomatic illness.

Since then, passing the Defence Mechanism Test has been mandatory for entry to the Swedish air force. So successful has it been as a selection procedure that the previous 60/40 ratio of failed to successful graduates from flight training has been reversed and the annual number of fatalities has dropped to near zero. So successful has it been that use of the test is now standard practice in many other countries.

There are at least three possible explanations of these remarkable results. Maybe those who fail the test become so despondent at their poor performance that they crash their aircraft out of sheer misery. Since they are presumably unaware of the discrepancies between the picture and their drawing, this seems inherently unlikely. After all, if they had been aware, why would they have drawn it in the way they did?

A second explanation is that the DMT does no more than test an individual's capacity for the rapid processing of visual information. So it may. But the sort of errors which are made suggest that something other than sheer inaccuracy is involved.

In my opinion the third and following explanation, based on the original rationale for the test, is the most convincing. It derives from the conjecture that among those youths who want to be fighter pilots there will always be some whose primary, albeit unconscious, motive is to reduce doubts they may have about their masculinity/virility. For such people hurtling across the sky with that ultimate in phallic symbols – a Tornado or Jaguar – jutting out in front of them, could well be reassuring.

But why should they have such doubts about their virility that they should need such a monstrously powerful prosthetic extension? The answer according to psychoanalytic theory is that bugbear of the Oedipus complex – castration anxiety. To put it very simply, because he desires a close physical relationship with his mother the small boy is terrified of retaliation by his jealous father, and given the nature of his 'crime' this retaliation can only take one form – the talion punishment of castration. For some children this alarming fantasy may well be reinforced by such remarks from mother as, 'If I catch you doing that again I'll tell your father and he'll cut it off!'

Confronted with this terrifying prospect, the helpless victim of a major conflict between his biological drives, what can the poor child do but resort to the simple expedient of putting the whole thing out of his mind? In the jargon of psychoanalytic theory, he uses the mechanisms of defence to prevent the conscious ego from being aware of, let alone troubled by, the tumultuous feelings and fantasies which surround his Oedipal strivings and consequent fears of parental retaliation.

And that would be the end of the matter but for one thing. Complexes may be relegated to the unconscious, but they don't go away. Rather do they smoulder on, an every-present threat to peace of mind. Thus it is that whenever the individual is placed in a potentially threatening situation old fears are reactivated, he feels anxious, and his defences go up. By itself this wouldn't matter too much were it not for the fact that, since they act like a sudden application of brakes to his normal thinking processes, they begin to interfere with other things he may be trying to do. And this is why, according to the theory, young men who join the air force to prove their virility are the very ones who crash their aircraft. In a sense they are self-fulfilling prophecies.

As to how the Defence Mechanism Test manages to detect these vulnerable creatures the answer is fairly obvious. The candidate identifies with the 'hero'. But here he is, playing with his 'attribute', when who should enter on the scene but the very person he dreads most – his father. No wonder he sees the 'hero' as a girl – someone to whom the worst has already happened, who can't be castrated because she's already lost her 'attribute', someone with whom he can identify only too easily.

But why should his performance on the test predict his performance in the air? After all a pilot's task does not involve being able to draw pictures of people (or anything else for that matter), nor does the sky contain 'threatening faces' (other than those of flying instructors). Here again, for those sympathetic to the Freudian theory the answer is fairly obvious. Just when he needs total concentration on the job in hand, rising anxiety from a variety of sources – fear of failure, fear of his flying instructor (the threatening father figure) and fear of his own demise including of course castration, alert his defences which, by their very nature, interfere with his capacity for processing information.

Solid arrows in Figure 7.1 depict the stages in information processing which are involved in competent performance on the Defence Mechanism Test *and* in piloting an aircraft. Under threat (dotted line), existing complexes are activated and generate anxiety. The resulting arousal of defence mechanisms may produce distraction and/or narrowing of attention, distortion of conscious perception, blocking of memory, biasing of decision-making and inhibition of responses.

He is like a tightrope walker who, just when the wind starts gusting and some large bird has decided to perch on one end of his balancing pole, remembers that he is only up there to overcome his fear of heights.

And so he hits another plane, or flies into a mountain, or tries to land short of the runway, or fails to notice that he's running out of fuel, or does any of those things which, in the end, reduce aeroplanes to piles of flaming wreckage.

Needless to say, there are those who find it hard to acknowledge that even fighter pilots may have once experienced something nasty in the woodshed.

Whatever the source of such scepticism, whether it be a general fear of psychoanalytic theorising, denial of their own castration anxiety, or simply that they are loath to accept that anything as simple as a perceptual test can predict something as complex as an aircraft accident, there are several points worth bearing in mind.

First, whether or not castration anxiety originates with a traumatic experience in childhood, there are good theoretical reasons, a number of findings from experimental research and plenty of real-life examples to support the view that men worry quite a lot about losing their ability to procreate. It makes good biological sense that they should. If they did not they probably wouldn't be here.

It is an obvious corollary of 'selfish gene' theory. It, in addition to, and sometimes rather than, modesty probably underlies the wearing of fig-leaves, loin-cloths, and sporrans. It explains the practice of airmen going into battle sitting on a steel plate. It explains the fact observed in the Falklands campaign that one of the first questions which the wounded asked when brought into a casualty clearing station was, 'Am I OK down below?'[3]

Researches reviewed by Kline[4] which support the Freudian theory of castration anxiety include an investigation[5] which found that out of 305 normal children who were asked to complete unfinished fables which could be taken to symbolise castration, 75 per cent showed signs of castration anxiety and significantly more boys showed this effect at the ages of five (the Oedipal period)

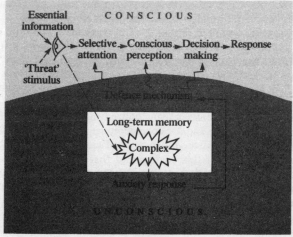

Figure 7.1

and thirteen (onset of puberty) than at other ages. Kline regards this as good evidence of the existence of a castration complex in boys.

A similar conclusion can be drawn from a study[6] which included a content analysis of different sorts of film material. Clear evidence of castration anxiety was also obtained in a study[7] of thirty males before and after genito-urinary surgery. That a castration complex can be induced by a traumatic experience was evident[8] from the effect of eugenic sterilisation upon prisoners convicted of sexual offences.

Strong support for the Freudian concept of the castration complex has also come from research[9] which found a significant relationship under high sexual arousal between fear of death and castration anxiety, and from an anthropological study[10] which, in Kline's opinion, constitutes 'the most important and powerful' evidence for the concept.

Given all this it is perhaps not so surprising that men with high scores on tests of castration anxiety tend to make errors in a situation which threatens to castrate them once and for all. For the writer's money the Freudian explanation is as good as any and better than most. It is also a potent (to use the appropriate word) illustration of the way in which an unconscious complex may drive someone towards behaviour which will kill him when he gets there.

For those interested in the survival of mankind it would be interesting to know whether the behaviour of political leaders is similarly affected by unconscious complexes. Are Reagan and Gorbachev plagued by castration anxiety and therefore anxious to prove their virility? In the case of Reagan, according to the psycho-historian Lloyd de Mause[11] this might well be so.

It seems that whereas Reagan idolised his mother, his feelings about his father were (and are) decidedly negative. Apparently the President's father drank too much and occasionally 'clobbered' him. It is in the context of this background that the title of Reagan's autobiography – *Where's the rest of me?* – takes on a particular significance; the phrase comes from a film in which Reagan played the part of a young man who wakes from an operation to find that both his legs have been amputated. The surgeon responsible for this unnecessarily harsh and vindictive act was motivated by the belief that the young man had been lusting after his daughter.

In his book Reagan dwells at length on the traumas he felt building up to saying this line. For de Mause such painful emotions are understandable since amputation is a symbol of castration.

Whether or not one subscribes to the psychoanalytic explanation of castration anxiety, there are in this instance certain other facts which, as Cohen in a review of de Mause's book, has pointed out, are curious (to say the least).

First, since he chose the phrase, 'Where's the rest of me?', as the title for the story of his life it evidently must have had some very special significance for Reagan; second, like the young man in the film, he himself married the daughter of a surgeon; third, he arrived for their first date on crutches, which, as Cohen says, is about as close to castration as one can comfortably get.

All this could, of course, be coincidental, but Reagan's frequent choice of words like cut, hit, kill, and so on, the vehemence of his hostility towards communism, his preoccupation with defence, his belligerent behaviour towards small nations and such politically inept *faux pas* as his joke about bombing the Soviet Union, support the notion that fear, anger and frustration, experienced at the hands of a drunk, 'clobbering' father, are now finding a legitimate outlet in the present role which he is acting out – that of the ageless, macho, super-virile American hero. This could be 'all balls', but perhaps in more senses than one!

Figure 7.2 Americans soared away from their inner problems on Reagan's MX phallus.

Presumably Mrs Thatcher is free from castration anxiety, but might conceivably suffer from its female counterpart – penis envy. (According to Freud,[12] some little girls are so dismayed when they discover their lack of an 'attribute' possessed by the opposite sex that they may spend the rest of their days trying to get even – either by emasculating men or by acquiring big phallic substitutes of their own – or by both these comforting activities).

Mercifully, perhaps, we don't know whether or not female political leaders would have failed the Defence Mechanism Test, but should perhaps ask if, at some level of the psyche, they are drawn for the wrong reason towards possessing, controlling and ultimately using such phallic substitutes as Cruise and Trident missiles. It is certainly on the cards.

There is, however, another unconscious complex which can be just as, if not more, destructive than that surrounding fears of castration. Because it has afflicted some top political leaders and may well have played a not inconsiderable part in initiating both world wars, it deserves discussion in the present context.

Named after the son of Phoebus, the sun god, it is called, by the French psychiatrist Maryse Choisy,[13] the Phaeton complex. According to the myth two things (other than castration anxiety) troubled the young Phaeton – did his father really love him? and was he, Phaeton, illegitimate?

When taxed with these questions, Phoebus was so shaken that he swore a solemn oath not only that he loved his son, but to prove it would grant him any wish he cared to make. Quick to exploit this rash promise, Phaeton, much as some young man might seek the ignition key of his father's car, asked to drive the sun itself. Phoebus, recognising the boy's limitations, was not enthusiastic, but a promise is a promise. So, with misgivings he handed over the reins of the fiery chariot. His doubts were soon justified. Phaeton was clearly unequal to the task. Fortunately the erratic behaviour of the sun as it swooped across the sky did not escape the notice of Jupiter, king of the gods. Alarmed at the possibility of a major conflagration as it plunged towards the earth, he loosed off a thunderbolt. The son of Phoebus fell to earth, or rather to water, for he plunged into the River Po, from which his charred body was retrieved by tidy-minded water nymphs and subsequently buried.

Several lessons may be learned from this tale. Never make rash promises. Don't take on tasks for which you are basically unfitted. Don't push father too far. Don't put too much faith in future movements of the heavenly bodies, and so on and so on.

But the most important feature of this myth is that it describes in suitably dramatic form one of the saddest, most common and ultimately destructive constellations of feelings, motives and behaviour known to man. It also provides us with a useful label for this well of misery and mayhem – the Phaeton complex.

In common with all the other topics discussed in this book, the Phaeton complex exemplifies how certain characteristics which evolved to ensure the survival of living organisms, may one day destroy them all. If there is one complex which, more than any other, supports the self-destruct hypothesis that we have built into ourselves the seeds of our own demise, it is this one.

Just how widespread may be the early acquisition and, thenceforth, lifelong possession of this canker remains a matter for conjecture. For our present purposes we will consider just four possible victims of this malaise – those who commit suicide, a certain type of murderer, fat women and British Prime Ministers.

For many species, physical survival depends upon a reciprocal relationship between parents and their young. Parents provide care, food, warmth and protection. And for their part, as a result of being imprinted on their parents, the offspring show attachment behaviour – that is to say they stay close to mother particularly when danger threatens.

Moreover, if they do not receive the requisite attention, the young take steps to rectify this state of affairs. Lambs bleat, piglets grunt and human babies cry.

Although, far down the animal scale, behaviour is motivated towards obtaining those things necessary for survival, their relative importance may vary. For example, according to the experiments of Harlow,[14] a baby monkey prefers a surrogate artificial mother made of soft towelling to one made of wire but equipped with a nipple connected to a supply of milk. Evidently the feel of terry towelling is more comforting than a drink. If lower animals feel 'loved' by their parents these experiences of warmth and softness could be the true origins of this emotion. Certainly, for humans, experiencing those caring responses which involve physical contact, cuddling, caressing and warm motherly smells are probably the beginnings of feeling loved. Later on the experience of feeling loved seems to necessitate two additional requirements – being made to feel one is a worthwhile person, and being secure in the knowledge that one is not just loved but loved by a particular person.

Presumably because parental care is essential for survival, frustration of the need for love, like frustration of the other basic drives, gives rise to some extremely unpleasant feelings – anxiety, fear, anger, jealousy and ultimately hate. And when the deprivation of love occurs in childhood the long-term effects of the Phaeton complex, which may by then be largely unconscious, can, as we shall see, be self-destructive for the individual, and could be cataclysmic for society.

As conceptualised by Choisy[15] the Phaeton complex refers to that painful collection of thoughts and feelings which result from lack of parental love. In the present context, however, it will be taken to include the possible consequences for a child of such eventualities as lack or loss of parents, having parents who are cold and unloving, and of specific traumatic experiences at the hands of such parents.

Whatever the immediate causes, whether it be insufficient social interaction, feelings of rejection, excessive anxiety, or simply the experience of not feeling loved, the results of these early tribulations may be long-lasting and destructive. Thenceforth, the individual so damaged in childhood, may, on the one hand, strive to achieve the love and approval of which he was deprived or, on the other hand, seek retaliation for the wrong done him.

The search for love and seeking for revenge are not, however, mutually exclusive. In accordance with the general principle that survival usually depends upon meeting frustration with aggression, so thwarted love turns to hate. The jealousy which drove Ruth Ellis to shoot her faithless lover, an act for which she subsequently hanged; the misery of Marilyn Monroe which drove her to suicide, and the widespread belief that 'Hell hath no fury like a woman (or man) scorned' may well have their origin in variations of the Phaeton complex.

One of the major dangers of the complex is that it is largely unconscious. Because the events from which it arose were *so* painful we prefer to forget them. There are two unfortunate consequences of this repression. Unawareness of the motives behind an individual's destructive or self-destructive behaviour forestalls their prevention by rational thought. Before he can stop it the damage is done. Secondly, because it is so denied in oneself, and submerged in others, society's belief in the reality of the Phaeton complex remains slight to non-existent. Like death itself, this possibility is one we prefer to ignore.

Be that as it may, it has become clear from a variety of researches[16] that whereas even short periods of parental absence may have adverse effects, albeit of a temporary nature, prolonged maternal deprivation, such as that experienced by children reared in orphanages and similar institutions, can result in permanent damage.

As Wolff says in her work on *Children under Stress*, 'Many investigators have related parent loss in childhood to various kinds of psychiatric and social disturbances in later life. Personality disorders, neurosis, delinquency, and attempted suicide in adult life are all statistically related to having experienced a disrupted family life during childhood.'[17]

The syndrome is not confined to humans. In the research, already mentioned, by Harlow, it has been shown that baby monkeys separated from their mothers may become physically and psychologically handicapped for the rest of their days.

While there is some controversy as to the life-long effects of parental loss in childhood, the main conclusion from studies of bereaved children[18] is that the traumatic experience of losing a parent may have profound and tragic consequences. Typical of specific evidence for this claim are the findings from research which compared different groups of children. In contrast to normals and those attending a dental clinic, twice as many of those attending a psychiatric clinic had suffered parental loss.[19] Of relevance to the supposed longevity of the Phaeton complex was the additional finding that the effects of bereavement in early childhood often became manifest several years later.

As to the claim that some varieties of the Phaeton complex may actually lead to self-destruction, people kill themselves in several ways, by 'accident', by adopting lethal life-styles such as those of drug addicts and alcoholics, and by deliberate suicide, often as an escape from the intolerable feelings of worthlessness which accompany severe depressive illness. While it is possible, if not highly probable, that the Phaeton complex may play a role in all these 'methods', one of the most common, to which it is probably linked, is that of eating oneself to death. By this is meant not some grotesque act of self cannibalism but rather the simple business of over-eating as a compensation for loss of love. That some people adopt this form of self-destruction as a result of events in very early childhood has been suggested by the findings from the following research.[20]

Each member of a class of students was asked to indicate, secretly and on paper, which of their class-mates they liked and which they did not. The experimenters then collected up the pieces of paper and pretended to sort them into two piles – the popular and the unpopular. On the basis of what had in fact, been a purely random allocation, each student was then informed as to whether he (or she) was generally popular or unpopular. Needless to say from that moment on there were two sorts of person sitting in the room – half of them smug, preening and self-congratulatory, the other half bowed, tight-lipped in their misery.

Everyone was then asked to indicate the extent to which they tended to deal with feelings of rejection by indulging in some sort of oral activity such as eating or drinking.

Finally, everyone was shown the subliminal word ·MILK· (presented so briefly that they were not conscious of it) and then asked to learn a list of words some of which were associated with 'milk'.

Then came the test – which words could they recall from the previously learned list? The result was consistent with the common-sense view that the machinery of human memory must have evolved for the gratification of needs. Of all the people who took part it was only those who, on the one hand, had been made to feel rejected and, on the other, used oral behaviour to deal with feelings of rejection, that not only recalled the most 'milk' related words but actually 'recalled' such infantile associations to milk as 'suck' and 'bottle' *which had not been on the learning list*! A hypothetical model to explain this interesting result is shown in Figure 7.3.

The findings from this experiment are consistent with the view that a complex of emotionally charged ideas about a deprivation experienced early in life, may be reactivated by subsequent experiences of a comparable nature, and that this reactivation of ancient memories may initiate behaviour (such as sucking sweets) of a compensatory kind. They are also consistent with the results from further research which suggest a link between an early complex and self-destructive eating.[21]

It is an odd paradox that while one half (at least) of the world tends to perish from malnourishment, the other half shows a predilection for dying from the effects of over-eating. While the under-nourished are victims of poverty and incompetent distribution, the over-fed tend to be victims of their own psychopathology – compulsive nibblers.

It has been estimated that in the United States alone there are over 125,000 tons of surplus adipose tissue. Sliced off the bodies to which it clings and rendered down, it might make enough bars of soap to wash everyone in the world several times over (particularly

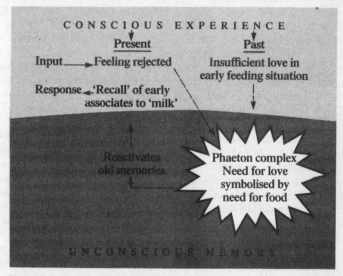

Figure 7.3 Contemporary feelings of rejection re-activate an infantile complex associated with feeling insufficiently loved while being fed in the very early years.

since many of the bodies would now be that much smaller). It would provide sufficient energy to light several major cities or to send a rocket to Venus. And, on the subject of Venus, the removal of all this fat from its present site would make a great many people more sexually attractive than they are at the moment.

Left where it is, the only individuals who benefit from these mountains of fat are those directors of so-called health farms who make a fortune from giving their clients nothing to eat, doctors who treat the multitudinous diseases of the overweight, and undertakers. In more ways than one, all this blubber in the wrong place constitutes an 'immense' problem.

It should occasion no surprise therefore that when Doctor Lloyd Silverman of New York University offered a free course of treatment to help obese women to become slim he did not go short of applicants. The treatment entailed eight weekly visits to his clinic. On each occasion the patients were given a four milli-second flash of a short sentence. For the experimental group the sentence was 'Mommy and I are one', and for the control group it was 'People are walking'. Silverman predicted that whereas the control sentence would have little effect, the huge women who had the symbiotic message would begin eating less and therefore lose weight.

By way of checking his prediction everyone was weighed at the outset and then periodically throughout the rest of the year. At the end of the eight weeks each subject was given this farewell advice, 'Every time you feel tempted to eat a cookie just remember that flash of light and you'll be able to resist the temptation.'

The results bore out his prediction. Whereas those in the control group were unaffected, those in the other showed, and maintained, a significant loss in weight.

The rationale for this experiment is consistent with other evidence for the Phaeton complex. For their survival babies need a close physical relationship with mother. Since thoughts are powered by needs, this gives rise to the fantasy that mother and child are one. This is the symbiotic wish.

It seems reasonable to assume that gratification of this wish is contingent on the fact that, at a very early age, being fed and being loved by mother are closely related if not identical experiences. Under the circumstances it is hardly surprising that stimulation of the mouth and lips becomes associated with being loved, from which it would follow that subsequent experiences of feeling unloved could, to some extent, be assuaged by oral activity – smoking, drinking, thumb-sucking and eating. This is the pattern suggested by the experiment of Spence and Gordon. But suppose that a legacy of the early feeding situation was one of intense frustration, with the symbiotic wish of being as one with mother so totally ungratified that the Phaeton complex becomes implanted as a constant source of anxiety and depression – what then?

One consequence might be a lifelong pattern of over-eating. It has been suggested that not only does over-eating keep at bay the sadness of being unlovable, but that the resulting obesity comes to constitute a sort of armour against the world – a defence against feelings of rejection. It also, as noted earlier, serves to confirm the underlying belief that they *are* unlovable.

When one considers their misery, not to mention the effort and money spent on attempts to lose weight, it is surely obvious that there must be very strong forces compelling the insatiable over-eating which results in rolls of fat. The very fact that Silverman's stout ladies puffed their way across New York in the faint hope of finding a 'cure' suggests that cutting down is no easy matter, which implies, in turn, that something very powerful has got them in its grip. Why not the search for love?

According to this reasoning, the only way to halt the self-destructive impulse to gorge would be to gratify the underlying symbiotic wish. Only by telling the unconscious that 'Mommy and I are one' could the anxiety and depression be allayed and the compulsion diminished. And this is exactly what the Silverman technique appears to achieve.

Dying under a self-inflicted mountain of fat may seem a pitiful waste of life, but in its effects might not be too unpleasant. Unfortunately, this cannot be said about some other outcomes of the Phaeton complex – outcomes which make the plight of huge American women seem (unlike their appearance) relatively slight.

In September 1941 Stephen and Anna Kallinger adopted a small boy.[22] Their ostensible reason for this act was to bring up a child of their own. At a deeper level, they were seeking an insurance for their old age by training up an apprentice to carry on Stephen's trade as a shoemaker. At a much deeper level they were probably, without any conscious insight, being driven by a 'complex' of emotionally charged ideas emanating from their own deranged sexuality. Their consequent behaviour towards the adopted child reflected all three motives.

Unencumbered by the slightest feelings of warmth or humanity, this grim pair set about rearing their adopted son with all the tender simple-mindedness of factory farmers. He was fed, clothed, cleaned and housed in a manner which would have done credit to the director of a Victorian workhouse.

It was a strictly contractual arrangement. In return for being 'rescued' from an orphanage, the boy had to spend his days learning how to be a shoemaker. This 'learning' consisted of collecting shoes, carrying leather and cleaning up the shop. To people like the Kallingers, time, money, work, sanctity and cleanliness are precious commodities. Play, idleness, mess, love, sex and happiness are not. These were the values they applied to the upbringing of the young Kallinger.

Because character formation was so important to the Kallingers, they paid particular attention to the matter of sex. Since for them sex was dirty and a constant threat to peace of mind, they tried to extinguish any sign of this tiresome drive in their adopted son. Not only did this gratify their basic prurience but promised, so they thought, to obviate any chance of the boy being distracted from the path of duty by amorous adventures. Besides imprisoning him in the family home and refusing him the companionship of other children, they taught him that his penis was the source of all evil. To emphasise this point the Kallingers made use of the fact that their adopted son had to undergo a minor operation for a hernia. By explaining that this surgery had been a form of castration they hoped to impress upon the child, that, given the evil nature of his anatomy, they were doing him a favour. Nothing if not appropriate in their methods of training, the instrument with which they illustrated how this operation had been performed was a shoemaker's knife. The knife they said had driven the devil from his 'little bird'. Thenceforth they said he would be impotent. But this was not to be.

Instead of becoming impotent, Joseph Kallinger emerged from these childhood experiences with a grotesque and malignant complex. Thereafter, and for ever more, thanks to the assiduous efforts of his 'parents', his hostility towards them and his sexuality were irrevocably welded together. Though they did not realise it at the time, the Kallingers' plan had gone terribly wrong. Rather than turning him into a psychological eunuch they had produced a psychiatric monstrosity. It is bad enough to be a paranoid schizophrenic. It is bad enough to be so psychologically damaged that sexual arousal can only occur when accompanied by fantasies of sexual mutilation. Thanks to Mr and Mrs Kallinger their adopted child had become both these things.* And this was most unfortunate for, when these two conditions co-exist in the same individual, the risk to society is very great indeed.

As the psychosis took hold the shoemaker's son 'heard' the voice of God telling him to rid the world of people by sexual mutilation. An inevitable part of his childhood experiences was that he had learnt obedience to authority, which is why he now obeyed the hallucinatory voice and tried to do its bidding. By the time he was caught and imprisoned for life, he had succeeded in killing his own child, killing and castrating another, and sexually mutilating, before murdering, a young woman. The Kallingers had a lot to answer for. But the case is not unique.

One of the dangers of unconscious complexes acquired in childhood is that the behaviour to which they give rise may be so appalling, so bizarre, so irrational and so apparently motiveless as to make apprehension of the perpetrator extremely difficult. Such was the case with Kallinger, with Peter Sutcliffe, the Yorkshire ripper, the necrophile John Christie and probably the Moors murderers. That it was not so with Denis Nilsen is simply because this mass murderer continued to live alongside the victims of his neurotic complex. When what was left of them was found, blocking his drains, he was there to provide an explanation.

But, though different in this respect, the crimes of this lonely, mild-mannered, sensitive civil servant, who in the four years up to February 9th, 1983, strangled fifteen young men in the privacy of his attic room, illustrates the fearful pressures which a complex of infantile origin can exert on adult behaviour. It seems, according to his biographer,[23] that events experienced before the age of six

---

* Given a biological predisposition towards schizophrenia, severe stress may well precipitate the disease.

culminating in the sight of the dead body of his grandfather, the only person he had ever really loved, forged a link in Nilsen's mind between love, sexuality and death. This it was which, abetted by loneliness and drink, led him to destroy those unfortunate drifters whose companionship he sought. Unlike Kallinger, who killed for hate, Nilsen killed for love. As revealed by the following excerpt from his account of what he did and why he did it, so overwhelming were the forces of Nilsen's childhood fantasies that they could turn most normal feelings on their head, substituting aesthetic pleasure for revulsion, and compassion for disgust.

Behind me sits Stephen Sinclair on the lazy chair. He was crashed out with drink and drugs. I sit and look at him. I stand up and approach him. My heart is pounding. I kneel down in from of him. I touch his leg and say, 'Are you awake?' There is no response. 'Oh Stephen,' I think, 'here I go again.' I get up and go slowly and casually through to the kitchen. I take some thick string from the drawer and put it on the stainless steel draining board. 'Not long enough,' I think, I go to the cupboard in the front room and search inside. On the floor therein I find an old tie. I cut a bit off and throw the rest away. I go back into the kitchen and make up the ligature. I look into the back room and Stephen has not stirred. Bleep comes in and I speak to her and scratch her head. 'Leave me just now, Bleep. Get your head down, everything's all right.' She wags her tail and slinks off into the front room. Her favourite place is on one of the armchairs in there, where she curls up. Looking back I think she knew what was to happen. Even she became resigned to it. If there was a violent struggle, she would always become excited and start barking. I was relaxed. I never contemplated morality. This was something which I had do to. I walked back into the room. I draped the ligature over one of his knees and poured myself another drink. My heart was pounding very fast. I sat on the edge of the bed and looked at Stephen. I thought to myself, 'All that potential, all that beauty, and all that pain that is his life. I have to stop him. It will soon be over.' He was wearing his white running shoes, very tight drain-pipe black jeans, a thick jersey, leather jacket and blue and white football scarf. I did not feel bad. I did not feel evil. I walked over to him. I removed the scarf. I picked up one of his wrists and let go. His limp arm flopped back on to his lap. I opened one of his eyes and there was no reflex. He was deeply unconscious. I took the ligature and put it around his neck. I knelt by the side of the chair and faced the wall. I took each loose end of the ligature and pulled it tight. He stopped breathing. His hands slowly reached for his neck as I held my grip. His legs stretched out in front of him. There was a very feeble struggle then his arms fell limp down in front of him. I held him there for a couple of minutes. He was limp and stayed that way. I released my hold and removed the string and tie. He had stopped breathing. I spoke to him. 'Stephen, that didn't hurt at all. Nothing can touch you now.'[24]

As pointed out at the beginning of this section, a feature of the unconscious forces which determine behaviour is that the deeds to which they give rise may be so bizarre as to be incorrigible, from which it is a short step to being unbelievable. And one of the reasons is not just that another human being could do such things, but that he should remain so apparently unaffected by the aftermath.

As Masters writes of Nilsen:

It is not *why* he dismembered bodies that bewilders, but *how* he could face himself having done so. The police photographs of human limbs and torn flesh found at Cranley Gardens would make any normally 'sane' person stagger and sweat. How is it possible to wake up in the morning to a man's head in a pot on the gas-stove? How can one place pieces of people in suitcases in the garden shed and leave them there for months at a time, then pick them up, rotting, for incineration? How was he able to tell me, with quasi-scientific curiosity, that the weight of a severed head, when you pick it up by the hair, is far greater than you would imagine? I confess I cannot even guess at answers to such questions, and as I said at the beginning, it is Nilsen's inhuman detachment, his invulnerability to the squalor of human remains, that makes him finally unrecognisable.[25]

There are parallels on a global scale. Despite the written and photographic evidence there are still those who refuse to believe that the Nazis could torture and starve to death millions of innocent people while continuing to live peaceful, well-fed lives amongst the rotting remnants of their crimes. Even though compelled to watch films of the concentration camps after the war was over, many German citizens still managed to convince themselves that none of this had ever happened. By itself such disbelief in past events that are horrific and inexplicable is understandable and not too serious. Society needs its defence mechanisms.

The danger is that if it is so hard to accept the reality of past events, how much harder will it be to accept the possibility of their recurrence.

As to the evidence of unconscious motivation in mass murderers, this could be dismissed as irrelevant to the survival of the species. After all, the Nilsens, Kallingers and Bradys of this world are comparatively rare monstrosities. Whether or not the law defines them as insane, in the eyes of most normal people they are mad as well as bad and of course mad people don't become political leaders.

There are really two issues here. Are so-called normal people sometimes driven to highly destructive acts of behaviour by unconscious motives? And can such 'normal' people ever achieve sufficient political power to bring about what Kallinger had so ardently desired – extermination of the human race? Regrettably the short answer to this question is 'Yes'.

If the Phaeton complex was confined to fat women and deranged murderers it would hardly constitute a serious hazard to the species. Unfortunately it is not.

Indeed, the first and certainly most dramatic evidence for the reality of the complex has come from a study of the last sort of people we would wish to see afflicted with this canker – Prime Ministers.

In the course of compiling biographies of Britain's twenty-four Prime Ministers, from Spencer Perceval in 1809 to Chamberlain in 1937, Lucille Iremonger was surprised to find that fifteen* of these men, that is to say 63 per cent had lost a parent in childhood.[26] Her subsequent examination of the 1921 census showed that for the rest of us, who don't become Prime Ministers, only about 2 per cent become bereaved in childhood. These figures are, to say the least, suggestive of a causal link between losing a parent and achieving the highest office in the land. Obviously there could be several explanations of this phenomenon – an extraordinary series of flukes, or maybe some congenitally ambitious babies seeing their parents as jealous obstacles on the path to Number 10, set about killing Mummy or Daddy by, say, excessive temper tantrums or putting cyanide in the port or some similar, lovable prank. But somehow neither of these hypotheses sounds terribly convincing.

* A sixteenth, born out of wedlock, knew no parents at all.

There is, however, another possibility, that Iremonger's Prime Ministers are what she called, Phaetons, and that their premierships were linked in some way to the complex of that name. Were this so one might expect to find evidence of the fact in the way they conducted their lives and the sort of personality characteristics which they displayed. After all, if losing a parent can have such profound effects as that of turning one into a Prime Minister it must surely have other discernible results. And this is exactly what she found.

According to their various biographers, of the sixteen Prime Ministers who, according to her, were deprived of normal parental love (fifteen through bereavement and one through bastardy), all showed abnormal sensitivity; all, bar one, showed a tendency towards solitariness and reserve, and a propensity for severe states of depression; all, bar two, manifested extreme reactions to subsequent bereavements; and all, with one accord, displayed an obsessive need for love and the achievement of total support. Other characteristics shared by all but one of these men (who was childless) included intense devotion to their own children, recklessness, and belief in the supernatural.

The possible relationships between loss of a parent and these character traits are outlined in Figure 7.4 (overleaf).

Of course there are other contributory factors which, given that the individual is sufficiently intelligent/well-connected/rich and/or a member of a politically orientated family, will facilitate his rise to the top. Not the least of these is the fact that loss of one parent may result in the greater undivided attention of the other, more adult society and more rapid maturing, itself encouraged by the tendency of a deprived child to try and assume the role of the missing parent.

Finally, there is that other feature of the syndrome, the ultimately self-destructive nature of the Phaeton character. Like their namesake in the myth these people appear to bring about their own downfall. Because they are fundamentally depressed, with an inner sense of worthlessness, they carry within them the seeds of their own destruction.

Prototypical of this unhappy band was, appropriately the last on Iremonger's list – Neville Chamberlain. Having, at the age of six, lost both his mother and his grandmother, Chamberlain was further disadvantaged by being left with a famous, formidable and successful father. If he needed an additional torment it was to be found in the goad of his elder brother, who, for most of Neville's life, was always out in front as the recipient of praise and status.

Chamberlain displayed all the characteristics of the severely damaged Phaeton – immature, ultra-sensitive, cold, secretive and depressed. Loathing games, his chronic unhappiness at school reached 'a peak of screaming misery' at Rugby.

The closing chapters of his life were as poignant as the beginnings. Not elected Prime Minister until 1937, by which time he was already sixty-seven, few could have been less well equipped to deal with the rising menace of Nazi Germany.

It is easy to be wise with hindsight, but the pattern which unfolded during the next (and last) three years of his life seems to epitomise the most doleful machinations of the Phaeton complex. First, there was the overwhelming ambition to become the great man of the

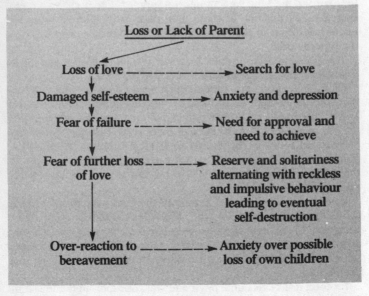

Figure 7.4   Because conflicting with the need to achieve, all this is poorly concealed behind a façade of false bonhomie and sociability.

hour, the beloved saviour of Europe; and then came the reckless
impulsivity – the fateful telegram to Hitler, despatched without even
informing fellow members of his Cabinet. Three times the gullible
Muhammad, umbrella in hand, flew off to meet the crafty 'mountain'
awaiting him in Munich. In his all-consuming search for love, he
deluded himself that even Hitler liked him and could be trusted.
In his life-long need for popularity, approval, love and acclaim he
returned from his third visit clutching the worthless 'piece of paper',
proclaiming to a credulous and congratulatory country, 'Peace in
our time'.

It was his greatest moment, but wretchedly shortlived. As
Iremonger puts it, 'No sooner the mighty triumph than the mighty
fall. No Phaeton ever had a greater one . . . Saint George had not
slain the dragon. Suddenly he wasn't Saint George at all, but a
sanguine old simpleton who had been bamboozled and bluffed by a
ruthless cynical dictator, and worse who had betrayed his country's
honour.'[27]

In May 1940, disgraced, humiliated, Chamberlain fell from power.
As he put it, 'All my world has tumbled to bits in a moment'. In
July of the same year he became ill with cancer and on November
9th he died.

Whether or not one is a dedicated Freudian, the material
considered in this chapter constitutes something of a cautionary
tale. Because of the almost infinite capacity of unconscious human
memory and the apparent inability of the brain to rid itself of the
effects of very early experiences, many of us go through life saddled
with various sorts of hidden complexes. Their consequences can be
deadly.

Because they are clearcut, well documented and fairly extreme,
the cases used to illustrate this thesis have been confined to five sorts
of people – accident-prone pilots, obese women, mad murderers,
Presidents and Prime Ministers. There is no reason to suppose, however, that there are not many others who are driven by unconscious
motives to achieve positions in life which will provide palliatives
for ancient hurts, and vengeful gratification of long-smouldering
resentments.

To take just one small example of how this might work in
practice, there is the sad matter of unnecessary surgery. Though
it now seems that there is little advantage to be gained from the

operation of radical mastectomy, 74 per cent of surgeons, despite the contrary evidence, persist in applying this procedure (as opposed to those which conserve the breast) to 100 per cent of women with breast cancer.[28] Obviously factors of time and expense may play a part (if wrongly) in mastectomy decisions, but could it also be that amongst these surgeons are some who derive a grim satisfaction from getting their revenge on a cold and frustrating mother by the talion punishment of lopping off a symbolic reminder of the person who, in his infancy, cost him so dear? This might well explain the petulance shown by some surgeons when the patient flatly refuses to fall in with their wishes? Of course this is only a hypothesis. But for any surgeon who reads this and blows his top it could well be true. Critics of this view may well say, 'Just because someone gets angry if you suggest he might be practising his profession for some reason of which he's unaware does not mean your hypothesis is necessarily correct'. They might add, 'Wouldn't you get mad if someone suggested that some people become psychologists for the wrong reason?' As to the first point, when it is suggested that a minority group (maybe just one or two individuals out of a population numbering some hundreds) might be driven by neurotic motives of a rather destructive kind, this is surely not going to release an explosion of wrath in those *not* so afflicted – why should it? But if and when the suggestion happens to be true, when it so to speak pricks a complex, then, because the complex had by definition to be repressed, angry denial may well be the favourite last-ditch defence against the threat of discovery.

On the question of sensitive psychologists; yes, of course many aspire to this profession for the 'wrong' reasons: out of voyeurism; or to be one up on the other people (which includes writing books about such pet hates as authoritarian personalities, pompous bullies masquerading as third-rate dignitaries, etc.); or, in the case of academic psychologists, because they are 'psycho-phobes' – people who become psychologists in order to prove to themselves, and hopefully everyone else, that there's no such thing as a psyche!

But what is the significance of all this in the context of this book?

If the world contains people who are driven by unconscious motives to achieve positions in which they can command an immense potential for the destruction of their fellow men, *and*, because unaware of the dark forces which propel them, cannot resist these motives or appreciate the infantile origins and irrationality of their behaviour, *and* are not only able through the defence of rationalisation to avoid the restraining influences of guilt or shame, but are actually encouraged by society to fulfil its aggressive fantasies, *and* are ultimately bent upon their own self-destruction, then, *if* it contains such people our days are truly numbered.

8

Murderous Morality

Whose conscience with injustice is corrupted.
Shakespeare, *King Henry VI, Part 2*

In 1935 a Mrs Alma Rattenbury and her chauffeur/handyman
were tried in the Central Criminal Court for the murder of Mrs
Rattenbury's husband. The jury acquitted Mrs Rattenbury, but her
lover, the chauffeur-handyman George Stoner, was found guilty.
Stoner's death sentence was later commuted to one of life
imprisonment. But for Mrs Rattenbury the future was less
fortunate. Some time after the trial, she took a knife and drove it
into her breast six times. Only after it had pierced her heart thrice
did she finally fall dead.

Of Stoner's guilt and Mrs Rattenbury's innocence there is no
possible doubt, so why did the woman vent such terrible aggression
upon herself? Judging from the impassioned notes she left behind,
it was not a simple matter of bereavement over her husband, or
anticipated bereavement over her lover, but largely because, in the
words of her biographer 'though her life was handed back to her [by
the court] it was handed back in such a shape that it was of no further
use to her'.[1] And why was this? In a way, the person best qualified
to answer this question would have been Mr Justice Humphreys –
the presiding judge.

Criminal courts are not moral courts, but Mr Humphreys evidently
thought otherwise. From the beginning to the end of the trial this
worthy, competent and learned judge did his best to ensure that Mrs
Rattenbury would, quite rightly, be acquitted, but at the same time

104

would be so irrevocably damaged by his words that it would have been kinder to have had her hanged.

According to Mr Humphreys, the silly, highly sexed, compassionate, amoral, warm-hearted Mrs Rattenbury – a woman who would not hurt a fly, who cared deeply for her husband, was 'a disgusting person'. And just in case this fact had escaped the notice of the court, he reiterated it with awful majesty at intervals throughout the trial. So why was she disgusting? Ostensibly, there were three reasons. First, sexually frustrated by her ageing and unresponsive husband, Mrs Rattenbury had not only fallen in love with another but had actually consummated this affection in the usual way. Second, the man she had taken to her bed was twenty years younger than herself; and third, the husband, who was as fond of his wife and concerned for her happiness as she was for him and his happiness, had evidently condoned the *ménage à trois*, which, had it not been for the jealous rage of George Stoner, might have continued indefinitely. As it was, in the course of the trial, Mr Humphreys took care to stigmatise the deceased Mr Rattenbury as a '*Mari complaisant*, not a nice character', but because this quiet, pleasant, generous man was not there to hear him, Mr Humphreys turned his righteous (self-righteous) scorn on the deceased's undoubtedly attractive widow. There was, of course, a fourth reason for Mr Humphreys's diatribe, but this was more to do with his psychology than that of Mrs Rattenbury. Mr Humphreys, scrupulously fair and highly competent in legal matters, took great pains to discover what, in modern parlance, we might describe as Mrs Rattenbury's guilt button, and then pressed it with unremitting heaviness throughout the trial. He did so, secure in the knowledge that the newspapers would so build upon his words that the frightful enormities of the Rattenbury's *modus vivendi* would be broadcast far and wide. To ensure total character assassination, Mr Justice Humphreys chose his words carefully, if without sufficient attention to the semantics of the English language. Much, for example, was made of the occasion when the two lovers (in the full knowledge of Mr Rattenbury) went up to London on a shopping spree. Between trips round Harrods they resided, ostensibly in separate rooms, in Kensington's Royal Palace Hotel. To the learned judge, however, this was an 'orgy' and he deliberately labelled it as such. Tennyson Jesse, from whose account of the case this tale is taken, was, however, clearly puzzled by the label:

It is difficult to imagine an orgy at the Royal Palace Hotel in Kensington, and indeed, I have never been able to discover of what an orgy consists. It is associated, more or less vaguely, in the popular mind with the 'historical' productions of Mr C de Mille; glasses of wine, dancing girls, tiger skins and cushions are some of its component parts. The private coming together of a pair of lovers and their normal physical ecstasies, however reprehensible these may be morally, do not seem well described by the word 'orgy'. Even shopping at Harrods does not quite come under this heading.[2]

But to Mr Humphreys, and therefore to the court and thence to the world at large, it was an 'orgy' and so this is how Mrs Rattenbury knew to what she had been party. And it was in this light she knew people would regard her.

So we have to ask another question. Why did Mr Humphreys, who was probably in all other respects a kindly and humane man, use his position to hound a woman to her death for sexual misdemeanours of a totally uncriminal kind? Unfortunately we cannot know exactly (or even inexactly) what was going on in Humphreys's mind and so must stick to some general principles which seem to fit the case.

At the beginning of Chapter 5 it was noted that the psyche of most mature civilised adults has three component parts – id, ego and superego. It is the last of these which we need to consider for an explanation of Mr Humphreys's behaviour in the case of the Crown v. Mrs Rattenbury.

The superego or conscience is not, unfortunately, a model of simplicity, for it too has three components. First, it comprises a set of moral principles, which are in fact taken over from the individual's parents. The so-called voice of conscience is in fact their voice, sometimes muted, sometimes strident, often hideously distorted, but unmistakably theirs. Unconsciously and involuntarily the child uses his internalised parents to police his id. Their rules and regulations, moralising and distinctions between right and wrong become his. If he breaks the rules he gets a sharp reminder in the form of guilt, which, underneath, so we are told, is largely fear of parental retribution. Depending on the 'crime' this may be castration or, even worse, abandonment by those upon whom his survival depends.

A second component of this mental system is something we touched on briefly when considering Hitler – an idealised image of the self to which we would like to measure up. Since attributes of this self-image may include not only notions of beauty, success and status, but also such aspects of morality as 'goodness', 'godliness', etc. we should perhaps conceive of it as overlapping both ego and superego. Since the materialistic motives of the ego may be irreconcilable with the spiritual aspirations of the superego (as exemplified in the old problem of rich men trying to enter heaven) there is room for internal conflict within the ego itself. One way of dealing with this conflict is to adopt the Protestant Work Ethic. Another might be to join the SDP. But there are others, like the time-honoured practice of committing murder in God's name.

David Yallop claims to have discovered the most recent case which may come within this particular practice. For hypocrisy, greed, corruption, megalomania and mayhem by men belonging to an organisation which purports to promulgate the teachings of Christ, whose luminaries busy themselves with purveying morality to the rest of mankind, there must be few better or nastier examples of collusion between components of the human psyche than that, adopted by those prelates and bankers within the Vatican, concerning the death of Pope John Paul I because it appeared he exposed their criminal activities.[3]

And finally there is the third component of the superego, which, to be unashamedly anthropomorphic, we might describe as the 'policeman' himself – the watching eye, which not only notes with unfailing vigilance any failure to measure up, but punishes accordingly.

So much for a brief rundown on the dynamics of conscience. What are their relevance to the subject matter of this book and Mr Justice Humphreys in particular? First, we must be quite clear about one thing – the evolution of a capacity for conscience was (and is) essential for survival. The corporate efforts of humanity and ultimately civilisation depended upon man's ability to acquire moral values – a sense of right and wrong. Without this capacity every other person would have to be a policeman and all the rest venereologists.

But unfortunately, like most products of our evolutionary history, superego can give rise to some unfortunate and sometimes lethal side-effects, just one of which is exemplified by Mr Humphreys's treatment of the wretched Mrs Rattenbury. In Chapter 9 we will examine the deeper reasons for aggressive persecution in the guise of sententious morality, but for the moment there are other issues which need to be pursued.

To most decent, well-behaved, civilised people the faintest suggestion that morality can be harmful is probably hard to accept. How
could manifestations of conscience, that set of principles without
which civilisation would be impossible, conceivably be wrong? In
several ways. First, they can give rise to gross incompetence. There
is hardly any sphere of human activity which does not from time to
time invite incompetence through the disturbance of rationality by
intrusive conscience. Typical are instances of bungling executioners.
Whatever one's views on capital punishment as a means of regulating
society, there are two things about it which are surely indisputable.
If it has to be done, then someone has to do it. If it has to be done,
then it should be done competently with minimum suffering to the
victim. Over the years these necessary, if not sufficient, criteria, for
efficient removal of unwanted transgressors have been met by the
appointment and training of executioners and the provision of the
means, be it an axe, rope, electrode or a gas chamber, for achieving
the desired end (of the victim).

So far so good. Why then, with everything provided and after a
long apprenticeship to the trade, should horrific cases of incompetence occur? One reason could be that the executioner is bringing
to his task the underlying thought that killing people is wrong. An
important component of this horrid business is a double conflict.
As a legitimate outlet for suppressed aggression, executing another
human being is an ideal pastime. Not only is it attractive to the id's
propensity for aggression, it also appeals to the ego. Public executioners are people of importance – prima donnas. They have rarity
value. There are not (fortunately) many of them about. At an ego
level they probably take pride in their job and are experts in such
technicalities as the optimal relationship between the weight of the
human body, the strength of rope and the extent of the drop. By
the same token there is probably not much they do not know about
honing a blade, or the ideal back swing. But both sets of motives
are in conflict with those aspects of the superego which have to do
with the inhibition of aggression and the moral precept 'Thou shalt
not kill'. So what can these unfortunates do? Either they must
resign their posts to become butchers of no importance, or keep on
hacking and slicing like indifferent golfers determined to master a
skill for which they are really quite unfitted. Of course, they employ
strategies to reduce the conflict – conscious thought that they are

rather special Civil Servants performing a necessary function for the state, and the wearing of a mask to hide their shame. But neither of these defences is of much comfort to the person whose half-severed head is still lying on the block.

Let us now move away from such grizzly matters to something less dramatic and rather more widespread; marital breakdown. Marriages fail for numerous reasons, but one of them is some form of sexual incompetence. For those without 'sexual hang-ups' it is probably difficult to imagine not being able to have a complete, intimate and satisfying physical relationship with the person you love. But every day and especially every night those triple demons of the bedroom – frigidity, impotence and premature ejaculation – erode the happiness of many loving couples. Whence do these problems come? Undoubtedly some derive from such parental injunctions, introjected long ago, as 'Sex is dirty', 'All men are beasts', and 'If I catch you doing that again Dad will cut it off'. So strongly embedded in the superego are these voices from the past that it is like having mother, with a frown, standing sentry by the bed. No wonder the unsuccessful lovers lie wrapped in misery.

None of this is lethal; a few public executioners and a million broken marriages will not terminate the human race. So are there other scenarios wherein intrusive conscience (unconscious superego) could result in disaster on a grander scale, claiming lives rather than just pain or unhappiness?

There are indeed. Both have to do with the superego. Both, together or apart, may ultimately destroy us all. Let us start with the simplest, the relationship between vocational choice and authoritarianism as a prime factor in military incompetence.

To summarise the thesis of my book[4] on this topic – military organisations may be likened to well-defended fortresses in an otherwise peaceful society. Since they constitute an enormous potential for destruction (id) they have to be constrained by the rigid rules of militarism (the superego) – that collection of rituals and regulations which ensures that no one steps out of line and begins, so to speak, loosing off at the wrong time and in the wrong direction.

Not surprisingly, military organisations tend to attract a minority of people who are themselves like little military organisations, people whose natural fund of aggression and sexuality is held down by an oppressive inhibitory counterforce. Such authoritarian characters are drawn towards hierarchical organisations as like unto like. This is all to the good. It is nice to see square pegs entering square holes and then developing satisfying symbiotic relations with the parent organisation. Military organisations require obedience, punctuality, cleanliness, and a readiness not to question orders from above, and these gifts are exactly what such people have to offer. So they get on well because they fit in so well.

But it is just because they fit in so well that they have an above average chance of reaching positions that they are ill-equipped to fill. Being a top military commander is one of the most difficult jobs in the world – flair, leadership, creativity, imagination, originality are just some of the traits required for inspiring one's own side and out-thinking the enemy. But these characteristics are the very opposite of those possessed by the rigid, close-minded conformists who, largely through not blotting their copy books, have, in days gone by, reached the highest levels of the military hierarchy. It is through such people that we lost 20,000 men in the first two hours of the Battle of the Somme. As Priestley remarked of this venture, the Generals at war might just as well have emerged from their headquarters with machine-guns blazing against the British soldiers.

Before leaving this vexatious matter of the role of superego in military incompetence, there are two final points. The first concerns an apparent inability to learn from past experience. It is a fact of history that the world's greatest commanders, men like Shaka, Wellington and Nelson, were significantly unencumbered by restrictive super-egos. Between them they displayed characteristics quite the opposite of those associated with authoritarianism – humour, sexiness, disobedience, assertiveness, unconventionality and, most important of all, they were able when the occasion demanded to display uninhibited aggression. Between them they provide a valid template of what one should be looking for if choosing professionals in violence – big uninhibited ids to fling against the foe. And so one would have expected that since the prime purpose of a military organisation is to win wars, care would be taken to select commanders to fit the historical mould. And yet, judging from a report by Graham Turner,[5] the ethos of the 1930s, when Montgomery-Massingberd (quite one of the worst Chiefs of the Imperial General Staff this country has ever had) pressed for the compulsory retirement of divorced officers, might possibly be with us still. From his study of Forces Chiefs Turner concludes:

> They also uphold a moral code which is a good deal less elastic than that which now obtains in many parts of the Church of England . . . as for divorce [opined one of the chiefs] the rate was lower in the army than in the outside world though, sadly, not much. But, whereas in other walks of life it was of no concern to an employer whether you were divorced, married, or even queer, it never went unconsidered in the services. Under certain circumstance it [presumably 'it' did not include married] could still provide grounds for chucking someone out. No, there had never been a Chief of Staff who's been divorced.

Let us be quite clear about all this. In no way are these words intended to cast aspersions on our present Chiefs of Staff. No doubt they are fine, dedicated and intelligent officers performing excellently their various and difficult roles. But, and this is the point, if present Chiefs of Staff have the stature of a Nelson or a Napoleon this is surely not because they have never been divorced. If the findings of Mr Turner reflect the criteria of military selection then society has got it wrong again.

As to why there should be such emphasis on moral standards in the armed services there are at least three non-mutually-exclusive reasons. First, at lower levels of the military hierarchy emotional entanglements with the wrong person could be very disruptive of good order and military discipline. Second, since the stock in trade of the military is violence and soldiers have the wherewithal to kill each other in large numbers, the possibility of murderous quarrels, *crimes passionnel*, blackmail and fragging of officers has to be reduced by the imposing of these rules and regulations. Finally, for people whose life's work is killing other people, for those who are, so to speak, professional breakers of the sixth commandment, it is surely understandable if they compensate by stricter observance of the seventh commandment.

Though illustrated in the context of military mistakes the present thesis obviously applies in many other walks of life. In the Church, in law, medicine, industry or the universities, there is much to attract people with an authoritarian superego. As a general rule of thumb the greater its potential for destructive behaviour the more authoritarian an organisation has to be, i.e. the greater the power the fiercer the brakes. Thus it is that the police, who from time to time shoot the wrong people, and the medical profession, who from time to time cut off the wrong leg or take out the wrong eye, are (have to be) far more authoritarian than, say, the Royal School of Needlework. I have singled out the military for special mention because the incompetence of military commanders constitutes a far greater threat to the future of mankind than does, say, that of authoritarian parsons, closed minded industrialists or prejudiced Professors.

However, incompetence brought about by too much superego is less to be feared than two other aberrations of man's moral structures – obedience to authority, however misguided, evil and/or dangerous that authority may be, and collusions between an individual's conscience and his id.

When Milgram wrote, 'This is a fatal flaw nature has designed into us and which in the long run gives our species only a moderate chance of survival',[6] he could have been referring to any of those obvious hazards to survival which we have so far considered. But he was not. He was in fact talking about something which many people would regard as a plus, even a necessity for survival – obedience.

Sometimes they are right, but there are exceptions to this rule. In 1952 the pilot of a Lockheed 60 returning from Nice made an unscheduled night stop. He complained of feeling tired. The company ordered him to continue the journey. While preparing the flight plan he reported feeling very tired and appeared to dread the impending take-off. He asked the local controller to prohibit him from flying. The controller refused. Shortly afterwards, in fine weather, he took off. Within minutes the Lockheed crashed, killing all seventeen people on board.[7]

Several reasons could be given for this pilot risking and then taking the lives of himself and his passengers. Whatever guided his behaviour, one thing is certain: without any physical coercion he felt compelled to carry out a potentially highly dangerous and, in the event, catastrophic task at the behest of people safely on the ground.

Clearly there are parallels between this case and that of government officials, who, from the safety of their offices, order men to risk their lives in battle for causes of sometimes very dubious validity. But Milgram's jaundiced view of obedience depended upon something other than such everyday examples, namely the results from a series of experiments in which 'ordinary, decent, law-abiding citizens' were asked to give what they believed to be near lethal electric shocks to 'helpless victims'.

For those unfamiliar with the work of this American Professor of Psychology, Milgram was interested in what has been called the Eichmann syndrome. On trial in Israel for the war crime of sending some millions of people to their deaths in the Nazi extermination camps, Eichmann's defence was that he was only obeying orders. This is an interesting plea against conviction for mass murder. If admissible it would exonerate all but one of those who played a part in the 'final solution'. From the guard on the train that carried Jews to the death camp to the man who tipped canisters of Zyklon B into the gas chamber, all were simply carrying out their orders. If admissible then it should, in principle, exonerate all but the man at the top of the liquidation programme. But it was not considered an adequate defence, and so Eichmann was hanged.

Though unsuccessful, Eichmann's plea does raise further questions. Did the 60,000 people whose job it was to exterminate six million Jews carry out their duties *because* they were obedient to orders from above or *because* they were sadists, glad of the excuse (the accepting of orders) to exercise their sadism, or was it because they were both obedient and sadistic? One approach to answering these questions would be to ask a further, simpler one – could obedience alone drive people who are not sadists into cold-blooded destruction of their fellow men? (The investigation of acts not committed in 'cold blood', i.e. as a consequence of some strong emotion, would not succeed in isolating obedience as the crucial variable). This was the question to which Milgram addressed himself. His subjects were those members of the general public – ordinary middle-class Americans, who responded to an advertisement (Figure 8.1, overleaf).

Note that the advertisement gave no details about the forthcoming experiment; nothing about punishment; not a word about electric shock.

Those who answered it were invited to act as teachers in an experiment which purported to investigate the extent to which punishment might facilitate learning. The 'learner' sat in one room, the 'teacher' in another. Every time the 'learner' made a mistake the 'teacher' had to administer an 'electric shock'. As the number of errors increased so the 'teacher' had to increase the severity of the shock.

Public Announcement

WE WILL PAY YOU $4.00 FOR
ONE HOUR OF YOUR TIME

Persons Needed for a Study of Memory

*We will pay five hundred New Haven men to help us complete a scientific study of memory and learning. The study is being done at Yale University.

*Each person who participates will be paid $4.00 (plus 50c carfare) for approximately 1 hour's time. We need you for only one hour: there are no further obligations. You may choose the time you would like to come (evenings, weekdays, or weekends).

*No special training, education, or experience is needed. We want:

Factory workers	Businessmen	Construction workers
City employees	Clerks	Salespeople
Laborers	Professional people	White-collar workers
Barbers	Telephone workers	Others

All persons must be between the ages of 20 and 50. High school and college students cannot be used.

*If you meet these qualifications, fill out the coupon below and mail it now to Professor Stanley Milgram, Department of Psychology, Yale University, New Haven. You will be notified later of the specific time and place of the study. We reserve the right to decline any application.

*You will be paid $4.00 (plus 50c carfare) as soon as you arrive at the laboratory.

TO:
PROF. STANLEY MILGRAM, DEPARTMENT OF PSYCHOLOGY, YALE UNIVERSITY, NEW HAVEN, CONN.
I want to take part in this study of memory and learning. I am between the ages of 20 and 50. I will be paid $4.00 (plus 50c carfare) if I participate.

NAME (Please Print) ....

ADDRESS ....

TELEPHONE No ....Best time to call you ....

AGE................... OCCUPATION ....SEX ....
CAN YOU COME:

WEEKDAYS .............EVENINGS.............WEEKENDS.............

Figure 8.1

The results from a number of such experiments were unequivocal in answering Milgram's question.

Despite the fact that the 'teachers' (the real subjects of the experiment) believed the 'shocks' were extremely painful and could hear the (simulated) screams of the learner, many of them had little hesitation about moving the shock-control lever to the further end of the dial, way past the point marked 'Danger 450 volts'.

From Milgram's account of the course and outcome of these studies there are several points germane to our present purpose. First, when there was no vocal feedback (e.g. grunts, screams) from the 'victim' most of his subjects went blithely up to the maximum punishment voltage. When vocal feedback was introduced some of the subjects became increasingly disturbed at what they believed they were doing to the 'learner'. The following excerpts from exchanges between Milgram and his subjects typify this state of affairs.

Morris Braverman is a thirty-nine-year-old social worker. He looks older than his years because of his bald pate and serious demeanor. His brow is furrowed, as if all the world's burdens were carried in his face. He appears intelligent and concerned. The impression he creates is that of enormous overcontrol, that of a repressed and serious man, whose finely modulated voice is not linked with his emotional life. He speaks impressively but with perceptible affectation. As the experiment proceeds, laughter intrudes into his performance. At first, it is a light snicker, then it becomes increasingly insistent and disruptive. The laughter seemed triggered by the learner's screams.

When the learner refuses to answer and the experimenter instructs him to treat the absence of an answer as equivalent to a wrong answer, he takes his instruction to heart.

Before administering 315 volts he asserts officiously to the victim, 'Mr Wallace, your silence has to be considered as a wrong answer'. Then he administers the shock. He offers halfheartedly to change places with the learner, then asks the experimenter, 'Do I have to follow these instructions literally?' He is satisfied with the experimenter's answer that he does. His very refined and authoritative manner of speaking is increasingly broken up by wheezing laughter.

The experimenter's notes on Mr Braverman at the last few shocks are:

Almost breaking up now each time gives shock. Rubbing face to hide laughter. Ratting eyes, trying to hide face with hand, still laughing. Cannot control his laughter at this point no matter what he does. Clenching fist pushing it onto table.

After the experiment, Mr Braverman, who regarded himself as 'a nice person', admitted that he had been in considerable conflict. He said, 'my impulse was to plead with him, talk with him, encourage him, try to ally myself with his feelings, work at this so we could get this through together and I wouldn't have to hurt him'. This may have been his 'impulse' but he did not in fact show any sign of, or mention, the possibility of disobedience.

A year later he told Milgram:

> What appalled me was that I could possess this capacity for obedience and compliance to a central idea, i.e. the value of a memory experiment even after it became clear that continued adherence to this value was at the expense of violation of another value, i.e. don't hurt someone else who is helpless and not hurting you. As my wife said, 'You can call yourself Eichmann'. I hope I can deal more effectively with any future conflicts of values I encounter.[8]

This subject, like several others, betrayed signs of conflict between obeying orders and feelings of compassion. Nevertheless, obedience to the instructions of an 'authority figure' triumphed over compassion *beyond the point at which he knew his victim was suffering pain*.

But there were others who, whatever they might have felt at some deeper level, showed neither conflict nor compassion. Stolid obedience carried them through.

> Jack Washington is a black subject, age thirty-five. . . He is a soft man, a bit heavy and balding, older-looking than his years. His pace is very slow and his manner impassive. . .
>
> When the victim's first protests are heard, he turns toward the experimenter, looks sadly at him, then continues reading the word pairs. The experimenter does not have to tell him to continue. Throughout the experiment he shows almost no emotion or bodily movement. He does what the experimenter tells him in a slow steady pace that is set off sharply against the strident cries of the victim. Throughout, a sad, dejected expression shows on his face. He continues to the 450-volt level, asks the experimenter what he is to do at that point, administers two additional shocks on command, and is relieved of his task.[9]

Interviewed after the experiment, this subject said he had guessed the shocks were 'extremely painful', but when taxed about who was to blame for the victim's suffering claimed that this was largely the responsibility of the experimenter, then the victim and least of all himself. He maintained, 'I was following orders. . . I was told to go on and did not get a cue to stop.'

If he felt any inner conflict he certainly didn't show it.

Evidence of conflict, in at least some of Milgram's subjects, when there was vocal feedback, suggested a further question – would close physical proximity of the victim curtail obedience? After all, it is one thing to damage people at a distance but quite another to see, perhaps actually feel, their suffering bodies. Even Haig, who sent thousands to their deaths, could not bear to visit military hospitals and so witness the consequences of his generalship. Even Eichmann and Himmler, who were quite happy to sign millions of death warrants in the remote seclusion of their offices, became physically ill when confronted with the effects of their bureaucratic antics.

Perhaps, under conditions of close proximity even the most obedient American citizens would disobey?

Mr Batta is a thirty-seven-year-old welder. . . He has a rough-hewn face that conveys a conspicuous lack of alertness. His over-all appearance is somewhat brutish. An observer described him as a 'crude mesomorph of obviously limited intelligence'. But . . . he relates to the experimenter with a submissive and deferential sweetness.

He has some difficulty in mastering the experimental procedure and needs to be corrected by the experimenter several times. He shows appreciation for the help and willingness to do what is required. The experiment is the Touch-Proximity variation. After the 150-volt level, Batta has to force the learner's hand down on the shock plate, since the learner himself refuses to touch it. When the learner first complains, Mr Batta pays no attention to him. His face remains impassive, as if to dissociate himself from the learner's disruptive behavior. When the experimenter instructs him to force the learner's hand down, he adopts a rigid mechanical procedure. He tests the generator switch. When it fails to function, he immediately forces the learner's hand onto the shock plate. All the while he maintains the same rigid mask. The learner, seated alongside him, begs him to stop, but with robotic impassivity, he continues the procedure. What is extraordinary is his apparent total indifference to the learner; he hardly takes cognizance of him as a human being. Meanwhile, he relates to the experimenter in a submissive and courteous fashion.

At the 330-volt level, the learner refuses not only to touch the shock plate but also to provide any answers. Annoyed, Batta turns to him, and chastises him: 'You better answer and get it over with. We can't stay here all night'. These are the only words he directs to the learner in the course of the hour. Never again does he speak to him. The scene is brutal and depressing: his hard, impassive face showing total indifference as he subdues the screaming learner and gives him shocks. He seems to derive no pleasure from the act himself, only quiet satisfaction at doing his job properly.

When he administers 450 volts, he turns to the experimenter and asks, 'Where do we go from here, Professor?' His tone is deferential and expresses his willingness to be a cooperative subject, in contrast to the learner's obstinacy.

Mr Batta's attitude, after the event, was distinctly extrapunitive. 'Well, we have more or less a stubborn person (the learner). If he understood what this here was, he would'a went along without getting the punishment'. In his opinion the learner brought punishment on himself.

Asked whether he felt tense or nervous during the experiment, he replied, 'The only time I got a little – I wouldn't say nervous – I got *disgusted*, is when he wouldn't cooperate'. As to the issue of responsibility, he did not seem to grasp the concept.

At the end of the post-experimental interview, he told Milgram how honoured he had been to help him adding, 'Sir, sorry it couldn't have been a full experiment'. He had done his honest best. It was only the deficient behaviour of the learner that had denied the experimenter full satisfaction. According to Milgram:

> In a questionnaire returned by Mr Batta several months later, he informs us that he followed the experimenter's instructions to the end, that he fully believed the learner was getting painful shocks, and that the experiment had not bothered him at all. He believes more experiments of this sort should be carried out, and he answers 'yes' to our question of whether he has learned something of personal value. But he does not tell us what.[10]

The evidence of eye-witnesses supports the view that far from enjoying their role these obedient subjects were in a state of considerable conflict: driven from within to perform acts which they knew to be wrong but were powerless to prevent. It is significant that when asked in a subsequent experiment[11] to give their time to a good cause – i.e. making calls in a campaign to save California's redwood trees – it was those subjects who believed they had been administering shocks who complied with the request.

The very act of guilt expiation that can, so to speak, pay tomorrow for what one does today suggests that as a keeper of morality conscience is unreliable to say the least. In a nuclear age we have to ask, what if there is no tomorrow?

Perhaps all this is being unduly pessimistic. After all, in one experiment only twenty-six of Milgram's forty subjects were prepared to deliver the maximum voltage shock of which the apparatus was capable. Provided society is run by people like the other fourteen subjects, we ought to be all right. But since obedience to authority remains one of the best ways of rising in a hierarchy it is unlikely that it would be. Even so, now that Milgram has put obedience on the map, surely we can guard against this particular threat to survival.

This notion that to be forewarned is to be forearmed assumes that people want to be forewarned – that society would, for example, be as grateful to Milgram as it would to any other scientist who discovers the nature of some other great danger to human health and happiness. Certainly there are some people, including the author of this book, who consider the investigation of obedience as one of the greatest contributions which experimental psychology has made. However, astonishingly, these were not the sort of attitudes expressed towards Milgram. In the house journal of the American Psychological Association he was taken to task.

This career-damaging criticism of Milgram by social psychologist Diana Baumrind[12] was based on three ethical considerations. First, he was wrong in deceiving his subjects as to the true purpose of the experiment. Second, as a necessary part of this deception, he was wrong in letting them believe they really were inflicting pain on another human being. And third, worst of all, he was wrong to put them in a conflict situation that some of them found stressful.

Counter-arguments, some of which Milgram included in his reply to Baumrind, may be summarised as follows:

1   His subjects *volunteered* to take part in the experiment.

2   Neither Milgram nor any of the psychologists whom he consulted *before* the investigation believed that these volunteers would behave in the way they did.

3   Apart from what turned out to be their inborn urge to obey an 'authority' figure, there was nothing to stop them refusing to comply with the instruction to deliver near-lethal shocks.

4   After the experiment all subjects were fully debriefed and assured that they had not in fact hurt anybody and had nothing to be ashamed of – that their behaviour was normal and understandable.

5   Far from criticising Milgram, his subjects maintained that, though stressed, they were glad to have taken part and discovered important aspects of their own psychology.

Typical are the following comments by one of the subjects, 'Participation in the "shock experiment" . . . has had a great impact on my life. . . When I was a subject in 1964, though I believed that I was hurting someone, I was totally unaware of why I was doing so. Few people ever realize when they are acting according to their own beliefs and when they are meekly submitting to authority. . .'

This same subject asked whether any other participants had reacted similarly, and whether, in Milgram's opinion, participation in the study could have this effect.

Milgram replied:

> The experiment does, of course, deal with the dilemma individuals face when they are confronted with conflicting demands of authority and conscience, and I am glad that your participation in the study has brought you to a deeper personal consideration of these issues. Several participants have informed me that their own sensitivity to the problem of submission to authority was increased as a result of their experience in the study. If the experiment has heightened your awareness of the problem of indiscriminate submission to authority, it will have performed an important function.

The subject went on:

'The experience of the interview doesn't lessen my strong belief of the great impact of the experiment on my life. . .

'You have discovered one of the most important causes of all the trouble in the world. . . I am grateful to have been able to provide you with a part of the information necessary for that discovery. . .

'With sincere thanks for your contribution to my life. . .'

Comments from other subjects included: 'This experiment has strengthened my belief that man should avoid harm to his fellow men even at the risk of violating authority', and 'I think people should think more deeply about themselves and their relation to their world and to other people. If this experiment serves to jar people out of their complacency, it will have served its end.'[13]

Most important of all is the fact that had Milgram not deceived his subjects into believing that they were hurting the 'learner' the whole experiment would have been worthless; in which case he would never have discovered that the need to obey can overcome the tugs of conscience and compassion. This has been substantiated by other work.

In 1972 Sheridan and King repeated Milgram's experiment, but this time the 'learner' was not a human but a puppy, and the shocks were real.[14] The results were similar to those obtained by Milgram, but there was an additional and disquieting discovery. Despite the fact that they could hear the yelps and howls of their canine victim, *all* the female subjects in this study used the maximum level of shock. It seems that, in this instance anyway, the need to comply with the instructions of an authority figure is not only stronger in women but can actually override the more maternal, compassionate feelings with which they are normally associated.

Fortunately for mankind the writer is not alone in taking the view that in these researches (unlike many others which have not attracted such opprobrium) the end more than justifies the means. Typical of the many favourable responses are the following comments.[15]

That [Milgram's] pioneer work in this field is attacked as being unethical, [is] simply because people like to shut their eyes to undesirable behavior, preferring to investigate memory, forgetting of nonsense syllables. . .

Milgram is making a momentous and meaningful contribution to our knowledge of human behavior. . . When Milgram's initial study appeared, he was already well aware that an area of scientific investigation was being opened up which would lead to reproaches and condemnation. . . To engage in such studies as Milgram has requires strong men with strong scientific faith and a willingness to discover that to man himself, not to 'the devil' belongs the responsibility for and the control of his inhumane actions.

Milgram's experiment seems to me one of the best carried out in this generation. It shows that the often stated opposition between meaningful, interesting humanistic study and accurate, empirical quantitative research is a false one: the two perspectives can be combined to the benefit of both. . .

Milgram, in exploring the conditions which produce such destructive obedience, and the psychological processes which lead to such attempted abdications of responsibility, seems to me to have done some of the most morally significant research in modern psychology.

So what are we to make of the hostility handed out to Milgram? Consider an analogous case. Suppose that, having surveyed the present highly dangerous scene of international politics, a social scientist makes the not unreasonable hypothesis that one of the main reasons for the election of disastrous leaders is that people tend to be swayed by the quantity rather than the quality of their verbal utterances. To test this idea he carries out the following experiment.

Four volunteers are invited to participate in a study of their ability to discuss an important topical issue. They are seated round a table. In front of each is a red and a green light bulb, so shielded that each person can only see his pair of lights. The experimenter then says, 'Your contribution to the discussion will be monitored. When you are doing well this will be signalled by a flash of your green light. But if you get a flash on the red light this means that you are not doing too well. In this way we hope to improve your performance as discussants.'

The experimenter then leaves the room and chooses at random which one of the four subjects he will make group leader. Without hearing a word of what they are saying he sets out to modify their behaviour by differential reinforcement, that is to say, the arbitrarily chosen leader is given significantly more green and fewer red flashes than the other subjects. The effects are quite dramatic. The verbal output and self-confidence of the unrewarded subjects steadily diminish while those of the 'leader' visibly increase which, in turn, further reduces the confidence of his companions. By the end of the experiment the chosen subject has indeed become leader and the others his followers. This study[16] has several features in common with the Milgram research. The problem being investigated has considerable social significance.

Its investigation involved deceiving the subjects as to the true purpose of the research. The effects were at least mildly stressing for the followers – they were made to feel inferior. Even the leader may have suffered after the debriefing; he was probably upset to find he had been fooled and that his growing self-confidence was quite unjustified. Finally, in a world which chooses its Presidents and Prime Ministers on the basis of shallow, irrelevant, and often inane criteria, the results are indeed important if not alarming.

But, unlike Milgram's, this research provoked no protest. Why? There could well be two, non mutually exclusive reasons. First, because the results were generally less sensational, they probably aroused less professional jealousy. Second, they did not conflict with an almost sacred belief in the importance of obedience. Obedience is the very cement of socialisation. From earliest childhood enormous emphasis is laid on its importance. Few things are more upsetting to parents than the disobedience of their children. Without obedience to authority there would be anarchy. Socialisation depends upon hierarchical organisation and corporate effort directed from above. Without obedience there could be no hierarchical organisation. Without obedience to authority we would still be back in the jungle. Under the circumstances it is hardly surprising that any move to denigrate obedience (and therefore threaten to lessen its power) meets with disapproval.

A curious feature of the criticisms heaped upon Milgram is that they do not include the obvious point that it is not obedience *per se* but the behaviour of some obedient people which threatens human survival. All Milgram did was to show that in certain contrived circumstances some people, like the egregious Mr Batta, would behave in a disagreeable way. Comparable research on sexual or drinking behaviour might well have shown that, while most people enjoy sex or drinking, a minority, when given the temptation, act rapaciously or drive when drunk. It would obviously be ridiculous to conclude from this that sex or drinking were dangerous in themselves. In other words, it is not just the tendency to obey which needs to be deplored but the combination of this with something else.

What is this something else? The short answer is the context in which the obedience occurs, that is to say, the personality make-up of the individual concerned and how this manifests itself in particular social situations. Consider the following two cases.

It is 1893. Two parallel lines of battleships, one led by the flagship HMS *Victoria*, the other by HMS *Camperdown*, were steaming peacefully through the calm blue waters of the Mediterranean. And then Vice-Admiral Tryon, Commander-in-Chief of this British fleet, issued the order that the fleet should reverse direction by turning *inwards*. It was intended as a good test of ship handling by his subordinate commanders. Unfortunately the distance between the two lines of ships was less than their combined turning circles. (Once before, earlier in his career, Tryon had narrowly escaped a major disaster by confusing the diameter of a turning circle with its radius. Geometry was not his strong suit.) Rear-Admiral Markham, aboard HMS *Camperdown*, received the order with dismay. No stranger to geometry, he knew it spelled disaster.

But, after momentary hesitation and some long-distance exhortation by his Commander-in-Chief, he put obedience before survival. The two great ships turned inwards. Tactful to the last he let the flagship draw ahead across his bows, before striking her amidships. HMS *Camperdown* sliced deeply into *Victoria*'s flank. In the interest of tidiness she then backed off, leaving behind a gaping hole. The sea poured in. The flagship rolled over. Tryon, and some hundreds of his sailors were drowned.

Apart from an understandable miscalculation there were two main contributors to this tragedy – the ethos of an hierarchical organisation, wherein it simply is not done to disobey orders from above, and the personalities of the two officers involved. Tryon was a venturesome, relatively uninhibited risk taker; Markham a hidebound, inhibited reactionary. Tryon was a hedonist, fond of wine and women (if not song), who could be explosively aggressive when the occasion demanded. Markham's only outlets for sex and aggression were pep talks on morality to his subordinates and (as a safe discharge for his suppressed hostility) the slaughtering of wildlife whenever he stepped ashore.

In terms of psychoanalytic concepts of tripartism, Tryon was well supplied with id, strong in ego, and relatively unconstrained by superego. Markham appears to have been the polar opposite. Unsupported by his weak ego, his id sagged beneath the weight of moral principles, the most relevant of which in the present instance being 'It is *always* wrong to disobey'.

Of course we cannot know for certain, but it is very likely that had their positions been reversed the Royal Navy's most embarrassing mishap would never have occurred.

Though they became victims of a fatal interaction between aspects of their respective personalities, neither Tryon nor Markham were villains. Though it proved expensive, Markham's obedience can in no way be seen as running counter to a set of moral principles. There was nothing immoral in Tryon's intention, nor in Markham's compliance with a foolish order.[17]

One might be tempted therefore to the comforting conclusion that when an order is perceived as basically immoral, obedience to that order will not occur. But in so thinking one would be mistaken. When Lieutenant Calley ordered the massacre at My Lai, a criminal act for which he was subsequently found guilty, the majority of his soldiers, as exemplified in the following interview with a participant by Mike Wallace of CBS News, did as they were bid:

Q. How many men aboard each chopper?

A. Five of us. And we landed next to the village, and we all got on line and we started walking toward the village. And there was one man, one gook in the shelter, and he was all huddled up down in there, and the man called out and said there's a gook over there.

Q. How old a man was this? I mean was this a fighting man or an older man?

A. An older man. And the man hauled out and said that there's a gook over here, and then Sergeant Mitchell hollered back and said shoot him.

Q. Sergeant Mitchell was in charge of the twenty of you?

A. He was in charge of the whole squad. And so then, the man shot him. So we moved into the village, and we started searching up the village and gathering people and running through the center of the village.

Q. How many people did you round up?

A. Well, there was about forty, fifty people that we gathered in the center of the village. And we placed them in there, and it was like a little island, right there in the center of the village, I'd say. . . And. . .

Q. What kind of people – men, women, children?

A. Men, women, children.

Q. Babies?

A. Babies. And we huddled them up. We made them squat down and Lieutenant Calley came over and said, 'You know what to do with them don't you?' And I said yes. So I took it for granted that he just wanted us to watch them. And he left, and came back about ten or fifteen minutes later and said, 'How come you ain't killed them yet?' And I told him that I didn't think you wanted us to kill them, that you

just wanted us to guard them. He said, 'No, I want them dead.'
So –

Q. He told this to all of you, or to you particularly?

A. Well, I was facing him. So, but the other three, four guys heard it and so he stepped back about ten, fifteen feet, and he started shooting them. And he told me to start shooting. So I started shooting, I poured about four clips into the group.

Q. You fired four clips from your . . .

A. M-16.

Q. And that's about how many clips – I mean how many –

A. I carried seventeen rounds to each clip.

Q. So you fired something like sixty-seven shots?

A. Right.

Q. And you killed how many? At that time?

A. Well, I fired them automatic, so you can't – You just spray the area on them and so you can't know how many you killed 'cause they were going fast. So I might have killed ten or fifteen of them.

Q. Men, women and children?

A. Men, women and children.

Q. And babies?

A. And babies.

Q. Okay. Then what?

A. So we started to gather them up, more people, and we had about seven or eight people, that we was gonna put into the hootch, and we dropped a hand grenade in there with them.

Q. Now, you're rounding up more?

A. We're rounding up more, and we had about seven or eight people. And we was going to throw them in the hootch, and well, we put them in the hootch and then we dropped a hand grenade down there with them. And somebody holed up in the ravine, and told us to bring them over to the ravine, so we took them back out, and led them over to – and by that time, we already had them over there, and they had about seventy–seventy-five people all gathered up. So we threw ours in with them and Lieutenant Calley told me, he said, 'Soldier, we got another job to do'. And so he walked over to the people, and he started pushing them off and started shooting. . .

Q. Started pushing them off into the ravine?

A. Off into the ravine. It was a ditch. And so we started pushing them off, and we started shooting them, so all together we just pushed them all off, and just started using automatics on them. And then. . .

Q. Again, men, women and children?

A. Men, women and children.

Q. And babies?

A. And babies. And so we started shooting them and somebody told us to switch off to single shot so that we could save ammo. So we switched off to single shot, and shot a few more rounds. . .

Q. Why did you do it?

A. Why did I do it? Because I felt like I was ordered to do it, and it seemed like that, at the time I felt like I was doing the right thing, because, like I said, I lost buddies. I lost a damn good buddy, Bobby Wilson, and it was on my conscience. So, after I done it, I felt good, but later on that day, it was getting to me.

Q. You're married?

A. Right.

Q. Children?

A. Two.

Q. How old?

A. The boy is two and a half, and the little girl is a year and a half.

Q. Obviously, the question comes to my mind . . . the father of two little kids like that . . . how can he shoot babies?

A. I didn't have the little girl. I just had the little boy at the time.

Q. Uh-huh . . . How do you shoot babies?

A. I don't know. It's just one of these things.

Q. How many people would you imagine were killed that day?

A. I'd say about three hundred and seventy.

Q. How do you arrive at that figure?

A. Just looking.

Q. You say you think that many people, and you yourself were responsible for how many?

A. I couldn't say.

Q. Twenty-five? Fifty?

A. I couldn't say. Just too many.

Q. And how many men did the actual shooting?

A. Well, I really couldn't say that either. There was other . . . there was another platoon in there, and . . . but I just couldn't say how many.

Q. But these civilians were lined up and shot? They weren't killed by cross fire?

A. They weren't lined up . . . They [were] just pushed in a ravine, or just sitting, squatting . . . and shot.

Q. What did these civilians – particularly the women and children, the old men – what did they do? What did they say to you?

A. They weren't much saying to them. They [were] just being pushed and they were doing what they was told to do.

Q. They weren't begging, or saying, 'No . . . no,' or . . .

A. Right. They were begging and saying, 'No, no'. And the mothers was hugging their children, and . . . but they kept right on firing. Well we kept right on firing. They were waving their arms and begging. . .[18]

In contemplating the content of this chapter we can, perhaps, begin to see what moved Milgram to suggest that obedience hazards our survival. Even without all the other dubious side effects of our evolutionary heritage there is enough here to warrant the gloomiest of prognostications.

We are, without doubt, the most aggressive animals on this planet – the only species which slaughters for pleasure rather than just for food, which relishes blood sports and regularly kills millions of its own kind. Amongst lower animals, aggressive behaviour towards members of the same species is kept within bounds by a complex unlearnt system of appeasement rituals. Members of species other than ourselves rarely fight to the death. As Milgram showed in his proximity experiment, potentially destructive behaviour towards another human *is* significantly reduced by his nearness – but it is not eliminated. Moreover, even if we do possess built-in safeguards against murdering each other, they are useless against technologies which can wipe out entire populations thousands of miles away.

Add to this a few leaders with the sensitivity of Lieutenant Calley, and sufficient Mr Battas, and we have all the ingredients for a speedy termination of all human life.

But perhaps all this is being unduly pessimistic. Having uncovered the special dangers of obedience, namely that people in hierarchical organisations can relinquish all personal responsibility for their actions and trade individual for group ideals, we can take steps to avert the ultimate calamity. But has Milgram's lesson been learnt?

It seems not. So deeply engrained is the need to obey authority that far from being acclaimed as one of the most important pieces of research in experimental social psychology his investigations have been condemned as unethical, and their progenitor villified.

All this leaves two haunting questions still unanswered. Suppose Dr Baumrind had been standing on the edge of that ravine which provided such sport for the obedient followers of Lieutenant Calley, would she have modified the tone of her attack in the *American Psychologist*? And why should obedience be so deeply engrained?

So deeply engrained that even individuals of a country which prides itself on freedom for the individual and vehemently resists being 'pushed around' can fall victim to its pressure?

9

' . . . Cometh Forth Hatred'

> The man who is able to assert himself is seldom vicious: it is the weak
> who are the most likely to stab one in the back.
>
> Anthony Storr

One conclusion to be drawn from Chapter 8 is that people whose obedience results in destruction of their fellow men fall into three groups – there are those who obey because they feel they have to, those who are emotionally indifferent, and those who do so because they want to *for some other reason.*

Amongst the latter are characters like Eichmann, Himmler and Lieutenant Calley, who demonstrate one of the most dangerous and depressing quirks of the human psyche – collusion between the aggressive tendencies of the id and the restraints of the superego. Locking people up 'for their own good', burning heretics, torturing dissidents, liquidating Jews to achieve racial purity or bombing the citizens of a small country to deter their leader from supporting terrorism are just some of the acts carried out by such people. Their common denominator is that they are murderous assaults carried out in the name of some moral code or principle which sanctions behaviour that would otherwise be constrained by guilt.

For a politically inspired collusion between id and superego there are few better examples than the South African government's policy of apartheid.

There may well be some members of President Botha's government and indeed of the general public who consciously and cynically defend their position against worldwide criticism and disgust by

130

claiming 'God is on our side', but there are probably many more who genuinely believe that they are morally justified in pursuing policies which in the eyes of the rest of the world are not only obscene but totally inexcusable on ethical grounds.

Since such features of apartheid as its arrogance, selfishness and cruelty run absolutely counter to the teachings of Christ, the attitudes and shamelessness of these self-professed devout Christians appear as bizarre and hypocritical as it would be for hypochondriacal vegetarians to claim that they eschew meat for moral reasons (for example, 'it is wrong to murder animals for the table') yet enjoy sacrificing live animals in the course of religious rituals.

Of the two sorts of people it is the unconsciously hypocritical who are the more to be feared.

But what are the origins of such collusion and why do they occur in the minds of particular people.

For many animals, including man, aggression serves two purposes: the obtaining of what is needed – food, territory, and mates – and the frightening off or destruction of predators. For lower animals and early man aggression spelt survival. For modern man human aggression is likely to spell his demise. There are two reasons, each a consequence of cultural evolution. The first is progress in technology. The second is what has been called 'poisonous pedagogy'. Either by itself is relatively harmless. In combination they are lethal. Together they provide the means whereby for the first time an entire species can be wiped out by its own kind.

In lower animals intraspecies aggression rarely involves a fight to the death. However furious and noisy a fight between two dogs, a point is usually reached where the one which is getting the worst of it (particularly if he happens to be on the other dog's territory), rolls over on his back, exposes vital parts of his anatomy to his opponent and, for good measure, may also urinate. By thus signalling, 'I've had enough, let's call it a day', the appeasing dog actually turns off aggression in the other. As a result nobody gets seriously hurt. A point has been made. Nothing is lost apart from face and a little urine. This life-preserving arrangement depends upon proximity. If dogs could kill at a distance by hurling things at each other, no amount of rolling over or peeing would have prevented a steady decline in populations of warring canine factions.

Although we have appeasement signals, like smiles and extending the open palm, their usefulness in preventing bloodshed has been nullified by such products of our superior intellects as slings, bows, gunpowder and nuclear missiles. Thanks to these cultural acquisitions, we are now able to kill each other at such great distances that there is not the slightest fear of being restrained by any sort of signals from the victim. For those whose job it is to eliminate as many of their fellow creatures as possible, technology is twice blessed. Not only are its products 'redder' than any natural tooth or claw, but they are also able to circumvent the undermining influences on an assailant of seeing or hearing the victim of his aggression.

The other lethal component of our aggression is our enormous capacity for hate and it is this which, Miller[1] and others have argued, results from 'poisonous pedagogy' – those traditional forms of child rearing which can turn babies with a potential for happy creative spontaneity into neurotic, vengeful adults.

The nature of this process hinges upon the relationship between aggression and hostility. Aggression, the reaction of an animal to any situation which threatens to frustrate its needs, is one of the great gifts which nature has bestowed upon her creatures. Aggressive behaviour evolved to overcome obstacles to survival. It is concerned with struggling against adversity. It is a component of exploration and a defence against attack. It is an ingredient of curiosity, maybe of shooting a rabbit for one's lunch, and of making a fuss if overcharged in a restaurant. It could play a useful part in beating a carpet, driving in a nail, or digging the garden.

Doubtless there are readers who, pursing their lips, will take exception to my views of aggression. They may say to themselves (and anyone else who happens to be near), 'beating carpets, banging in nails, whatever next? Any theory which tries to explain so much explains nothing!' However, in this case this tired old criticism of unpopular theories is unwarranted.

All these instances have in common two salient features. All involve the use of force, either verbal or muscular, to make the environment more suited to one's needs, and all, as exemplified in the following passage, may lead eventually to anger, even murderous hostility towards that part of the environment which the behaviour was trying to change:

. . . When George drew out a tin of pineapple from the bottom of the hamper, and rolled it into the middle of the boat, we felt that life was worth living after all. We are very fond of pineapple, all three of us. We looked at the picture on the tin; we thought of the juice. We smiled at one another, and Harris got a spoon ready. Then we looked for the knife to open the tin with. We turned out everything in the hamper. We turned out the bags. We pulled up the boards at the bottom of the boat. We took everything out on to the bank and shook it. There was no tin-opener to be found. Then Harris tried to open the tin with a pocket-knife, and broke the knife and cut himself badly; and George tried a pair of scissors, and the scissors flew up, and nearly put his eye out. While they were dressing their wounds, I tried to make a hole in the thing with the spiky end of the hitcher, and the hitcher slipped and jerked me out between the boat and the bank into two feet of muddy water, and the tin rolled over, uninjured, and broke a teacup. Then we all got mad. We took that tin out on the bank, and Harris went up into a field and got a big sharp stone, and I went back into the boat and brought out the mast, and George held the tin and Harris held the sharp end of his stone against the top of it, and I took the mast and poised it high up in the air, and gathered up all my strength and brought it down.

It was George's straw hat that saved his life that day. He keeps that hat now (what is left of it), and, of a winter's evening, when the pipes are lit and the boys are telling stretchers about the dangers they have passed through, George brings it down and shows it round, and the stirring tale is told anew, with fresh exaggerations every time. Harris got off with merely a flesh wound. After that I took the tin off myself, and hammered at it with the mast till I was worn out and sick at heart, whereupon Harris took it in hand. We beat it out flat; we beat it back square; we battered it into every form known to geometry – but we could not make a hole in it. George went at it, and knocked it into a shape, so strange, so weird, so unearthly in its wild hideousness, that he got frightened and threw away the mast. Then we all three sat round it on the grass and looked at it. There was one great dent across the top that had the appearance of a mocking grin, and it drove us furious, so that Harris rushed at the thing, and caught it up, and flung it far into the middle of the river, and as it sank we hurled our curses at it, and we got into the boat and rowed away from the spot, and never paused till we reached Maidenhead.[2]

One hesitates to be heavy about anything so delightful as the anecdotes of Mr Jerome, but the story of Harris and the pineapple is probably one of the most complete and palatable accounts ever written of the time course of aggression.

It starts with the pleasant anticipation of gratifying several needs – hunger, thirst and the reduction of boredom. Stage one of the behaviour is both destructive and exploratory, yet totally free of animosity (there may even be a twinge of affection for the object being attacked). At stage two, however, two sources of frustration begin to arise – frustration of the need to reduce hunger and, even more unpleasant, frustration of attempts to gratify this need.

As a result behaviour becomes increasingly violent and varied. It is at stage three, however, that something new appears. The original needs become overtaken and then supplanted by a third, the need to discharge mounting rage towards the obdurate object. In the last and final stage of this saga the urge to discharge rage finds its gratification in the object itself becoming a focus of such intense hatred that it changes from a battered tin of pineapple into the leering mocking face of an entity that has to be murdered – in this case by drowning. By this last act any possible gratification of the original needs has been sacrificed for that of a much greater one.

So much for progressive stages in the manifestation of normal 'benign' aggression. Only in the last, as prolonged frustration evokes hatred, do they even begin to approach that malignant aggression which results from 'poisonous pedagogy'.

Where it differs is that the hatred is immediately discharged in an attack on the source of frustration. Nothing is bottled up.

In contrast, the distinguishing feature of malignant or neurotic aggression is that instead of being discharged onto the offending object (or person) the hatred is repressed, stored up, until such time as it can be safely unloaded onto some other, innocent and undeserving target. It is this state of affairs which results from poisonous pedagogy.

According to Miller, advice on how to raise children has been based on a number of attitudes and beliefs which, when translated into actual parental behaviour, succeed in turning some infants into neurotic, unhappy, anxious, depressed adults. Some of these people become extremely dangerous. Given the technological power which is now to hand, it only needs one or two such individuals to precipitate a global catastrophe.

The following excerpts from the grim manuals to which Miller refers* exemplify their general flavour.

On obedience:

> One of the vile products of a misguided philanthropy is the idea that, in order to obey gladly, the child has to understand the reasons why an order is given and that blind obedience offends human dignity. I do not know how we can continue to speak of obedience once reasons are given. These are meant to convince the child, and, once convinced, he is not obeying us but merely the reasons we have given him. Respect for a higher intelligence is then replaced by a self-satisfied allegiance to his own cleverness. The adult who gives reasons for his orders opens up the field to argument and thus alters the relationship to his charge. The latter starts to negotiate, thereby placing himself on the same level as the adult; this equality is incompatible with the respect required for successful education. Anyone who believes he can win love only if he is obeyed as a result of explanations is sorely mistaken, for he fails to recognize the nature of the child and his need to submit to someone stronger than himself. . . . We have defined obedience as submission of the will to the legitimate will of another person . . . The will of the adult must be a fortress, inaccessible to duplicity or defiance and granting admittance only when obedience knocks at the gates.

On discipline:

> Discipline is an essential part of learning. This must be kept in mind when administering discipline. Discipline is, as stated above, not primarily words but deeds; if presented in words, it is not instruction but commands . . . It proceeds from this that discipline, as the Old Testament word indicates, is basically chastisement (musar). The perverse will, which to its own and others' detriment is not in command of itself, must be broken. Discipline is, as Schleiermacher puts it, life-inhibiting, is at the very least curtailment of vital activity insofar as the latter cannot develop as it wishes but is confined within specific limits and subjected to specific rules. Depending on the circumstances, however, it can also mean restraint; in other words, partial suppression of enjoyment, of the joy of living . . .
>
> With the most forceful form of punishment, corporal chastisement, we come to the ultimate in punishment. Just as the rod serves as the

---

* Some of the worst of these extracts were by a man called Schreber. So popular were his books in Germany that many went through forty printings and were translated into several languages. It is not without significance that his own child was a paranoid patient referred to by Freud.

symbol of paternal discipline in the home, the stick is the primary emblem of school discipline. There was a time when the stick was the cure-all for any mischief in school as the rod was in the home. It is an age-old 'indirect way of speaking from the soul', common to all nations. What can be more obvious than the rule, 'He who won't hear must be made to feel'? Pedagogical blows provide a forceful accompaniment to words and intensify their effect. The most direct and natural way of administering them is by that box on the ears, preceded by a strong pulling on the ear, which we will remember from our own youth. This is an unmistakable reminder of the existence of an organ of hearing and of its intended use. It obviously has symbolic significance, as does a slap on the mouth, which is a reminder that there is an organ of speech and a warning to put it to better use . . . The tried and true blow to the head and hair-pulling still convey a certain symbolism, too.[3]

On sex:

If a child is caught in the act, then it isn't difficult to coax a confession from him. It would be very easy to say to him, so-and-so saw you do this or that. I prefer to take a detour, however, and there are a variety of them. You have questioned the child about his peeked appearance. You have even gotten him to confess to certain aches and pains that you describe to him. I would then continue: 'You see, my child, that I am aware of your present ailments; I have even enumerated them. You see, then, that I know about your condition, I know even more: I know how you are going to suffer in the future, and I'll tell you about it. Listen. Your face will shrivel, you hair will turn brown; your hands will tremble, your face will be covered with pustules; your eyes will grow dim, your memory weak, your brain dull. You will lose all your good spirits, you won't be able to sleep, and you'll lose your appetite etc.'* It is hard to find a child who will not be dismayed by this.[4]

According to Miller, through corporal punishment, threats of divine retribution, threatened and actual withdrawal of love, odious comparisons between the child who is 'bad' and some other paragon, real or fictitious, who is 'good'; by trickery, ridicule, humiliation, lies and deception – all under the mantle of that adult hypocrisy,

---

* There is a grim irony in the fact that since this was written onanism has become the only safe form of sex!

'It's for your own good' – children of all ages have been systematically manipulated, crushed and frustrated. And for some of them their lives were permanently spoilt:

> Punishment followed on a grand scale. For ten days, an unconscionable length of time, my father blessed the palms of his child's outstretched four-year-old hands with a sharp switch. Seven strokes a day on each hand: that makes one hundred forty strokes and then some. This put an end to the child's innocence. Whatever it was that happened in Paradise involving Adam, Eve, Lilith, the serpent, and the apple, the well-deserved Biblical thunderbolt of prehistoric times, the roar of the Almighty and His pointed finger signifying expulsion – I know nothing about all that. It was my father who drove me out of Paradise.[5]

Because, along with all the other lies with which the child is fed there lurks the all-pervasive deception that his parents are saintly omniscient demi-gods who only have his interests at heart (usually put across as 'This hurts me more than it hurts you'), the child is effectively prevented from expressing, let alone seeking redress for the painful feelings he is made to experience. But because the bad feelings and the helpless rage do not come out does not mean they go away. On the contrary, in the course of time they become transformed into a more or less conscious hatred towards a variety of often quite undeserving individuals and groups.

It is this after-effect of 'poisonous pedagogy' which poses the greatest danger to mankind.

To be more specific, adults who were victims of the sorts of treatment prescribed by Dr Schreber have an above average chance of becoming neurotically depressive, possibly suicidal, or of manifesting what has come to be called an authoritarian personality.[6] In the first case the hatred which they could not express towards their parents becomes turned back upon themselves. In the second case it is turned outwards on to others. The one place where it rarely, if ever, goes is its rightful target – the parents who engendered it.

Because the offspring of such parents cannot recall and therefore face up to the humiliations which they suffered as children, such people tend to idealise their parents and their childhood. When they go on about how *wonderful* mother and father were, and how absolutely idyllic their childhood was, the chances are that they weren't and that it wasn't.

By itself this may not matter too much. The trouble is that when bad feelings fail to reach their rightful target they seek another. For authoritarian personalities the focus of their hostility may be any individual or group which it is socially acceptable to hate – Jews, Asians, homosexuals, communists, drug addicts, negroes, trades unionists, Argentinians, Catholics, Protestants – anyone in short whom society under the direction of some deranged political leader (who is him- or herself a product of an authoritarian upbringing) has decided is 'bad'. It is on to this 'bad' group that the victim of poisonous pedagogy thankfully projects those parts of himself which his parents had so assiduously taught him to hate.

Given these dynamics it is not surprising to discover that one of the favourite targets of authoritarian aggression (suitably concealed beneath a cloak of hypocritical 'good intentions') will be the individual's own children. He hates in them what he so hated and still hates in himself and so they, because they cannot answer back, and cannot see through the hypocrisy, and are – let's face it – 'legitimate' targets, become the helpless recipients of traditional child-rearing practices.

Thus it is that the ways of poisonous pedagogy become perpetuated over the years, spreading like a virus from one generation to the next.

All this is very sad and rather nasty. It certainly makes for a lot of human misery. But how could it possibly threaten our survival as a species?

The answer is quite easily!

Put the technology of modern warfare at the disposal of an authoritarian personality, then find him a scapegoat, and one is asking for trouble. Not only are such people rigid, dogmatic, closed minded and therefore incompetent at handling complex situations,[7] but they also retain from their childhood almost inexhaustible reserves of hostility which they are eager to discharge. Elsewhere in this book the point has been made that one of the major risks to mankind is his readiness to trade survival for peace of mind. For authoritarian personalities peace of mind is at least partly achieved by the discharge of hate.

All this is bad enough, but what is worse is that authoritarian people are probably the last to see anything wrong in unleashing their aggression upon their fellow men. Such people are 'always right'. They always 'know best'. What they do to other people is 'always justified'. Even as the world might, largely through their own doing, come crashing about their ears they would manage to remain protected from guilt and shame by an impenetrable shield of self-righteous indignation. Part of their plight is that the shield precludes anything approaching a meaningful *rapport* with their fellow men. For an extreme example of this disability there is the abysmal incompetence of those who persist in trying, on the one hand, to extract information from, and, on the other, change the belief system of, their victims through torture and/or brainwashing. In fact, neither of these techniques is likely to produce either true and useful information or effect any permanent change in the victim's ideology. On the contrary, such primitive methods only serve to harden resistance and intensify the need for revenge.

The point was made most forcibly in 1972 by the following advice on how to deal with terrorists in Northern Ireland:

> The whole technique of skilled interrogation is to build up an atmosphere in which the initial desire to remain silent is replaced by an urge to confide in the questioner. This does not involve cruel or degrading treatment . . . such treatment is . . . counter-productive . . .[8]

But if the methods of torturers are *so* unproductive why are they not abandoned? The answer is that though sanctioned by morality they are fuelled by desire. The fact that they involve extreme pain and slow destruction of the human body, coupled with the most obscene of sexual assaults, is quite consistent with the notion that they provide legitimate outlets for otherwise suppressed hostility and sexual excitement.

Any authoritarian reader who, having somehow managed to get thus far in this chapter, is experiencing doubts about the suggested infantile origins and possible consequences of 'poisonous pedagogy' might like to consider these heartfelt and sincere sentiments:

> It was constantly impressed upon me in forceful terms that I must obey promptly the wishes and commands of my parents, teachers, and priests, and indeed of all grown-up people, including servants, and that nothing must distract me from this duty. Whatever they said was always right. These basic principles by which I was brought up became second nature to me.
>
> Rudolf Höss, Commandant at Auschwitz

And if one still doubts the possibility (let alone probability) of the relationship between an upbringing spiced by punitive morality and such subsequent vindictive aggression as the gassing and incineration of some millions of one's fellow men, it might be interesting to consider the fact that 60 per cent of German terrorists were the children of Protestant ministers. The following is a description by a minister's daughter of what it's like for children to be brought up in a minister's family.

> They are told that their values, by virtue of their nonmaterial nature, are superior to all tangible values. The possession of hidden values encourages conceit and self-righteousness, which quickly and imperceptibly blend in with the required humility. No one can undo this, not even they themselves. No matter what they do, they have to deal not only with their physical parents but with the omnipresent super-Father, whom they cannot offend without paying for it with a guilty conscience. It is less painful to give in, to 'be a dear'. One does not say 'love' in these families, but rather 'like' and 'be a dear'. By avoiding use of the verb 'love', they take the sting away from Eros' arrow, bending it into a wedding ring and family ties. Warmth is prevented from becoming dangerous by being relegated to the home fire. Those who have warmed themselves by it will be cold ever after wherever they may be.[9]

Even if one accepts the arguments and evidence put forward in this chapter it might still be legitimately objected that it is largely irrelevant to the present state of the world. The problem is not that parents are too harsh but too lax. Hooliganism, drug addiction, the crime rate, empty churches and a general lowering of moral standards all testify to the fact that nowadays it is the absence rather than presence of a 'poisonous pedagogy' which we need to worry about.

Fair enough! But there are three points which we need to consider before leaving this vexatious topic.

First, most, if not all, of today's political and military leaders belong to an age group with an above-average chance of having undergone traditional child-rearing practices. Second, the 'grievous faults' of those young people who were brought up by more permissive and liberal parents may cause a lot of problems in present-day society but are not of such a kind as to precipitate a Third World War. Indeed, it could be claimed that the only hope for the world is that it will last long enough under its existing rulers for the present generation of young 'hooligans', Greenham Commonites, and other thorns in the flesh of the establishment to come to power before it is too late.

Third, one has only to consider the politics of South Africa and some Latin American countries to arrive at the hypothesis that, if there is a Third World War it could well be triggered off by the intolerable tensions created within such authoritarian regimes.

Before continuing there is one last issue, the relationship between possessing lethal technology and that likely consequence of poisonous pedagogy, the paranoid reaction. As illustrated in the following example of a recent international crisis, when these two factors interact the risk of a bloody confrontation becomes very great indeed.

Like the other characteristics discussed in this book, a predisposition to distrust potential sources of danger, whether these be geographical, meteorological, biological or social, obviously had and in this case still has survival value. People who value their lives don't build their houses on the edge of active volcanoes, stroke hungry tigers, or pick quarrels with psychopathic 'bouncers'. A certain amount of suspiciousness and a modicum of wariness is healthy and useful.

But, when this predisposition is strengthened by particularly painful experiences in childhood and accompanied by a tendency to project one's hostile feelings on to others, the resulting paranoid reaction may prove more of a burden than a blessing.

Particularly is this so, as the following example suggests, when the paranoid reaction becomes so automatic yet delusional that no amount of contrary evidence will convince the individual concerned that he might, just might, be misjudging the other party. If both parties to a conflict behave this way then hopes of a bloodless reconciliation begin to fade.

Critics of this viewpoint might well object that it pays to feel paranoid about a huge and menacing enemy. Look what happened to Chamberlain. If this 'gullible old fool' had been a bit more distrustful, it might have saved the world a lot of trouble.

The point is well taken but, surely, somewhere between the gullibility of Mr Chamberlain and the paranoid reactions of some present world leaders there is a middle ground called objectivity. There is a sense in which being overtrusting and over-suspicious are very similar – both lead to irrational behaviour. They do so because both spring from beliefs which resist being changed by contrary evidence. In both cases the resistance is a manifestation of some underlying complex of emotionally charged ideas which, being unconscious, is chronic and unalterable. According to this argument, Chamberlain's gullibility like Reagan's paranoia are products of unhappy experiences in childhood. In Chamberlain's case this manifested itself in a persistent search for love and approval, in Reagan's for the need to discharge on to others the hatred which he had felt for his father.

To the extent that the positive decisions of these two men were (or are) determined by feelings belonging to earlier and now irrelevant events they were (and are) irrational. In both cases objectivity becomes sacrificed for neurotic gratification. As happened with Chamberlain, and could happen with Reagan, their lack of objectivity was (could be) very dangerous for the rest of us.

On September 1st, 1983 a 747 of Korean Airlines, flying from Anchorage to Seoul, deviated so far from its scheduled route that it entered Russian air space. As a result it was shot down by a Soviet fighter into the Sea of Japan. The crash killed 29 air crew and all 240 passengers. Since wreckage of the plane and therefore the cockpit voice recorder have never been found, establishing the precise cause of this tragedy has been difficult. However, given the undisputed facts – that the plane was off course, entered Russian air space and was shot down – several questions may be asked. First, why was it off course? There are three possible reasons: failure of all its navigational systems, incompetence on the part of the air crew, or a deliberate intention to enter Russian air space. As to the first, since the 747 (Flight 007) had, in addition to three Inertial Navigation Systems (INS), a facility for picking up the signals from Radar Beacons on the ground, LORAN (Long range air navigation), ground radar, and radioed information from air traffic controllers monitoring the position of the aircraft by radar, this possibility is so unlikely that it can be discounted.

A second possible reason for Flight 007 being 'off course', was that this was intentional, either because it was being used as a spy plane or because it had been decided, for political reasons, to provoke the Russians and/or test their defences of Sakhalin Island. If only because the Americans already have a number of spy planes, specially converted 707s, any one of which could have been used to provoke a Russian response, this hypothesis may be dismissed as the most unlikely of the three.

After the event the Reagan administration made political capital out of the fact that the 'evil' Russians had deliberately 'murdered' 269 innocent civilians. But taking advantage of a serendipitous accident is a far cry from arranging the whole thing beforehand. After all, why choose a planeload of passengers which included a number of influential Americans?

The third and most likely possibility is that the crew of Flight 007 misread or misprogrammed (e.g. entered incorrect figures into the INS) their equipment, or failed to make use of navigational information that was available from their numerous other sources of information. Of the three possibilities this seems the most likely. Through what is known as 'finger trouble' it is very likely that the wrong co-ordinates were entered into the Captain's INS at Anchorage. It is known that flight crews often fail to check for agreement between their three INSs. By the same token, so confident are flight crews of the extraordinary accuracy and sensitivity of INS that they may well fail to check it against their other sources of navigational information.

In support of this contention Hersh cites two 'horror' stories. When an inspector of the Federal Aviation Authority, travelling on the national airline of a North African country, visited the flight deck he found all three members of the crew in their duty position but fast asleep. To block the sun their navigational charts had been carefully taped over the cockpit windows. This happened *after* the shoot down of Flight 007! In another incident the voice recorder recovered from a wreckage of an East European airliner which had hit a mountain disclosed that the pilot and a stewardess had been engaged in sex at the moment of impact.[10]

In the case of the Korean 747 there is reason to believe that Captain Chun Byung-in spent much of his last flight talking to passengers and was therefore neglectful of events on the flight deck. It is known that junior flight crew are extremely diffident about challenging decisions made by the Captain. This is particularly true of Asian airlines. In the words of an American pilot who had served in the Korean Air Force, 'Those Korean Captains and Second Officers don't say boo, they just sit there like vegetables.'[11]

All in all then, the evidence suggests that the Korean airliner was off course through over-reliance on and/or misuse of available technology.

And so we come to the second question. Did the Soviets shoot down Flight 007, after due warning, because they genuinely mistook it for a spy plane or as a deliberate act of aggression after identifying it as a civilian airliner? "

To this day, according to Seymour Hersh, the Reagan administration, in the face of overwhelming evidence to the contrary (including military intelligence which they preferred to ignore), maintains the myth that the Soviets, having identified Flight 007 as a civilian 747 airliner knowingly and wittingly shot it down. For their part the Russians continued to maintain that the 747 was a spy plane and that it was only shot down after it had ignored a warning that it should land.

In the mischief they have tried to make out of this tragic accident both sides displayed a paranoid reaction which could have started the Third World War.

As to the latter supposition, when they heard of the shoot down some senior officers immediately started planning for a retaliatory strike against the Soviet Union, an act which, in the opinion of another officer, 'could have started World War III'. According to Hersh, this same officer, then stationed in the Pacific, was 'approached by an Air Force General and asked to forward an essentially fraudulent intelligence report to the Pentagon that was designed to justify acts of provocation against the Soviet Union. The General wanted me to corrupt intelligence', the officer recalled. 'I told him to go to hell.'[12]

Before the advent of nuclear weapons a concatenation of the three factors responsible for the destruction of Flight 007 – over-reliance on the 'reliability' of 'fool-proof' technology which is neither fool-proof nor reliable, a paucity of facts regarding what the other side is up to (despite the multi-billion dollar/rouble intelligence services which the Super Powers maintain) and the aggressive paranoid reactions of antagonistic humans may not have mattered too much, but now it could matter quite a lot.

Part Three

The Big Decision

When the sun sets, shadows that showed at noon
But small, appear most long and terrible

Nathaniel Lee, *Oedipus, IV*

10

Options

... for on his choice depends
The safety and the health of the whole State.
Shakespeare, *Hamlet*

Whether or not we, as a species, survive depends on what we decide to do. If we do nothing but carry on as we are, then it could all be over within the foreseeable future. If we decide to accelerate the arms race and increase our present exploitation of the Third World, then the time left will probably be shortened. Only if we called a halt to our present self-destructive ways of thinking and acting could we extend our use of this planet as a place in which we and future generations might enjoy reasonable prospects of survival.

This is the Big Decision. Which way it will go depends on how we make decisions. We have already seen several reasons for believing that the prospects are not rosy. To reiterate, since decisions are based on conscious plans, and the content of consciousness at the moment of choosing between various courses of action is extremely limited, the chances of ignoring vital pieces of information or accurate long-term predictions of future outcomes are immense. Sheer absent mindedness, the running off of routine habits outside conscious control, and the exclusion from consciousness of unpleasant facts and feelings are just some of the hazards. While we go on trading survival for peace of mind our days are numbered.

It has been pointed out how interactions between those components of the human psyche – basic biological drives (particularly that of aggression), the ego, that pragmatic master of expedience,

147

and moral conscience, aided and abetted by an elaborate system of largely autonomous defence mechanisms – can result in a wide range of self-destructive tendencies. Together or apart they pose problems for survival. They do so because, together or apart, they contribute to our *penchant* for making irrational decisions. But they are not the only contributors to this fatal flaw in human thinking.

Let's look at this more closely.

Figure 10.1, believe it or not, depicts the way in which that mythical creature, rational man, arrives at his decisions.

To make the best choice between possible courses of action, he must first know what he aims to achieve – his goal. Secondly, he must possess as much information as possible about the various options. If putting money on a horse, he should know its pedigree, whether it is arthritic and how many races it has won. Most such information comes via the eyes or ears, some occasionally via the nose.

But necessary information is of little use if he can't hold it in his head, and so optimal decision–making is also dependent upon an efficient memory. Four things in particular should be stored in memory: information about the courses open, the goal or what he is aiming at, the probabilities of each choice being successful and the

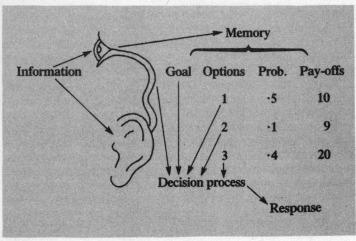

Figure 10.1

pay-offs – those likely benefits of success and penalties of failure – for each option.

Because nothing is ever certain, because the favourite can fall at the first fence, no one can ever be 100 per cent sure that what he chooses to do will turn out for the best. But at least, in principle, it is possible to act rationally, to make the best possible choice, even if it is only the best of a bad bunch. If, for example, his goal is to come away from the races with more money than he started with, then, assuming he is capable of multiplying the pay-offs by the probabilities, his rational choice would be number 3. This is rational decision-making. It hardly ever, if ever, occurs. As one expert has remarked, 'I do not think we can be satisfied with the assurance that most people act rationally most of the time.'[1] Why should this be?

There are in fact several reasons. The most important are depicted in Figure 10.2 (overleaf).

About the first of these various sources – Input Deficiency – there are just four points.

Obviously one cannot hope to make a rational decision on the basis of inadequate information. Ironically, this is likely to occur in those very situations wherein it is most important that it should not, i.e. during times say of international crisis. It is at such times that each side does its best to conceal information from the other. This particular obstacle to rational decision-making is itself a product of the irrational urge towards secrecy for its own sake. Just how ridiculous this preoccupation towards maintaining secrecy can be is exemplified by the following excerpt from the editorial columns of the *Physician*.

It must be a hundred years since a Prussian statesman contemptuously described an official secret as a scrap of paper passed between low-grade government clerks. Such a view was not taken by the Department of Health and Social Security when a distinguished panel was convened to advise on the limited list of drugs. The five professors (representing clinical pharmacology, general practice, paediatrics, geriatrics, and psychiatry), one consultant physician, one general practitioner, and one pharmacist were expected to sign the Official Secrets Act. The United Kingdom has now become one of the most secretive societies in the West, and, an ominous sign of pre-conditioning, only two members objected. The Minister of Health put it mildly when he admitted that the request was 'excessive'. The hastily drafted and debated Official Secrets Act of 1911 was concerned with the defence of the realm and, in particular, spying by the Germans in Great Britain. Those who drafted the Act could not have conceived that it would be applied to academic discussions about balsams, cordials, teas, elixirs, herbs, cough medicines, indigestion mixtures and laxatives. Indeed such matters are not even confidential, and reliance should have been placed on that discretion which is not only the prerogative of doctors and civil servants; an equal understanding of 'secrecy' is shown, for example, by clergymen, bankers, stockbrokers, lawyers and, not least, by members of the oldest profession. The official secrets syndrome, long endemic, is now an epidemic. It is fostered by fear of indefinable, unquantifiable, and non-existent threats. It often affects the insecure and inadequate in whom the possession of special knowledge (however trivial and inconsequential) confers a sense, or even the reality, of power. In 31 pages of appendix B, the DHSS lists drugs and other substances 'not to be available at NHS expense'. Pages 25

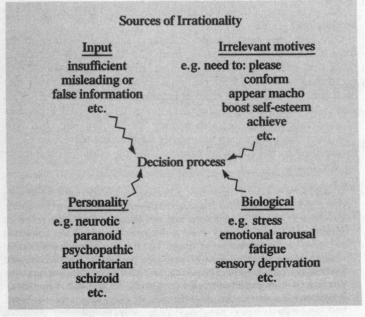

Figure 10.2

to 28 are mainly devoted to tablets with a formula only described by a code name. Is it unrealistic or paranoid to ask if details of their contents have been suppressed by the Official Secrets Act?[2]

In a world infested with 'moles', congregating most densely in places like Foreign Offices, Defence Ministries, cabinets and counter-espionage agencies, the Official Secrets Act is something of a laughing matter. The big problem now is that with a plethora of spies there are not enough secrets to go round, hence hecatombs of 'moles' are in danger of adding to the present unemployment figures. The main purpose of the Official Secrets Act appears to be that of rationalising redundant spies, flattering the egos of self-important officials, and providing a uniquely bogus screen behind which to hide bureaucratic incompetence. One thing is for sure, it does little for rational decision-making.

The greatest hazard of input deficiency is that it provides much more scope for the creative talents of the decision-maker. Unconstrained by tiresome facts he can give full rein to his imagination. A lack of solid evidence from outside leaves a fertile breeding ground for prejudice, bigotry, paranoia and wish fulfilment fantasies. These are not the handmaidens of rational decision-making.

About the next source of error: such irrelevant motives as the need to please and the wish to cut a macho figure have been dealt with in preceding chapters: suffice it to say that any decision which is influenced by an irrelevant motive runs the risk of being irrational. This is true whether the motive is personal greed, to appear young and spritely, or to obtain a passport to heaven.

As with irrelevant motives, we have already considered evidence for the biasing role of personality characteristics in decision-making. In any given situation decisions made by psychopaths, authoritarians, paranoiacs and people of a schizoid temperament would probably differ markedly from each other. Since there can only be one *best* decision we have to accept that it, whether or not it occurs, would depend more upon the psychopathology of the person who was making it than upon reality. Hence the outcome may be far from what is best for all of us. Since, for reasons examined elsewhere in this book, political leaders have an above average chance of being extrovert, paranoid, egomaniacal and neurotic, this particular source of error is almost inescapable.

Coming now to the items on the far right of Figure 10.2, it is worth noting that they have a common denominator. They all relate, in one way or another, to the state of arousal of the brain. One of many ways in which brains differ from computers is that they are not either on or off but vary in their state of 'on-ness' from just barely ticking over to buzzing with activity.

This continuum of arousal plays an important part in the making of irrational decisions. For every task there is an optimal level of arousal. Generally, the more complex the task the lower the optimum point. Thus simple decisions like what I shall have for breakfast can be made at higher levels of arousal than complex ones such as how to get along with the Russians. Another and related point is that extremes of arousal whether very low as in, say, sleep deprivation or boredom, or very high, as in states of severe stress, reduce any possibility of rational decision-making.

Since the most complex problems are also likely to be the most emotionally arousing, we are left with the disturbing paradox that the more important a decision the poorer the state of mind for making it. However inept someone may be, it is virtually certain he will be even worse when stressed. Chapter 11 takes up this theme.

11

Stress

> . . . the only thing we have to fear is fear itself.
> Franklin Delano Roosevelt

It has been suggested that one of the reasons we have become our own worst enemies is because anything added to a system to protect, modify or enhance its main effect invariably produces undesirable side effects. Lead in petrol, preservatives in jam, contraceptives in bed – always a price is paid. There are few better examples than the human stress response – that collection of emergency reactions which occur when physical well-being and/or psychological peace of mind are threatened from without.

As reiterated *ad nauseam* throughout this book, the survival of living organisms depends upon their relationship with the environment. Too little of what they need, or too much of what they don't, constitute threats to the good life. Too much or too little food, drink, heat, excitement, information, work, leisure, praise, punishment, even money, wives and children, may prove injurious. Carried to excess some discrepancies between what we require and what we get may threaten life itself. The stress response is part of nature's answer to this problem. It is the extreme manifestation of those self-regulating reactions whereby animals attempt to cope with the demands made upon them. When the demands exceed their normal resources, the stress response attempts to make up the shortfall.

For those who wish to know more about the psychology of stress there are plenty of good textbooks.[1] For those who don't, Figure 11.1

outlines such features of the stress response as are pertinent to the ensuing discussion.

As depicted in Figure 11.1 the stress response evolved to handle environmental situations which are perceived as threats to physical well-being. In this capacity it was (and is) highly efficient.

For early man who, as he sauntered down a jungle path, came face to face with a sabre-toothed tiger, the components of the stress response were just what was needed if he was not going to end up inside the animal. His was an extreme but short-term emergency which could only be resolved successfully by the rapid expenditure of muscular energy.

He *had* to feel alarmed, for that was the spur to action. He *had* to think quickly and act swiftly, and all this without becoming unduly overheated. But most of all he needed lots of blood sugar in his blood and lots of blood to the muscles of his arms and legs.

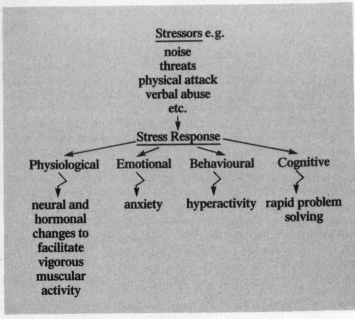

Figure 11.1

The trouble is that the workings of this remarkable piece of protective machinery, so suited to the problems which confronted our distant forebears, are inappropriate to most of those with which modern man has to contend. This is hardly surprising, for the latter were not the sort of problems which brought about their evolution.

Whereas the stress response still seems to operate on the principle that the main threats to survival can be dealt with by vigorous behaviour, most stressful situations with which *we* are confronted require thought rather than muscle for their solution.

For coping with industrial disputes, marital discord, information overload, bereavement and alien ideologies, the stress response is about as satisfactory as shaving with a blowlamp. It is not just useless but downright harmful. Why?

There are several reasons. First, nine times out of ten it does absolutely nothing to reduce the cause of stress. No amount of sweating, raised blood pressure, increased heart rate, etc. – all those reactions which enabled primitive man to get the better of a wild animal – is going to help in coping with a tiresome boss or the awkward questions of an inquisitive tax inspector. None of the stress reactions so well suited to dealing with the one would be of much use in coping with the other.

There is a more serious side to all this, which relates to what has been called the General Adaptation Syndrome[2] or GAS for short. The final stage of GAS is, in effect, a disease of stress – a major malaise of our time. It occurs when the internal responses to a stressful situation are unsuccessful or overly prolonged; instead of being discharged in removal of the stressor, they boomerang upon the body which they were originally designed to protect. It occurs through misapplication of a physiological anachronism. The stress response has, in many respects, outlived its usefulness. Very rarely does modern man have to run for his life, but there are many occasions when his brain gets it wrong and his body behaves as if it had to.

In the late 1960s British Airways carried out research[3] on just one of the normal responses to stress which they thought might be afflicting their airline pilots – changes in heart rate. For people about to embark on a long flight the results of this inquiry are not encouraging. When he boards his aircraft at Heathrow the Captain's heart-rate is nice and steady at around 60 to 65 beats a minute.

On take-off it rises to around 80. Over the Atlantic it drops back again, *BUT* when he joins the 'stack' over Kennedy Airport it soars to the incredible rate of 150 beats a minute.

It's not pleasant hovering about in the skies above New York – slightly anxiety-making and certainly frustrating. Deep down the pilot may well feel like running away from the whole situation. He can't, but that doesn't stop his heart from trying to.

Fortunately, for the hundreds of passengers sitting comfortably in a big jet miles above the earth, when that reassuring voice from somewhere up front says, 'This is your captain speaking. We will shortly be starting our descent to Kennedy Airport. The weather over New York is fine and clear. The temperature is around 50 degrees Fahrenheit etc. etc.', he doesn't add, 'my heart has just doubled its usual rate, my blood pressure has already risen well above what is considered normal for a man of my age. By the way I am in fact fifty-five and will probably be retiring fairly soon. It's not that I'm unfit but, well, I do have a slight tendency towards occlusion of the coronary artery and – oh yes – an above-average chance of having a stroke. But don't worry, my inexperienced young co-pilot is very keen to try his hand at driving one of these things. I hope you have enjoyed flying with us'.

At least the 118 people who met their death aboard the BEA Trident which crashed at Staines on June 18th, 1972 were spared comparable details about those factors which contributed to *their* demise. The immediate cause of this disaster was 'premature retraction of the leading edge droop'.[4] To the uninitiated this may well sound like some sort of sexual dysfunction, but reflects in fact a failure on the part of the crew to fly the plane properly, as a result of which it fell out of the sky.* The factors which contributed to this human error included: the necessity of adhering to a complicated noise abatement procedure which, although officially 'safe', nevertheless reduced the performance safety margin; the fact that two inexperienced co-pilots had been rostered to fly together; *the distinct possibility that the pilot had suffered a heart attack shortly after take-off* and, finally, judging from such graffiti as 'No to Keyline management' (a reference to the dead pilot, Captain Key) and 'Grim Jim for the chop' subsequently found scrawled on the navigation table in the cockpit, the very

---

* The droop is a piece of the wing which, when lowered, assists the plane to climb and prevents stalling at slow speeds.

strong suspicion that the morale of the flight crew was not all that it should have been.

Altogether there was quite enough here to produce a stress reaction with fatal consequences for all on board.

But the human stress response does not have to precipitate anything as dramatic as a major air disaster in order to qualify as at the best unhelpful and at the worst highly destructive in many social situations.

Being interviewed for a new job, being unfairly (or even fairly) criticised, being threatened with the sack, discovering that one may have the symptoms of a fatal disease, trying to hold down a job for which one knows one is basically unfitted, knowing one is responsible for the lives of others yet fearing that one will fail in one's responsibility, and so on: all these and many other similar situations have three things in common. They pose a threat to physical well-being and/or psychological peace of mind. They generate anxiety, fear, even terror, and, because they pose a threat, they trigger off the body's stress-response system. But in not one of these and many comparable situations does the response reduce the stress. On the contrary, it only serves to make matters worse. A dry mouth, pounding heart, trembling hands, a face pouring with sweat, are no help when being interviewed by a potential employer or, when already late for an appointment, your car runs out of petrol. Flushing with shame when caught out doing something you shouldn't, falling over your words, or forgetting someone's name when having to introduce them, all serve to increase the original unease – piling misery upon misery. With every second the downward path grows steeper. For man the descent is hastened by awareness of what his body is doing. The victim knows he's sweating and experiences the shame of knowing that others know he is afraid, that they know he knows they know, which only makes him sweat the more.

Being aware of one's own stress response is like being kicked when one is already down. Soldiers at moments of great danger may experience the infantile sensations of involuntary incontinence, a not uncommon symptom of extreme stress, symptoms which they cannot help but which they take as proof of their cowardice. This faulty attribution results in shame, which only serves to increase stress. It is a downwards spiral.

But, if slower and more insidious in its onset, the price of prolonged chronic stress may be even more destructive. Thwarted in its attempts to master or remove the stressor, the body turns upon itself. Table 11.1 shows there is hardly a single symptom of physical or mental disease which cannot be laid at the door of stress.

Bodily	Mental
Tiredness	Anxiety
Aches and pains	Irritation
Indigestion	Fear
Migraine	Rage
Tachycardia (rapid heart rate)	Guilt
Disorders of the gastro-intestinal tract	Paranoid feelings
Skin disorders	Insomnia
Asthma and other respiratory disorders	Disorders of eating
Disorders of the cardio-vascular system	Sexual dysfunction
Failure of the immune response system	Delusions
Arthritis	Hallucinations
Cancer	Emotional flattening
	Alcoholism
	Drug addiction
	Phobias
	Other neurotic symptoms
	Psychosis

Table 11.1 The Effects of Stress

The effects of prolonged chronic stress may long outlast the events which brought them about. Studies of bereavements [5] and of the survivors from the concentration camps and the Hiroshima bomb[6] suggest that the effects of extreme stress are probably irreversible, certainly maladaptive and ultimately lethal. Depression culminating in suicide, the early onset of cancer or heart disease following the loss of a loved one, and even psychosomatic symptoms brought on by guilt at having survived when so many died are just some of our self-destructive reactions.

Not only is the victim of stress prone to a variety of psychosomatic disorders but, through the stress-induced failure of the immune system, vulnerable to a wide range of pathogens. This paradox, that those very mechanisms which evolved to get us out of trouble have now become the most destructive of positive feedbacks – the effects of which can be summarised by saying that the more stressed the more physically incapable, the more physically incapable the less competent and the less competent the more stressed and so on until death (mercifully) intervenes – prompts the uncomfortable thought that politicians stressed by an international crisis are likely to become increasingly inept as the days or hours slip by.

Equally worthy of consideration are some of the consequences of trying to deal with stress by medication. The world is full of people hopelessly addicted to substances, the intended use of which was to reduce such unpleasant accompaniments of stress as tension, anxiety and depression.

A related problem, with serious implications for the survival of the species, concerns the treatment of actual physical disorders brought about by stress.

As documented by L'Etang,[7] those very people who by reason of their age, abilities and personality become top leaders – Generals, Presidents, Prime Ministers, and so on, have an above average chance, through the stresses of the job, of adding to their problems because of some physical disorder. In a nuclear age the prospect is not encouraging. But there are two additional hazards. Now that world leaders are in a position to bring about mass genocide, it has become rather important (to put it mildly) that their psychological and physical disorders are not concealed. In fact, few people are more motivated and more able, with or without the collusion of their doctors, to conceal their disabilities. Secondly, whatever *their* motives, the doctors may prescribe remedies with side effects which could well render the patient even more unfit to govern than would the disease which they are trying to cure. Such was apparently the case with Hitler's Dr Morell, who prescribed for his patient a large and curious range of medications, of which the worst were Dr Köster's antigas pills and the notorious Vitamultin tablets.

The purpose of Dr Köster's invention was to reduce intestinal discomfort not, as the name might seem to imply, Hitler's verbal outpourings. In the event, since their main ingredients were the two poisons strychnine and belladonna, the antigas pills probably inclined the German warlord towards being even more restless, confused, excited, deluded, and noisily delirious than he was already.[8]

As for the other nostrum, since this consisted largely of caffeine and methylamphetamine in (according to Dr Schenk of the Reich Health Department) a truly horrifying concentration, it was likely to produce disorientation, irritability, convulsions and hallucinations.[9]

If the following impression which Hitler made on one of his generals (Heinz Guderian) is anything to go by, one cannot help feeling that Hitler's friends and advisers could have well done without the good offices of Köster and Morell.

His fists raised, his cheeks flushed with rage, his whole body trembling, the man stood there in front of me, beside himself with fury and having lost all self control. After each outburst of rage, Hitler would stride up and down the carpet–edge, then suddenly stop immediately before me and hurl his next accusation in my face. He was almost screaming, his eyes seemed about to pop out of his head and the veins stood out on his temples.[10]

Take another example. There have been speculations as to why a politician as experienced as Anthony Eden should have precipitated anything so crass as 'Great Britain's last disastrous imperial adventure' – the Suez 'war' of 1956. Certainly a contributory reason was that Eden, by his own admission, had been living on amphetamine – a drug which in large doses is known to produce excitement, distractability and, most seriously in Eden's case, *unfounded suspicions and delusions of persecution*.[11]

Intoxicated by this stimulant, taken presumably to counter the stress of information overload, Eden's already paranoid hatred for Nasser assumed such psychotic proportions that Britain suddenly found herself embroiled in one of the most ridiculously embarrassing military fiascos of all time.

More recently, so it has been suggested, the monumental error of judgement which resulted in the 'Bay of Pigs' was at least partly the result of Kennedy's medication with Cortisone. This treatment for Addison's disease has the side effect of making the patient more optimistic, even euphoric, and therefore presumably readier to take risks.[12]

What does all this add up to? Assuming that the most important decisions are likely to be made under the most stressful circumstances and that the very making of them is itself likely to be a highly stressful process, then those people like airline pilots or political leaders who can least afford to be unwell are the very ones most likely to be physically impaired by the job they are trying to do.

This is bad enough, but worse is the fact that long before any physical manifestations of the full-blown stress response, emotional arousal may have profoundly disturbing effects on the mental processes which precede the making of a decision.

Consider once again (provided you are not about to fly from London to New York) the hearts of airline pilots who are waiting for permission to land at Kennedy Airport. Beating at 150 to the minute indicates emotional arousal and a superfluity of adrenalin in the bloodstream. Could it also indicate reduced mental efficiency? Judging from a couple of experiments[13] the answer is yes. In one study, it was found that, whereas injecting normal subjects with one part in a thousand of adrenalin chloride increased muscular performance (which is exactly what the stress response is designed to do), it also significantly *decreased* the ability to carry out simple problems in mental arithmetic.

In a second experiment, use was made of the public address system whereby pilots can talk to their passengers. Through it being 'inadvertently' left switched on, a planeload of servicemen heard snatches of conversation from the flight deck, the gist of which was that, due to serious mechanical problems, they were about to ditch in the sea. With this news fresh in their minds, the passengers were then required to carry out some simple mental tasks which included recalling a previously learned emergency escape sequence. In comparison with a control group in a plane which did *not* have a 'faulty' address system the stressed servicemen showed serious impairment of memory and reasoning. Of particular significance was the fact that recall of the escape sequence became impossible just when it was most needed.

In the light of these experiments it is not perhaps surprising that the majority of aircraft accidents occur during landing. It is ironic that just when he most needs to think clearly a pilot's judgement should be at its poorest, and this through the effects of an emotional response so totally inappropriate to the task by which it was provoked.

Figure 11.2 shows the sequence of psychological processes that occur between receipt of information and the making of a response. Each one of these stages is vulnerable to the effects of emotional arousal.

As the following examples show, disruption, blocking or distortion anywhere along the line hazards the ultimate decision. Take the matter of attention. For early man there was survival value in being able to narrow attention upon the sorts of problem he was likely to encounter. Confronted by a cobra poised to strike, it was policy to divert attention from more attractive objects and focus on the immediate danger. Overtures to desirable bedmates hovering nearby could wait until later. It was a matter of first things first. But, as the following example shows, the sort of problems facing modern man are often of a very different sort.

On a clear moonlit night in 1972 a Lockheed 1011 of Eastern Airlines was about to land at Miami Airport. On the approach the pilot noticed that a green light, which would indicate that the nose-wheel strut was extended and locked down, had failed to come on. A decision was taken to overshoot and the aircraft cleared by Miami to circle at 2,000 feet. Control of the plane was switched to the autopilot while the crew attempted to discover the cause of the problem. But then the untoward happened: somehow the altitude-hold switch on the control column became disengaged. Presumably someone had unwittingly leant against the column. How it happened is less important than the fact that nobody noticed. *So narrowed was their attention* on the relatively minor problem of the unresponsive light that no one became aware of the fact that the plane was losing height.[14] Nor did they heed a warning signal from a radar operator on the ground. No one saw the trees of the Everglades, now clearly

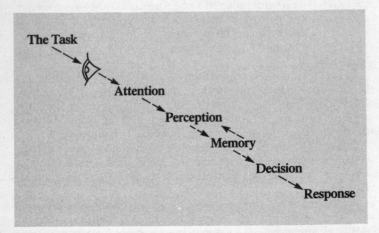

Figure 11.2   Sequence of Mental Processes Involved in Making a Decision

visible through the flight-deck windows, and no one heard the C-chord alert (ground proximity warning signal) – their last warning of the approaching plunge into the alligator-ridden swamps below. This quite unnecessary disaster, which cost many lives, can be traced to the effects of mild stress on the cognitive processing of otherwise competent, professional, conscientious men.

It is, incidentally, a good illustration of the fact that, for most humans, the greatest sources of stress are themselves, or rather their appraisal of what is otherwise a harmless event. There is nothing inherently stressing about the non-appearance of a green light and there is a sad irony about the fact that had the Captain of the Eastern Airlines jet been less experienced and/or more psychopathic the accident might never have happened. He might not have even noticed the absence of the light, or, if he had, might have taken a chance and risked a landing. After all, one can land a jumbo jet without that little wheel in front. It might grind away a bit of the nose of the aircraft or leave a groove in the runway as it ploughs along the ground, but at least most airports are free of water and alligators. Those who died were victims more of the flight crew's sense of responsibility than of a failure in the nose-wheel monitoring system. They were victims of the fact that how a situation is appraised may determine how stressful it becomes.

By way of an example there is an anecdote from the First World War. A soldier was blown up by a shell. As luck would have it, a large part of him sailed through the air and landed in a stew which an army cook was preparing for the midday meal. The cook's immediate impulse was to fish out the foreign (or perhaps one should say 'allied') body – but then, being of a creative nature, he changed his mind. Having removed bits of uniform and the odd button from this new ingredient, he stirred it in with the stew. Later, when lunch was served, a strange thing happened. For the first and probably the last time in his life the cook found himself the object of a standing ovation – 'Thought you couldn't f. . . . . . well cook – best f. . . . . . stew since we left Blighty.' One enthusiastic trooper with more accuracy than he realised shouted out, 'At last some nosh with a bit of body in it.'

It was an opening the cook could not resist. 'Yer dead right, mate, it 'as – Private 'ardcastle's!' Warming to this theme he gave them the details. For a moment there was stunned silence and then they fell upon him. They threw away what they hadn't eaten and one vomited. The cook was posted to another unit, but his reputation followed him and he was never allowed to cook again. And all that had been changed, since the first delicious mouthful, was their *appraisal* of what it had contained.

Even more hazardous than the effects of stress upon attention is its influence upon perception. If perceptual experiences are considered as lying along a continuum from veridical at one end to hallucinatory at the other, then it is generally true to say that under stress there is a tendency for perception to move from true to false. As reality grows ever more painful to behold, perceptual experience becomes an increasing function of what the percipient would *like* to be the case rather than what really *is* the case. As they draw on past experience which may now be totally inappropriate, 'perceptual hypotheses' become increasingly invalid. As a potential for self-destructive calamities this vulnerability to stress has three special features. First, it is the nature of perception that, while vividness and clarity may remain unimpaired, the actual information received and transmitted diminishes to zero. Second (because of this), no one remains more oblivious of his shortcomings as a perceiver than the percipient himself. Finally, steps, either chemical or psychological, which might tend to make him *feel* better may not only reduce still further the chances of any constructive self-criticism, but will probably succeed in making his perception even less valid than it was already.

For an example of what *can* happen there is the case of a certain railway signalman. The job of signalman, like that of an air traffic controller, is not one for which we are naturally fitted. High levels of responsibility, loneliness, long spells of boring inactivity, a limited repertoire of possible responses, and appalling consequences if one makes a mistake add up to the ingredients for a state of chronic stress. (In the case of air traffic controllers for whom the stressors are similar only worse, because the task is more complex, it is possible that life expectancy may be considerably shorter than that for most other occupations.* In the circumstances it is not surprising that some signalmen resort to alcohol. One such, the case in question, became a victim of that positive feedback sequence – boredom

---

*In the United States according to figures published in 1979, eight out of every nine ATCs have to retire for medical reasons before reaching the normal retiring age of fifty–five.[16]

plus responsibility → stress → resort to alcohol → incompetence → greater stress → more drink and so on. Fortunately for the travelling public this particular signalman was discovered before it was too late and removed to hospital where he showed the following symptoms of alcoholic hallucinosis. At 11.53 each night he would leap from his bed, pull imaginary levers and peer anxiously down the line (of beds) muttering, 'It's coming, it's coming.'

When peace of mind depends on sustaining a preferred hypothesis, there appear to be no limits to what can be done with awkward information. For the immense cost in lives and human misery which have resulted from this quirk, there are few better examples than that of Montgomery's attempt to capture the bridges at Arnhem (Operation Market Garden) in the face of overwhelming evidence against the advisability of such a move.[15] But for a case which might have resulted in an even worse disaster there is that of Three Mile Island. The incident involved an interaction (perhaps one should say a lack of interaction) between three sets of facts. First, there were those to do with the nature and inherent dangers of a water-cooled nuclear reactor; second, the extensive and highly elaborate mechanisms for monitoring the workings of such a reactor, and for warning of dysfunctions in its component parts; third, there was the human element, those presumably knowledgeable and well-trained engineers, technicians and managers whose job was to run the plant. On the day in question the first stage of the crisis concerned events within the reactor itself. Through the failure of its pump, the 'cool' side of the heat exchanger became starved of water. However, the near occurrence, from this small start, of a melt-down which could have destroyed the state of Pennsylvania was due less to failure of a pump than to the fact that those in charge refused to believe the warning signals from their own monitoring system. It was a situation analogous to that of a nurse in an intensive care unit whose reaction to heart failure of the patient might be to blame the electrocardiograph for giving 'false' information.

Paradoxically, it seems that out of possible explanations for a given turn of events there is a preference for that which is least threatening to survival.

So intertwined are perception and memory that it is not surprising to find both failing under stress. Just as perceptual hypothesising becomes biased towards unjustified wish fulfilment, so do memory processes begin operating in such a way as to reduce anxiety but increase ineptitude. Repression and its more primitive counterpart denial, selective recall, unrealistic appraisal, confabulation, fugue and secondary elaboration all serve to drive a wedge between past experience (reality as it really was) and what the subject now recalls. It could be argued of course that, as with all the other mechanisms which are geared towards preserving peace of mind, some 'dimmings' of memory have in the past had considerable survival value. Without them how could people have 'picked up the pieces' after such appalling setbacks as the Black Death, the Tangshan and Tokyo earthquakes which together killed over a million people,[17] and the crash of Wall Street, immediately after which (but only for a very limited time) people committed suicide in droves. Without them what mother just recovered from the agonies of childbirth would ever risk doing it all again, and what escapee from a hideous marriage would ever contemplate another matrimonial entanglement?

But there *is* another side to this particular coin. Even minor lapses of memory due to anxiety (as in stage fright) may have appalling consequences.

Take the case of a signalman called Tinsley who, in 1915, brought about the worst accident in the history of British railways.[18]

It happened to the north of Carlisle. Thanks to a private arrangement between the two men who worked the signal box at Quintinshill, the day-shift signalman, Tinsley, arrived for duty thirty minutes after he was due to take over from his friend, Meakin, who looked after the night shift. While waiting for Tinsley, Meakin had noted down all traffic movements.

With Tinsley's arrival, Meakin settled down to read the paper. Meanwhile Tinsley busied himself with entering into the official register all those movements which his friend had kindly jotted down, thereby concealing the fact that he had been late reporting for duty.

Both men knew that, in addition to their loop lines being occupied by stationary goods trains, a slow northbound passenger train had been temporarily shunted on to the southbound mainline in order to give the shortly expected Euston-Perth express a clear run through. Not only could Tinsley see the stationary passenger train, standing at signals on the line to London less than sixty-five yards from where he was sitting and not only was the shunting of this train one of the movements which he had now to enter in the register, but he was actually visited, in accordance with normal railway regulations, by the driver of this stationary train. Yet, despite all this knowledge, when, a few minutes later, he received a phone call asking whether he would accept a special troop train from the north, he not only said he would but cleared all his southbound mainline signals. In due course the troop train, travelling fast on an easy downhill gradient, arrived at Quintinshill. When the driver and fireman of the stationary passenger train saw what was bearing down on them they jumped for their lives. In the ensuing crash the 'special' and the leading coaches of the other train were totally destroyed. But worse was to follow. Seconds too late Meakin recalled the imminent arrival of the London-Perth express. He threw the northbound signals to danger, but nothing now could halt the express. Weighing 600 tons, drawn by two large locomotives and travelling very fast, it burst upon the scene. Unable to stop, even with full emergency braking, it ploughed into the wreckage from the first collision, thereby also damaging the two goods trains that had been waiting patiently on the loop lines. All in all Tinsley's lapse of memory, occasioned one supposes by the slight anxiety of having to falsify his time of arrival in the train register, totally destroyed one train and severely damaged four others. And in so doing it killed 230 people, most of them soldiers on their way to France.

Doubtless, incurable optimists about the indefinite survival of mankind will shake their heads and say accidents like that at Quintinshill are pretty rare events, hardly worth getting worked up about. Two points – such carnage on railways may be fairly rare; lapses of memory under mild degrees of stress are not. Tinsley's error cost hundreds of lives. A comparable lapse of memory in the nuclear age need only happen once, to cost hundreds of millions of lives.

Momentary lapses, as when one cannot recall a person's name, are not the only way in which emotion can play havoc with memory. Equally embarrassing and sometimes fatal is the phenomenon of 'negative transfer'.

This harmless sounding quirk of the human mind refers to the fact that something learned in one situation may be inappropriately applied to the handling of some other, later, situation. This could occur as a result of simple absent-mindedness (see Chapter 3), but there are reasons to believe that the tendency to fall back upon an earlier mode of response – a form of regression – may be induced by even mild degrees of stress. In the following example the precipitating emotion could possibly have been social in origin.[19]

It is a feature of authoritarian hierarchical organisations that career prospects depend, amongst other things, upon swift obedience to orders from above. So, if you are asked to do something, you jump to it. Unlike the exercise of power, which is generally satisfying, such immediate obedience may not always be enjoyable to the person who does the obeying. Some people may love to obey and may be whole-hearted in their readiness to act in accordance with the dictates of another. But there are others who obey only because forced to do so by reason of the fact that their career depends on it. For such individuals manifestations of obedience may well engender considerable conflict. They obey, but underneath seem to be saying, 'Why the hell should I?' Now since airlines *are* of necessity authoritarian organisations, it is possible that some members of their flight crews, despite knowing obedience is essential for reasons of safety, are subject to this conflict. For such people it could constitute a source of stress and might possibly explain the following curious incident.

In 1979 the Captain of a Boeing 747, *en route* from Boston to London, told his flight engineer to turn on the fuel heaters. Thereupon the engineer tried to do as he was bid.

Now it so happened that though relatively new to 747s, this engineer had served for many years on 707s. This should have been no great problem, since the flight decks of the two Boeings have much in common. There is, however, at least one small difference between them. On 707s the four fuel-heater switches are protected by a safety guard, but on 747s they are not. On 747s the safety guard is reserved for the four fuel supply switches. Need one say more? Obediently the engineer lifted the safety guard and switched off the supply to the engines. One by one the great turbo-fans ceased to spin. An amazing quiet descended on the aircraft as it began gliding down to the Atlantic 39,000 feet below.

'What have you done?' asked the Captain (though he probably did not put it quite like that). Even as he posed this searching question he switched over to standby-power. Thereupon the engineer, no doubt chastened by his error, made his second mistake. He moved all the engine switches to 'flight start', thereby running the risk of draining the batteries before anything would start – other than dismay amongst the passengers – as they plunged towards the sea.

Fortunately, however, the Captain remained master of what had become a delicate situation. With commendable *sang-froid* he 'persuaded' the engineer to be less ambitious and just concentrate on starting No. 2 engine. When this was done the electrical power from *its* generator enabled the other engines to restart. With this new lease of life the 747 levelled out some way above the waves and so continued on its journey.

In the past the occasional disaster, as when a diver who gets into trouble *forgets* to release his weight belt (a not uncommon occurrence apparently), or a signalman *forgets* about the existence of a train, or a flight engineer *forgets* that not all flight decks are identical, may have seemed a small price to pay for a stress sensitive memory system. But in a nuclear age the possibility of such errors should be taken rather more seriously.

Not surprisingly, an inappropriate stress response system is equally unhelpful when it comes to the more central processes of thinking, planning and decision-making. Even without narrowed attention, perceptual distortion and lapses of memory, the making of a rational choice when confronted with different courses of action is often quite exceptional.

Why should this be? Again the short answer is that, since our capacities for perceiving, remembering and thinking evolved for the gratification of bodily and social needs, they are forever at the mercy of the emotions to which these needs give rise. This state of affairs sounds bad enough, but what is worse is the disturbing paradox that the more emotionally important the decision that has to be made, the less rational our approach to making it.

Compare holidays with marriage. In the case of holidays most people start planning months in advance. They pore over brochures, consult friends and remember past holidays. There is much weighing of odds. What is the probability of snow in the Alps at particular times of the year? What is the likelihood of sun on the Costa Brava? Which is worse, a broken ankle on the nursery slopes or tummy ache in Tunis? How much will it cost? Whom are we likely to meet? Whom can we be sure of avoiding? Which is more unfaceable, endless veal in an Austrian guesthouse or interminable spaghetti on the Italian Riviera? And so on.

How does marriage compare? Is there a similar sifting of evidence and weighing of probabilities? Probably not. One falls in love and then, having plunged into this vortex of the heart, irrationality takes over.

Your future spouse may be cold and selfish. Your future mother-in-law may resemble a cottage loaf with a blue rinse. She may exude hostility with a voice like a buzzsaw, but do these facts feature in the decision? Probably not. And supposing your beloved's father looks about as cheerful as someone who's swallowed the breadknife, does this constitute a negative pay-off? Not at all. Do you even consider the possibility that your angel will grow to be like Mama, and you'll be the one with the breadknife? Not at all. As the divorce statistics suggest, the decision to marry X rather than Y, this emotionally important decision, probably the most important of your life, has about it as much rationality as the forays of an intoxicated woodlouse.

Why should feelings so cloud reason? How does it come about that, when in the grip of strong emotions, even the coolest brain may show tendencies verging on the psychotic?

One answer probably lies in the dark mists of our evolutionary past. Animals that waited too long studying form and weighing probabilities would have perished. Put yourself in their position. If you saw your lunch galloping away from you, would you hang about wrapped in thought? If the nubile doe with the limpid brown eyes, peeping coyly from behind glistening lashes, is going to dart away to that leering buck in the next glade, are you likely to sit around pondering on her mother? Of course not!

In other words we are paying the price for the fact that long ago speed of response was then the very essence of survival.

This dangerous relationship between decision-making, emotional importance and time has in fact turned out to be one of the most ridiculous legacies of our evolutionary past. Thanks to the dubious benefits of high-tech cultures, more people than ever before have too *much* time on their hands. Even with the help of TV, video recorders, and package-deal holidays to the Costa del Sol, lots of people simply don't know how to fill their days. But they still run their lives as if every second counted, pelting home impervious to fog, speed limits, and the daily toll of road accidents, only to spend a listless evening watching the box, or at some excruciatingly boring dinner party. Far from diminishing the compulsive preoccupation with time, our culture emphasises it quite early in life. Now you'll be fed, now you'll sit on the potty, now you'll finish sitting on the potty, you'll be late for school, and so on. Most people's working lives are regimented by the clock.

I.Q., the very yardstick by which we attempt to measure intellectual ability, is often measured in terms of performance against time. It is as if we are determined to pit ourselves against computers, the one great virtue of which is that they can do lots of very simple things very quickly, and are ignoring the fact that, although electronic devices may indeed be able to process information at something approaching the speed of light, our brains do not and cannot ever approach such celerity of action. But not one of our present silicon-based computers, left to its own devices, could write the plays of Shakespeare or successfully remove a brain tumour or solve the problems of East–West tension. The human brain, like the mills of God, seems designed to grind slowly on problems of enormous complexity. To try and measure its intellectual ability with the yardstick of speed of response is as absurd as it would be to estimate the excellence of a Bishop by popping him on the bathroom scales. And yet we continue to assess mental prowess by such ridiculous contests as *Mastermind*.

A particular hazard of this preoccupation with time is that it seduces people into taking short cuts. So eager are they to give an answer in five seconds rather than ten that they tend to ignore, bypass or leap over something which should have claimed their attention. Investigators[20] of this foible asked people questions like this: 'Here is a description of a personality – he is solemn, orderly, meek, and introverted. Is he more likely to be a farmer or a librarian?'

The majority replied, incorrectly 'librarian'. In fact this 'solemn etc.' person is more likely to be a farmer (and not just because of the weather we've been having this year). He's more likely to be a farmer for the very simple reason that there are more farmers than librarians. But they were in so much of a hurry to answer the question that the subjects in this experiment took a fatal short cut, completely ignoring a vital component of statistical problems of this kind – base-rate probabilities.

The example given may seem banal, even trivial, but take the case of a diagnostician trying to decide whether a collection of symptoms that are common to many illnesses (in their early stages) were due to diseases A, B or C. How could he maximise his chances of coming up with the right answer without taking into account the general incidence of the maladies in question?

Back in the jungle, years ago, simple decisions as to whether to hide or make a run for it when danger loomed had to be made very quickly, but the sort of decisions required of modern man necessitate more careful and prolonged cerebration. And yet, paradoxically, the more hazardous the content and complex the issue the greater the tendency to make snap judgements and wild guesses.

Take the job of teaching people to fly. Like teaching people to drive (as Bob Newhart has illustrated in his sketch 'The Driving Instructor'), teaching people to fly is a serious and sometimes nerve-racking experience. Hence it is not surprising to discover that some flying instructors, because they are involved in a fairly high-risk venture, take irrational short cuts in their thinking. One such is the unjustified assumption that students respond better to punishment than to reward. It is based on the observation that if someone does a brilliant landing and is rewarded with praise he tends to do less well next time. If however, one of their students lands his plane like a sack of potatoes falling off a ten-foot wall, and they lay about him with blistering invective, he tends to do better next time. So they go away scratching their heads and muttering, 'There you are – it just goes to show – punishment is the only language these so-and-sos understand'.

It may be, but this conclusion certainly does not follow from the observations of the flying instructors. All they have witnessed is the statistical phenomenon of regression to the mean. Very good or very bad landings are, by definition, events of considerable rarity lying at the two extremes of normal flying behaviour. If someone has come down with exceptional skill then, by chance alone, he will tend to do less well next time. Similarly, the man who crash-lands his long-suffering aircraft will, when he's out of plaster and back on the airfield, probably do better. By chance alone he will probably regress nearer to the mean of normal flying behaviour.

Needless to say, the motives to save time receive support from other motives – laziness, resistance to altering a course of behaviour on which one has already embarked, and the decision to terminate a boring activity for something more enjoyable. It is likely that all these were occupying the mind of a Boeing 727 pilot approaching Funchal, Madeira on November 19th, 1972.[21] Having been cleared to land, the pilot of the Portuguese airliner was then given new instructions. Owing, he was told, to a sudden change of wind, he should now approach from the opposite direction. The pilot replied, 'I am on finals and intend to land.' And this he did, 2,000 feet beyond the runway threshold. The 727 completed the remaining 3,000 feet of the runway in record time, shot off the end, down a bank and burst into flames: 125 people died because the pilot couldn't bear to change his mind.

Unseemly haste is not the only consequence of trying to make important decisions. Equally damaging is the symptom of indecision caused by conflict. If every time a rat approaches a piece of food he receives an electric shock, a state of indecision will be forced upon him by incompatible needs. He may not know it, but he is in the grip of an approach-avoidance conflict. The situation is not immediately lethal. Provided the shock is not too severe, or the need for food too acute, he may well spend a long time just rocking to and fro. Nothing is running out except possibly the patience of the experimenter. But supposing he *has* to make a decision one way or another? What then?

The runway of the Harry S. Truman airport at St Thomas in the Virgin Islands, like its famous namesake, does not suffer fools gladly. It is not one of the world's longest and at its far end stands a mountain.

On a warm day in 1976 the pilot of an American Airlines 727 encountered another hazard of this place.[22] As it neared the ground, the Boeing was suddenly wafted upwards by hot air rising from the tarmac.

With his aircraft floating rather than flying, the pilot fought to regain control. By the time he had done so it would still have been possible to make a safe landing. Using flaps and reverse thrust he could still have brought the plane to a halt before the end of the runway. But he changed his mind in favour of going round again.

The 727 began to rise but then, presumably because increasingly aware of the mountain looming up at him, the pilot changed his mind again and attempted to land.

This time, however it really was too late. Now, no amount of braking could prevent the plane streaking off the end of the runway, up a bank, through a chain-link fence, and into a petrol filling station. Amongst the pumps of this thoughtfully placed hazard it burst into flames. There were no survivors.

The indecision of this otherwise competent pilot killed quite a lot of people. Indecision by politicians or military commanders can be immeasurably more devastating in its effects. The indecision of Marshal Bazaine, who locked up himself and his army in the fortress of Metz because he couldn't decide what to do next, cost France the Franco-Prussian War, while the indecision of the two commanders in the following rather longer example in Chapter 12 cost close on a million French and German lives.

12

Verdun

A monster fearful and hideous, vast and eyeless.
                                                    Virgil

In the course of this book many examples have been given of our self-destructive tendencies, but for the most part they have been minor incidents – 230 people killed in a railway accident, 582 in an air disaster, 1,400 in the sinking of a ship, a few hundred dying prematurely from cancer, a dozen or so murders, and so on. Apart from the millions who died in the last holocaust they are all small beer. Each of these examples, moreover, served to illustrate only one or two of our shortcomings. As such it is hoped that they fulfilled their purpose, but what we need now by way of an interim summary is one single catastrophe of epic proportions. It would need to be an episode which, in terms of human destruction, comes as near as possible to what might, what could, what probably will come to pass within the foreseeable future.

Doubtless there are other examples, but what happened at Verdun in 1916 fits the bill most neatly. Verdun exemplifies what can happen when decisions about whether or not to use the technology of mass destruction are influenced by the sources of error that were outlined earlier (page 150). Stress, deranged personalities, irrelevant motives, the denial of unpalatable information, egomania, unconscious conflict and inordinate morality all played their part in this ten-month destruction of over one million people.

In 1916 the German Commander-in-Chief, von Falkenhayn, for want of a better idea, decided to try and win the war by 'bleeding

175

the French white'. To do this he chose the salient of Verdun. He reasoned that Joffre would, if necessary, sacrifice his whole army to defend this emotionally significant though strategically unimportant place. His reasoning proved correct.

The battle which followed lasted ten months. It has been described as the worst in history. It consumed 420,000 people. Another 800,000 were gassed or wounded. To these costs must be added the genetic loss to France and Germany, apparently permanent damage to the French countryside, and the tragic consequences for France, in the Second World War, of attitudes and beliefs generated by the experience of Verdun. Since the cost to Germany was also enormous, it must indeed be reckoned a bad battle – a ridiculous, stupid, monstrously wasteful battle.

If political differences *must* be settled by armed conflict, then at least the operation should be conducted competently with as little mess as possible. By these lights the 'surgery' at Verdun was inept. It resembled the blundering of a drunken quack, trying to amputate someone's leg with a blunt bread knife.

Why? Ordinary stupidity is clearly not the answer. So intellectually able was von Falkenhayn and so adequately provided with those traits which take an officer to the top of his profession that he achieved the unique distinction of being, at one and the same time, Minister of Defence and Chief of the General Staff. Even his appearance was reassuring. With his close-cropped hair and aristocratic features he looked 'the typical Prussian General',[1] a man of steel, stern and ruthless. But beneath his encouraging exterior were character traits which, as we shall see, did not accord with the sort of war he liked to wage.

Falkenhayn's problem was one of conflict and indecision. More than most, he seemed to epitomise that abiding problem of professionalising violence – the inner conflict between boundless hostility and fear of the consequences. On the one hand, he opposed the practice of duelling but, on the other, rationalised it as necessary for the honour of the army. He was responsible for the first use of poison gas, but when ordering its use at Verdun was too mean in the amount of phosgene which his artillery was allowed to deliver. Though more impervious to casualty lists than even Joffre or Haig, and a ready advocate of such disagreeable policies as those of unrestricted submarine warfare, and promiscuous bombing in reprisal for Allied raids, he would nervously call off a potentially successful offensive as too risky and ambitious.

Given the nature of this cold, secretive, hostile, cordially disliked yet nervously prudent individual, the prospect of 'bleeding the French white' must have seemed extraordinarily attractive to him. It would be fun to amass secretly, in the forests to the east of Verdun, the biggest collection of cannons the world had ever seen (and beside each piece, the neatly ordered piles of shells). He probably relished the thought that, when the time came, he would be able to liquidate, from a safe vantage point, hundreds of thousands of Frenchmen. He could hardly have devised a more orderly and methodical piece of bloodletting. But some people are never satisfied.

Having assembled his 1,220 guns and 2,500,000 shells, Falkenhayn began to falter. Evidently, delight at the thought of the impending holocaust was not the only thing going on inside his bullet head. There seemed to be another voice which said, 'Take care, make sure you don't weaken yourself elsewhere – and what if things go wrong?' Though it may seem inappropriate to use the word 'conscience' in connection with such a man, there was, at this stage, in the behaviour of this 'gentle' creature the suggestion of an impulse quite contrary to that of unbridled destructiveness. It showed itself in three ways. First, despite the opportunities offered by his mighty arsenal, he seemed to forget the golden principle of concentration of force. Deaf to the entreaties of his underlings that he should attack the French simultaneously from both sides of the Meuse, he insisted on restricting his assault to the right, or eastern, bank. He must, he felt, keep sufficient troops in reserve and in other places, to meet the possibility of an Allied counter-offensive. His typically obsessive concern was to be secure at all points at all times.

Second, Falkenhayn seemed suddenly indecisive about the object of the exercise. Having planned the attack with the express purpose of bleeding the French white, he was now happily accepting his Fifth Army's plans for a *Blitzkrieg* victory at Verdun. Since a rapid capturing of Verdun would effectively prevent this place from becoming a centre for slow blood letting, he seemed to be having second thoughts.

Let's leave Falkenhayn for the moment, uneasily poised to eliminate a million of his fellow men, and consider his adversaries, the French. In a way, their situation was the exact opposite of that occupied by the Germans – it can be summed up as one of gross unreadiness. In accordance with the current philosophy of the French military establishment, Joffre had reduced the great fortifications of Verdun to little more than impotent memorials to the foresight and prudence with which an earlier generation of Frenchmen had countered external threats. Using the recent fate of Belgian forts as their excuse, the French High Command opined that burying oneself (and one's honour) under mountains of concrete was no way to fight a war. Soldiers, they said, should be out in the open where they could be seen, not cowering underground like moles.

In the luxury of their palace at Chantilly, Joffre and his staff had managed to remain buoyant and optimistic about the virtues of unmolelike behaviour despite the events of 1915. During this expensive year they had pursued their policy of 'grignotage' or 'nibbling away' at the enemy. This simple, cosy-sounding activity which, according to Horne, has been likened to 'trying to bite through a steel door with badly fitting false teeth' cost France 50 per cent of her regular officers, and approximately the same number of lives as Britain lost in the entire four years of the war. (And no one could accuse Britain of being miserly in her expenditure of soldiers' lives.)

As the following description of grignotage in action suggests, the staff did well to keep their spirits up when confronted with the realities of their doctrine:

> Officers declined to make themselves inconspicuous by carrying a rifle: instead they led the way brandishing a cane and were picked off by the hundred. The attacks assumed a drearily stereotyped pattern. First came the preliminary bombardment and the agonizing wait in the front lines; then the attack, with perhaps a fortunate few, generally very few, reaching the first German trenches to bayonet the survivors there; a brief pause, then the enemy's deadly barrage on their own captured position, followed by the inevitable counter-attack; finally, the attackers, too few to hold their ground, driven back to their own trenches, decimated relics of the original force; the remaining three-quarters to nine-tenths, dead, or dying with their bowels hooked on the wire of No-Man's-Land . . . hoping only to attract the merciful attention of an enemy machine-gunner.[2]

The lesson which Joffre drew from these grisly events was not that they represented a murderously uneconomical way of waging war, but that their artillery was too old and too sparse to carry out an effective preliminary bombardment. Thus it was that he found a second reason to dismantle the forts of Verdun – to lay his hands on the many guns that lay there mouldering.

Meanwhile, in accordance with the principle that none are so deaf as those who do not wish to hear, not a whisper of German intentions percolated through to the minds of those who controlled France's military machine. At lower levels of the military hierarchy, however, some forebodings of the approaching storm were beginning to be felt. The first to voice his fear was General Coutançeau, Governor of Verdun. As the man on the spot, he gave his opinion that it was wrong to denude Verdun of guns. He was promptly sacked for daring to criticise the High Command. His replacement, the elderly General Herr, though equally dismayed by the total unpreparedness of Verdun, took a softer line. He merely pleaded for reinforcements to carry out the necessary task of strengthening the fortress. Joffre's reply was to withdraw more batteries of guns with the reassuring comment, 'You will not be attacked. Verdun is not the point of attack. The Germans don't know that Verdun has been disarmed.'[3]

The next applicant for help was made of stronger stuff. Lieutenant Colonel Emile Driant, who had been entrusted with the defence of a key position at Verdun, wrote to the Minister of Defence:

The sledgehammer blow will be delivered on the line of Verdun – Nancy. What moral effect would be created by the capture of one of these cities! . . . we are doing everything, day and night, to make our front inviolable . . . but there is one thing about which we can do nothing; *the shortage of hands*. And it is to this that I beg to call the attention of the Minister. If our first line is carried by a massive attack, our second line is inadequate and we are not succeeding in establishing it; *lack of workers* and I add: lack of barbed wire.[4]

In response to Driant's letter the Minister of Defence, Galliéni, sent a delegation to Verdun. In due course they reported back. Everything that Driant had said was true. The report was sent to Joffre, who promptly flew into a rage. Of his eventual reply Liddell Hart said, 'It might well be framed and hung up in all the bureaux of officialdom the world over – to serve as the mummy at the feast.'[5]

I cannot be a party [said Joffre] to soldiers under my command bringing before the Government, by channels other than the hierarchic channel, complaints or protests concerning the execution of my orders . . . It is calculated to disturb profoundly discipline in the Army . . . to sum up, I consider nothing justifies the fear which, in the name of the Government, you express in your dispatch of December 16 . . .

Since Driant died heroically not long after these events, he was saved from the humiliation of a court martial.

In the days that followed, despite their poor facilities for gathering military intelligence, despite the half-heartedness of their aerial reconnaissance, despite the absence of anyone on General Herr's staff who could analyse air photographs and despite their lethargic approach to discovering the enemy's intentions, the French obtained so many scraps of evidence for what was to come that there must have been few soldiers (or civilians) at Verdun who did not fear the worst. But somehow, like the three wise monkeys, Joffre and his staff remained wrapped in ignorance and innocence. The fact that their aerial photography showed no new 'jumping-off' trenches was seized upon (as the Germans had hoped it would be) as proof that no attack was about to be launched.

Almost within hours of Falkenhayn's attack, Joffre was telling Haig that an attack on Russia was the next item on the German agenda. Not to be outdone, French Operations offered the pontification that any offensive against France would occur at Artois or in the Champagne.

Thanks to the monumental complacency of their leaders, the future for France looked very black indeed. But then, just as Falkenhayn was to give the signal for his great barrage to begin, destiny (or whatever it is that watches over bad Generals) stepped in – the weather broke. It was a temporary respite. A week later, during which time the French made some belated minor improvements to their position, the skies cleared and the battle of Verdun began.

Within minutes a hurricane of high-explosive shells was falling on the French positions. The earth seemed to erupt as trees, trenches, concrete pill-boxes and men disintegrated into unrecognisable heaps of debris. On one section alone the deluge of steel and high explosive was fed by a steady forty shells a minute. Into just one area of 500 by 1,000 yards, Falkenhayn's artillery pumped no fewer than 80,000 heavy shells. And then, quite suddenly, the barrage ceased. Those who had not been buried alive or ripped open by the flying shell fragments, emerged cautiously from what was left of their trenches and dugouts. For many, however, the pleasure they derived from finding themselves alive was short-lived as the Germans switched to a new more appropriate form of destruction – short-range mortar shells. Meanwhile, the long-range guns opened up once more on targets farther back.

During a second lull, in what was intended to be a systematic annihilation of the French army, German patrols advanced upon the remains of the French positions. The latter had certainly changed out of all recognition:

> It looked as if a giant sledgehammer had pounded every inch of the ground over and over again. Most of the fine oaks and beeches had been reduced to jagged stumps a few feet high . . . from the few branches that remained hung the usual horrible testimony of a heavy bombardment in the woods; the shredded uniforms, dangling gravid with some unnamable human remnant still within; sometimes just the entrails of a man, product of a direct hit. It seemed impossible that any human being could have survived in the methodically worked-over, thrashed and ploughed up wood.[6]

But some did survive, which only goes to show that however hard one tries, however conscientious and dedicated to the task of mass extermination, there will always be a tiresome few who, by some freak of chance, escape destruction. The Germans now learned this to their cost as the impossible happened and French bullets brought them to a bloody halt. Ever resourceful, some of the German patrols introduced an exciting new variant into intra species war – flame throwers. But even these, though fearful in what they could do to eyes and mouths, and pain-receptors in the human skin, failed to achieve the successes that had been hoped for. And sometimes, if the operator was shot, he might swing round on his colleagues and hose them down with liquid fire.

But the main reason for the Germans' failure, on the first day of the ten-month battle, lay in the pusillanimous mind of their leader, Falkenhayn. Like a nervous surgeon who, half-way through making the first incision, develops paralysis of the hand, he held back his main assault until it was too late. After suffering appalling casualties, the undermanned patrols were left that night stranded in no man's land. This was the prelude to a succession of similar disappointments for the Germans.

On the second day of the battle the French doctrine that every inch of ground lost must be retaken by immediate riposte, combined with Joffre's failure to provide what was required for the defence of Verdun, played into the hands of Falkenhayn. Amongst those who paid with their lives for the negligence of the French General Staff, were the redoubtable Colonel Driant and all but a handful of his two battalions of valiant Chasseurs.

Meanwhile a sixty-year-old divisional commander, General Bapst, was having troubles of his own. Aware that his position was about to be encircled and that, if it was, he would have insufficient troops to defend two other equally important sections, he sought permission to withdraw. At first his superior, General Chretien, said 'No', but then after two hours of indecision ordered Bapst to make up his own mind. Bapst, his own HQ rendered uninhabitable by a large shell, ordered the withdrawal. Three hours later he received a peremptory order from his indecisive superior, 'The Brabant position should not have been evacuated without permission from the superior command.' Bapst was ordered to retake it. Half an hour later he received yet a third order from the same source telling him not to use too many men.

Obediently, Bapst ordered the impossible. But by this time there was no one left to carry out the counter-attack so the order was countermanded. Though Bapst's behaviour had been perfectly correct and had saved two regiments from annihilation, he narrowly missed being court martialled and was never again given an active command.

And so the courageous, futile, French attacks went on until whole battalions, divisions, even corps of the French army simply ceased to be and were replaced by others who in their turn were devoured by the remorseless mincing machine of Verdun. Eating well and sleeping well, in far-off Chantilly, General Joseph Jacques Césaire Joffre maintained his usual monumental calm. Provided he was never kept waiting for his lunch or dinner and provided he could take his afternoon nap and have a good night's sleep, he remained a source of great confidence and fount of optimism for all those who had the good fortune to be with him and not amongst those who, for days at a time, had had no sleep at all, whose rations of greasy meat, when they arrived at all, were scarcely distinguishable in smell or texture from the muddy putrescence of the battlefield, who, as often as not, were reduced to drinking water from craters in which floated the bits and pieces of their dismembered comrades.

It was only when the Germans eventually broke through and the whole French position was in danger of collapse that Joffre suffered any serious discomfort. Against his express order that on no account was he to be woken from his night's sleep, General de Castelnau had him roused from his slumbers for a word of advice. Such are the horrors of war!

Joffre's response to the crisis was to appoint Pétain as the new commander of the Verdun forces.

Amongst war lords like Haig, Joffre and Falkenhayn, Pétain was the odd man out – he cared about his solders, he visited units, impressed his personality upon all under his command, visited the wounded and when things went wrong did not try to shift the blame on to someone else.* He believed in attrition by expending shells rather than lives. Deploring the murderously wasteful methods of his predecessors, he believed that a properly organised defence and defensive tactics could usually stop an attack long before it reached its objective. Not very surprisingly these beliefs, and therefore their proponent, were such anathema to the closed minds of French High Command that Pétain's rise had been slow until such time as he could put his theories into practice following the total collapse and discrediting of Joffre's Plan XVII. In the great retreat of 1914 and later, on the Marne, it was the concentrated devastating firepower of Pétain's troops which made his critics eat their words. Judging from its results, Pétain's arrival at Verdun had far more effect upon the efficiency and morale of the fortress's defenders than all the exhortations to 'Resist whatever the cost; let yourselves be cut to pieces on the spit rather than fall back' which they had received so many times before.

At this stage in the ten-month battle the stiffening of French resistance, consequent upon the arrival of France's best General, was not the only problem which began to occupy the minds of the German High Command. For its success their plan had depended upon

* It could be argued that Pétain's concern to avoid unnecessary bloodshed contributed to his fall from grace during the Second World War.

a gradual moving forward of the hundreds of guns and mortars upon which their 'bleeding white' depended. But nobody had foreseen the near impossibility of shifting all this hardware across a terrain that their own shells had converted into a roadless blood-soaked quagmire. As scores of horses and men slipped and struggled to heave the gigantic cannons from the tenacious slime into which they sank, the French steadily improved their defences. It was then, with this dilemma, and with mounting casualties, at the very moment when his forces had come nearest to capturing Verdun, that Falkenhayn added to their misery by holding back those very reserves which could have tipped the balance.

One of Falkenhayn's half-measures had been his steady refusal, in the face of strong contrary advice, to attack Verdun from both banks of the Meuse. Like a man who insists on fighting with one hand tied behind his back, he had confined the attention of his artillery and armies to the right bank. His excuse had been lack of available troops and the necessity for holding on to his reserves. Now, belatedly, under pressure from his Chief of Staff and commander of the Fifth Army he changed his mind. An attack would go in on the left bank even though it now required more troops than would have been necessary a month earlier. So began the three-month battle for a small hill with the appropriate name of Mort Homme.

Within a fortnight French casualties had reached 89,000 and German 81,607. Week after week the contest swayed back and forth with what had once been French villages, but were now unrecognisable conglomerates of mud and decomposing flesh, changing hands over a dozen times. In one small area of this hideous battlefield 10,000 French alone lay protruding from the mud, their rotting broken corpses producing such a miasma of putrefaction that the Germans had to issue a double ration of tobacco to those who fought there.

By the end of May German losses were even greater than those suffered by the French. Somewhere along the line the policy of 'bleeding white' had become a fatal boomerang.

While all this was going on, those on the right bank of the Meuse had their share of problems. So intense and so continuous was the shelling that there was little opportunity to bury the dead. Attempts to dig graves invariably meant that the diggers too would need a grave before their task was completed. Craters and gullies were used instead – 'there were few of these in which did not float some ghastly, stinking fragment of humanity' – but even here even the dead did not rest undisturbed. Of one gully nicknamed La Ravaine de la Mort, Horne writes

> Day after day the German heavies pounded the corpses in this gully, until they were quartered and re-quartered, to one eye-witness it seemed as if it were filled with dismembered limbs that no one could or would bury. Even when buried, shells exhume the bodies, then reinter them, chop them to pieces, play with them as a cat plays with a mouse. As the weather grew warmer and the numbers of dead multiplied, the horror reached new peaks. The compressed area of the battlefield became an open cemetery in which each square foot contained some decomposed piece of flesh - you found the dead embedded in the walls of trenches, heads, legs, and half-bodies, just as they had been shovelled out of the way by the picks and shovels of the working party.[7]

Far behind the lines the two High Commands, German and French, though insulated from the squalid stresses of the battlefield, had troubles of their own. On the German side the Commander-in-Chief, von Falkenhayn, and Crown Prince William commanding the Fifth Army were losing interest in the 'bleeding white' experiment and the capture of Verdun respectively. But General Knobelsdorf, Prince William's Chief-of-Staff, thought differently. By working on the weak-minded Falkenhayn and removing from the Fifth Army those senior officers who supported Prince William's view that it was time to call a half, Knoblesdorf achieved his purpose. The German offensive would go on.

On the French side a comparable difference of opinions was evident between Pétain and Joffre. Left to himself Pétain, in accordance with the principle of saving casualties while at the same time using defensive fire power to destroy the attacker, would have withdrawn from Verdun and the lethal salient on the right bank. He had already prepared highly secret plans for luring the German army through a succession of carefully prepared lines upon which they, not the French, would be bled white. But Pétain was not a free agent. He knew if he tried to implement his plans he would be sacked and an *attaque à outrance* General appointed in his place. From Pétain's experience such a man would be spendthrift with the lives of his soldiers. And so he compromised, first by a reduction in French counter-attacks, second, by persuading Joffre that, after so many days, divisions should be taken out of the fighting zone and sent to rear areas for rest and recuperation. In contrast to the German practice of either keeping units in the front line until they were annihilated or 'topping up' with replacements as these were needed, Pétain's method, besides being infinitely more humane, stood a far better chance of maintaining morale. It also had two valuable, if somewhat paradoxical side effects – while the German troops became demoralised by France's apparently inexhaustible supply of fresh troops, German intelligence, in pursuit of their particular wish-fulfilling fantasy, managed to view the same data as proving that French losses were much higher than they really were! This of course only encouraged Knobelsdorf to continue his offensive with renewed obstinacy.

The beauty of these serendipitous consequences was lost on Joffre, whose single-track mind got no further than the fact that, for Pétain, yielding ground seemed to take precedence over launching counter offensives. Just as Falkenhayn was deceived by *his* gatherers of military intelligence into overestimating French losses, so too was Joffre misled by totally false information about the magnitude of German casualties. In Joffre's case the heaven-sent belief that Germany was running out of men made him increasingly impatient with Pétain's lack of offensive spirit, but at the same time quite unable to part with those reserves which Pétain needed. Like Falkenhayn, Joffre shared the obsessive trait of having to keep something back – in this case it was soldiers for the next place of execution – the Somme.

Joffre was growing restive. It's reasonable to suppose that as he contemplated Pétain's handling of Verdun he experienced a spectrum of emotions not one of which was enjoyable. Here was this military heretic enormously popular with his men, considered by the French public as a national hero, but acting in a way quite contrary to the book. How galling that a man who preferred defence to attack, who cared about husbanding lives, should now be proclaimed as Saviour of Verdun. And how exquisitely painful that he, Joffre, his reputation already sunk to low ebb in the public mind, should be unable to sack Pétain because of the public outcry this would evoke.

But happily for Joffre he belonged to that group of Generals who, rather than use up their imagination on the battlefield, reserve this valuable commodity for their political manoeuvrings. It now came to his aid. He would not sack Pétain, but propel him upstairs or more precisely to the job of commanding Army Group Centre. This move, while still in theory allowing Pétain some say in events at Verdun, would effectively deprive him of direct control. For the man on the spot, the new commander of the Second Army, Joffre chose Robert Nivelle, an individual regarded by posterity as probably one of the worst Generals France has ever had. And just in case Nivelle, by himself, was not bad enough he brought with him two terrible assistants – his Chief-of-Staff, Major d'Alenson and his Chief Executive, General Mangin.

As a team to destroy what was left of the French army, they could not have been better chosen. If Nivelle needed any encouragement to squander lives in wasteful counter-strokes, then the cadaverous d'Alenson, a sort of military Rasputin, was there to give it. Since he himself was dying of consumption, the wholesale slaughter of his fellow countrymen meant little, provided they achieved victory for France before he died.

By themselves ambition and resolve are not enough, if there is no one to execute the deeds. Here again, Nivelle was well served. In General 'butcher' Mangin he possessed the toughest, roughest 'gorilla' in the French army – the perfect hatchet man. Whether Mangin suffered from excess of aggressive drive, a surfeit of what Freud called the 'death instinct' or was merely trying to compensate for whatever it was (or wasn't) that gave him a high-pitched and squeaky voice remains a matter for debate. Suffice it to say that for this amiable creature the preservation of life, whether it was his own or others, counted for absolutely nothing. Trying to restrain him from attacking the enemy on every possible occasion would have been like trying to contain a hungry leopard within a paper bag. But Nivelle did not even try. On the contrary he and Mangin set about the Germans with a ferocity hitherto undreamt of. The results were catastrophic for both sides. Take the case of Fort Douaumont. Owing to a succession of unbelievable errors and incredible shortsightedness this massive, fairly hideous, pile of stone and concrete, the pride of France, 'the world's most powerful fortress', had fallen accidentally into the hands of a German Sergeant and his ten obedient if nonplussed men. The consternation and dismay produced by this military *faux pas* was immediate and far reaching. Had it been taken by a posse of charladies, French embarrassment and humiliation could hardly have been more acute.

No wonder then that now, when Mangin's burning gaze lit upon the provocative contours of Fort Douaumont, he vowed to get it back. While Pétain was reluctant to try and recapture the fortress with insufficient men, Nivelle and Joffre were delighted for Mangin to have a go. Rarely has glory exacted such a price.

Consistent with Nivelle's persistent inability to keep vital information from reaching German ears the enemy knew all about his plans within forty-eight hours of these being issued. Understandably, they prepared to receive the French invasions.

Mangin deployed his mortars. For five days they bombarded Douaumont. But, as the Commandant of another fort had predicted, they were not enough. Though they killed a lot of Germans and sacrificed the last shreds of surprise, not a crack did they make in the main body of the fort.

Assured by Mangin that his bombardment had 'completely flattened' their objective, the French Battalion Commanders prepared for zero hour. Before it struck, however, two German shells fell fair and square on the French 'jumping off' trenches. To those sophisticated in such matters, they conveyed a simple message 'We have your range and are just waiting for you to show yourselves'.

The French did so. As they emerged from their trenches they were greeted by the carefully sited German artillery. Within minutes the 129th Regiment, which had been detailed to take the fort, was reduced to forty-five men. One entire company had diminished to a Lieutenant and twenty-seven men. Of the flanking 74th Regiment, one battalion was completely wiped out and another, pinned down by the murderously accurate German fire, never left the trenches. A few broke through and reached the fort. But after a day of inglorious activity during which reinforcements, ordered up by Mangin, were annihilated before they even reached their objectives, Douaumont remained firmly in German hands.

An appropriate comment was found in the diary of a young Second Lieutenant. Unlike his usually rather flippant observations on the military scene, he wrote of his last day of life; 'Humanity is mad! It must be mad to do what it is doing. What a massacre! What scenes of horror and carnage! I cannot find words to translate my impressions. Hell cannot be so terrible. Men are mad!' [8]

Having lost far more than the Germans, including a thousand prisoners left in enemy hands, Mangin had succeeded in leaving a

500-yard gap in the French front. Somewhat late in the day, some may think, he was removed from the section by his Corps Commander and passed 'for neither the first nor last time into temporary disgrace'.[9]

It was typical of the man that Pétain, in his account of the battle, took full responsibility for the disaster and, with a magnanimity rarely to be found in the afterthoughts of war leaders, laid no blame upon Nivelle and Mangin. And as a measure of the rightness, purely from the standpoint of military efficiency, of his concern for morale and husbanding lives, there is the fact that the abortive attempt to recapture Douaumont produced those first cracks in discipline of the French army which culminated in the widespread mutinies of 1917. It was these rather than the loss of the fort which most nearly cost France the war.

From this awesome sequence of events it might be thought that Nivelle had learned a lesson. But he had not.

This was clear from what happened when the Germans turned their attentions to another important buttress in the French defensive system – Fort Vaux. Like the other forts at Verdun, Vaux had long ago been deprived of its main armaments by Joffre. Hence it was a remarkable testimony to the fortitude and courage of the Fort Commander, Major Raynal and his small garrison, that for a week they held out against four German battalions. With nothing more than machine-guns and grenades, a cocker spaniel and four pigeons, they withstood gas and flame throwers and an artillery barrage which, at its worst, reached a crescendo of 2,000 shells an hour. What defeated them in the end was thirst. Despite earlier warnings, the High Command had neglected to do anything about the supply or storage of water in this key defence position. As a result, before finally capitulating, Raynal's men had been reduced to licking the slime from the walls and drinking their own urine.

During the week-long siege Fort Vaux's defenders had only one source of communication with the outside world, their pigeons. Drugged with the toxic fumes from inside the fort these wretched birds staggered into the air with desperate messages for a relief attacking force. The last of them, bedraggled and half gassed, fulfilled its mission, was relieved of its message and then dropped dead. It can be seen to this day, stuffed, in a Paris museum, the only member of its species to be awarded the Légion d'Honneur.

Nivelle's part in the fall of Fort Vaux was not auspicious. While it was still in French hands he launched five relief attacks. Each failed for the same reason, an insufficient number of troops engaged. Losses in these inadequate attempts had been terrible. But when Raynal and his survivors eventually capitulated, Nivelle steadfastly denied that the fort had passed into German hands. Even an enemy broadcast confirming their victory was dismissed by him as a hoax. His honour was at stake so, as if to prove that black was white, he then ordered a sixth attack to relieve a garrison that was in fact no longer there to be relieved. The Generals under him protested at this madness but even his evil genius d'Alenson could not deter him. The consequences were predictable. The German machine-gunners concealed in their embrasures held their fire until the French were within yards of their positions then mowed them down at point-blank range.

Disappointed yet not totally dismayed, Nivelle sought consolation in other futile counter-offensives. Once again his allegiance to the doctrine, 'Attack, attack and never yield ground', combined with Joffre's miserly withholding of reserves for later sacrifice on the Somme, produced nothing but death for the forces in his care. But now a new factor began making itself felt, a not wholly surprising failure in morale. Their feelings lowered by the disaster at Douaumont and Fort Vaux, some French soldiers began to doubt the wisdom of continuing with this insane battle. The first flickerings of mutiny appeared. High Command, ever resourceful, had a remedy.

When a young Second Lieutenant saw his company, already reduced to thirty-five men, was about to be encircled and annihilated he broke the rules and ordered a retreat. This act had not gone unnoticed by other members of the 347th Regiment. Having been subjected to intense shelling they broke for it and ran.

The Second Lieutenant and a young ensign (evidently thrown in for good measure) were promptly shot – without trial – for 'cowardice'. Since these two young officers had a fine reputation in their regiment for bravery under fire, it is not altogether surprising that the story of their fall from grace and ultimate demise was not made public until after the war was over.

Meanwhile, Pétain, rightly concerned by the loss of Fort Vaux, the deteriorating morale, and the renewed German offensive, conveyed his anxieties to GQG. Since this occurred during Joffre's absence in London, some gloom and consternation began to permeate the top levels of the French military staff. Depression and anxiety, however, were dissipated by 'father's' return. Outwardly unmoved by the dire news from Verdun, Joffre blamed Pétain for being an alarmist, adding that there was absolutely nothing to worry about. The fact that he promptly sent General de Castelneau to Verdun, for an on-the-spot assessment, suggests this apparent *sang-froid* was (to mix our anatomical metaphors) only skin deep. There was too, a slightly anxious note in his latest Order of the Day, 'Soldiers of Verdun! . . . I make one more appeal to your courage, your ardour, your spirit of sacrifice, your love of country . . .'

Unfortunately, if not unbelievably, even these valuable sentiments were not enough to turn the tide in France's favour. What saved Verdun, and indeed France in her darkest hour, were not the platitudes of her Commander-in-Chief, but shortcomings on the other side.

Critics of the thesis expounded in this book, anxious to defend humanity against the faintest breath of criticism, might make the point that incompetence is only relative. If, in a battle, or indeed a war, one side loses and the other wins, then at least one side must have been competent. Warming to their theme, such critics would (indeed have) gone on to say that in all probability both sides were competent but one a little more so than the other. Verdun gives the lie to this charitable viewpoint. Neither side won, in any meaningful sense of this word, and both sides took an appallingly long time to achieve their mutual destruction. If this spells competence then this word too has lost its meaning.

To get back to the battle, just when errors by the French General Staff seemed about to culminate in victory for Germany, a long history of curious behaviour by the German Commander-in-Chief turned the tide once more.

As we have seen, Falkenhayn had a number of personality traits which were not conducive to military success. He vacillated. He was hesitant and indecisive. He was over-cautious and obsessive. And when it came to providing reinforcements and concentrating his efforts in one place he was niggardly. But in the end the trait which cost Germany Verdun and ultimately the war, was something other – his overwhelming and repellent arrogance. Like many arrogant people with marked authoritarian traits, Falkenhayn harboured and expressed enormous contempt for peoples and races that were different from himself. In terms of modern psychological jargon, he, a member of the 'in-group', projected on to outgroups the weaknesses of his own mixed-up personality. Now, unfortunately for Germany, one of these outgroups particularly despised by Falkenhayn was her ally, Austria. Even worse was the fact that the Austrian Commander-in-Chief, Field-Marshal Conrad von Hotzendorf, had still not recovered from the fact that the Austrian military had been subordinated to the Prussians since their defeat in 1866. For Conrad this humiliation was sharpened by the knowledge that his troops were inferior to those of Germany. Under the circumstances it was hardly surprising that Conrad should have been sensitive to slighting comments by his Prussian colleague in arms. However, the fact that Germany and Austria were now united in a desperate struggle for existence would, one might suppose, have produced some burying of the hatchet – at least for the duration. Not a bit of it. Neither Falkenhayn nor Conrad would subordinate their feelings to the reality of the military situation. Far from concealing his contempt for the Austrian army, Falkenhayn went out of his way to be unpleasant. Pounding the table he shouted at the Austrian Archduke Karl, 'What is your Imperial Highness thinking of? Whom do you think you have in front of you? I am an experienced Prussian General!' And just for good measure he assured the Archduke on another occasion that Austrian troops were disorganised, inadequate and unmilitary.

Carefully recorded in Conrad's diary, these unkind sentiments did not evoke warm and friendly feelings. By themselves of course such symptoms of mutual antipathy need not have mattered. Unfortunately, however, they found expression in military behaviour that was not only incompetent but in the end, disastrous for both protagonists.

Hostile and secretive, Falkenhayn expressed his contempt by concealing his military intentions from Conrad, and rejecting such military suggestions as were put forward by his Austrian ally. Conrad's response was to look sulky, say nothing, and then go off and follow his own wishes. This pattern of behaviour reached a climax over the matter of Verdun. True to his principles Falkenhayn planned and opened Germany's major offensive for 1916 without a word to Conrad. When Conrad learned of the attack on Verdun he was not amused. By way of retaliation, and without consulting Falkenhayn, he thereupon withdrew troops from the Russian front for the purpose of attacking Italy. (For Conrad the piquancy of this little exercise resided in the fact that Falkenhayn had earlier, and sneeringly, rejected his suggestion that they should jointly attack Italy.) Unfortunately for Conrad his plans miscarried. Owing to inclement weather the attack on Italy was delayed, surprise was lost and so, when his new offensive did eventually begin, it was checked by the Italians.

Worse was to follow. With Austria's eastern front denuded, Russia chose this moment to launch an attack on what was now the weakest point of the Austrian front. Their offensive proved successful. Taken by surprise, the Austrian front collapsed and 400,000 soldiers were captured. For the wretched Conrad these calamities produced the ultimate humiliation as, cap in hand, he confessed his errors to Falkenhayn and sought the latter's help. While no doubt making the most of Conrad's discomfiture, the German Commander-in-Chief nevertheless realised that he had no option but to take three divisions from the Western Front to plug the Austrian gap.

The effect of all this on Verdun was complex, but in the end saved the day for France. For a week Falkenhayn was torn between the conflicting advice of the cautious but realistic Crown Prince and the belligerent Knobelsdorf, but then, consistent with the nature of his personality, gave way to the stronger of these two men. A new 'big push' was launched against the French.

Nivelle had had a precious week in which to scrape together more men and to repair his defences. Nevertheless, the German offensive fought its way to within two and a half miles of Verdun before petering out. That the Germans got as far as they did was partly because they introduced a new factor in the Verdun battle – phosgene gas. This novel way of destroying people, animals and plants was delivered by artillery shells. It effectively silenced those French batteries which lay within its path. Whatever else they did, French gas masks did not seem to hinder the effects of this new irritant.

However, despite the encouraging effects of their new weapon the German offensive was a failure. There were several reasons but one in particular was the Germans' mistrust of novelty. They decided not to risk their all on phosgene. As a consequence there was only sufficient gas to knock out guns in the centre of the French line. Those on the flanks remained to inflict fearful punishment on the German attackers. It was yet another instance of too little used too soon.

In a subsequent attack Knobelsdorf once again used phosgene for his preliminary barrage. As on the previous occasion, those French artillery positions which had been saturated grew silent beneath the swirling toxic fumes. Confidently the German infantry emerged from their trenches and began to move upon the French. Their euphoria, however, was short-lived, for suddenly the full weight of the 'asphyxiated' French artillery opened up with devastating force and accuracy. Nivelle's gunners had apparently risen from the dead. By wisely concealing their possession of a new invention, a phosgene-proof gas mask, the French had turned the tables on their adversary.

With the failure of both their gas attacks the Germans forfeited for ever their chance of capturing Verdun. Apart from one further, futile, costly attack, forced upon his long-suffering countrymen by the incorrigible Knobelsdorf, German forces were from that time onwards on the defensive. For month after month they were pushed further and further back, gradually conceding all the ground that they had gained at such appalling cost.

Once again, however, the reversal of fortunes at Verdun could not be wholly attributed to shifts in competence by the opposing forces. Once again, an event elsewhere – Haig's opening of the battle of the Somme – proved the decisive issue.

French and German readers who feel that this chapter has been unduly critical of continental military commanders may be mollified to learn that those British troops who fought at the Somme fared in some respects even worse under *their* Commander-in-Chief than had the armies of Joffre and Falkenhayn. If, over the port in some Valhalla for dead Generals, there are moments of good-humoured bragging, then the reminiscence by Haig that in the space of a few hours he managed to expend 57,000 of his troops would more than cap any comparable boast by either of his continental counterparts.

Of the day, Haig's chronicler, Colonel Borastyn wrote that it 'bore out the conclusions of the British Higher Command, and amply justified the tactical methods employed'. It would have been more accurate to call it, as did a recent British writer, 'probably the biggest disaster to British arms since Hastings . . . Certainly never before, nor since, had such wanton, pointless carnage been seen; not even at Verdun, where in the worst month of all (June) the total French casualty list barely exceeded what Britain lost on her *one day*'.[10]

Despite the Somme, fighting at Verdun, like the symptoms of some hideous disease, smouldered on for another five months, until the very ground itself could hold no more. 'On my arrival, the corpse of an infantry man in a blue cap partially emerges from this compound of earth, stones and unidentifiable debris. But a few hours later, it is no longer the same; he has disappeared and has been replaced by a Tirailleur in khaki. And successively there appear other corpses in other uniforms. The shell that buries one disinters another.'[11]

On the German side, Falkenhayn and Knobelsdorf were dismissed by a disillusioned Kaiser. On the French side Nivelle's ability as an artillery man combined with Mangin's uninhibited lust for killing secured Verdun for France. It was the end of an expensive venture. France and Germany's combined losses for their ten months' contest approached one and a half million killed or maimed.

Two questions might be asked. Given that a political problem coupled with a military deadlock could only be solved by force of arms, could this solution have been achieved with greater economy? Was the cost of Verdun unavoidable merely because the two sides were equally matched, or was there something in the minds of those who directed the battle which added quite unnecessarily to the slaughter? Did the victims of the battle pay a price for the indecisiveness of their leaders? I take the view that there was and they did.

Competent generalship involves the ability to calculate the outcomes of a plan. As events proved, both Falkenhayn and Joffre miscalculated the respective outcomes of throwing down and taking up the gauntlet of Verdun. They did so because they were governed by motives and attitudes that were irrelevant to the military realities of the situation. They did so because those very personality characteristics which had taken them to the pinnacles of their respective military organisations were ill-tuned to the tasks they had undertaken.

In their unconscious collusion to fight the battle of Verdun, Falkenhayn and Joffre, aided and abetted by such relatively minor figures as the Kaiser and Knobelsdorf, as Nivelle and Mangin, had continued a situation which, at incalculable cost to their fellow men, enabled them to act out deep undercurrents of their respective personalities.

In some ways analogous to a husband and wife who use their sado-masochistic partnership, their children and their possessions, their talents and their friends, to turn their home into a battlefield for the resolution of their own internal conflicts, the warlords at Verdun used the machinery of battle, the personalities of their underlings, and the bodies of their men to express *their* inner needs.

This somewhat psychoanalytic interpretation of why the Falkenhayns and Joffres of this world behave as they do may not suit everyone. Moreover, since they (Falkenhayn and Joffre) are not (fortunately) the sort of people one meets every day of the week, it might be objected that as a 'species' they are probably extinct and therefore irrelevant to a thesis on contemporary man. Two points. First, people like that lovable pair are certainly not extinct. There are still enough of them about to create a lot of misery for everyone else. If there is a striking difference between them and their contemporary equivalents it is only that nowadays top leaders of that ilk are probably more circumspect about revealing their idiosyncracies until it is far too late for anyone to do anything about stopping them.

The second point is this. Two of the prime characteristics of the men who ran Verdun – their compulsion to go on and on blowing people to pieces and their apparent lack of compassion towards their fellow men – may be at least partly attributed to two more products of evolutionary progress, the effects of which are certainly *not* confined to the warlords of Verdun. The first of these is boredom or rather the need to avoid this dreariest of feelings. For Falkenhayn and Joffre it could well have been unboring if not actually exciting to go on killing people. No one could deny that, whatever else it might be, murder on such a scale has about it a certain degree of novelty.

13

Boredom

Of course boredom may lead you to anything. It is boredom sets one
sticking gold pins into people.

Fyodor Dostoevsky[1]

The scene of their crime was Chicago and the year 1923. Nathan
Leopold was nineteen and his friend Richard Loeb eighteen. Both
were rich, spoilt, good looking and intelligent. They wanted for
nothing, beyond some further excitement to liven up their lives. They
hit on an unusual, if not entirely original, idea – that of planning and
carrying out a 'perfect crime' – an apparently motiveless murder.

On the day in question they waited, in a hired car, outside one
of Chicago's fashionable schools. Amongst the children leaving
for home at the end of the day was a distant cousin of Loeb's,
fourteen-year-old Bobby Franks. They decided he would do. They
had nothing against him. Franks was the victim of bad luck. Had
he left school five minutes earlier or five minutes later it could just
have easily been some other child. Their selection of a victim was
capricious.

They enticed him into the car, killed him, then dumped his body
by a culvert in a wooded area on the outskirts of the city.

Unfortunately for the murderers, theirs was not the perfect crime.
The first hint of its imperfection came with Leopold's discovery that
he had lost his glasses. These were subsequently found lying on the
ground by the corpse in the culvert. Whether or not this clue was
the result of a Freudian error inspired by guilt, remains a matter for
conjecture. Suffice to say that it sealed their fate. Both received life

197

sentences. Loeb died in gaol. Leopold was freed thirty-three years later.

Since there seemed no other motive for the crime, and psychiatrists who examined the boys could find no possible case for a plea of insanity or diminished responsibility, it may be concluded that what they did they did for 'kicks'.

It is the present writer's contention that the Leopold-Loeb murder exemplifies what can on occasions be one of our most self-destructive motives – the reduction of boredom. Other less dramatic but ultimately no less lethal consequences of the same motive are to be seen in smoking, heroin addiction and football hooliganism. Escape from its unpleasant effects, including those of tension and depression, may well be one of the motives which leads people to break their necks climbing or pot-holing or motor racing. It contributes to most sorts of risk taking, sexual promiscuity and gambling. There is little doubt that it plays a part in terrorism, brinkmanship and going to war. Together with alcohol it accounts for many of the 7,000 deaths which occur annually on the roads. Boredom is a potential killer.

But why are we saddled with it? What are its likely origins?

Curiously, academic psychologists other than followers of Freud have surprisingly little to say about boredom. But they do have a lot to say about four very clearly related concepts – arousal, curiosity, exploratory activity and information load. All are relevant to a theory of boredom.

Since survival depends upon knowledge of the environment, animals that spent time exploring the terrain had an advantage over those which sat 'twiddling their thumbs'. Hence it is reasonable to suppose that natural selection favoured two sorts of tendency in living creatures. The first was to reduce ignorance about the world in which they lived. To this end natural selection and mutations favoured the evolution of eyes, ears, noses and all the other sensory devices whereby knowledge is gleaned. But all this would be of little use unless it was moved around. And so a second tendency evolved – to be active, to explore the environment. But this conflicted with another useful characteristic – a tendency to be lazy and so conserve energy. It is not unreasonable to suppose that it was the conflict of these two tendencies which gave rise to the evolution of the capacity for boredom.

The argument hinges on the fact that the acquisition of knowledge is synonymous with reduction of ignorance, which may be rewritten as the reduction of uncertainty. Hence the greatest reduction of ignorance is provided by those experiences which are least expected, because, of course, a novel, strange, improbable or unanticipated event reduces more uncertainty than one which the animal had half expected. Viewed in this way we would expect the most successful information gatherers to be those with a special sensitivity for the novel and unexpected, and a liking for those sorts of activities (like wandering around looking under flat stones and peering into dark holes) which could lead to big, and hopefully pleasant, surprises.

All this makes good sense, but suppose, for one reason or another, an animal is on the lazy side, or over-indulged or for some other reason disinclined to explore its environment. How might nature 'persuade' it to get off its backside? One answer would be to make it very unpleasant to do nothing.

Several experimental observations support this conclusion.

1   Even when satiated (i.e. neither hungry nor thirsty) rats will explore a new maze and subsequently put this knowledge to good use when running through the maze for food in the goal box.[2]

2   Many animals including humans will seek stimulation and prefer novel to familiar stimuli. They will also spend more time and energy on looking at complex as opposed to simple patterns.[3]

3   The young of many species including man show signs of intensified stimulus hunger if they have been confined in a sensorily impoverished environment. If deprived for too long the damage done may be irreparable.[4]

In one respect at least information is much like food. We need an optimum amount. Too much or too little and we begin to suffer the consequences. As with other aspects of our genetic make-up which have become inappropriate to the consequences of cultural evolution, the need for stimulation leading to adaptive exploration has become not just redundant but highly destructive. Three groups of people are particularly afflicted. First, there is the growing population of jobless adults and unemployed school leavers. For them there is little left to explore and finding new sources of stimulation is difficult and expensive. The second victims of boredom are those who fit the psycho-analytic theory of the malaise. According to its chief proponent, Fenichel,[5] boredom is the result of the inhibition of drive aims. It is the effect of an over-strict superego which, by preventing unconscious wishes (presumably of a sexual nature) from surfacing, denies their gratification in a bit of activity of the appropriate kind. Born of an age wherein observance of the Sabbath was synonymous with doing nothing that was enjoyable, it is not surprising that Fenichel called boredom 'Sunday neurosis'. Nowadays any other day of the week would be equally appropriate.

Whether or not boredom occurs on Sundays, the most extreme manifestations of this unpleasant state can be induced under experimental conditions. In the early 1950s three Canadian psychologists[6] decided to find out what would happen to people who were deprived of normal sensory stimulation. The volunteers for this experiment were male college students. Each was paid twenty dollars to spend twenty-four hours lying on a comfortable bed in a soundproofed room. Throughout the experiment they had to wear translucent goggles and, to reduce the possibility of tactile stimulation, cardboard tubes along their arms (except when eating, or using the toilet).

The student volunteers were not deterred by these constraints. Indeed to be actually paid for staying in bed seemed too good to be true. It sounded like an enjoyable way of earning money. But they were wrong. Having spent the first few hours making up for lost sleep they then became increasingly restless, agitated and anxious. As time dragged by they began to experience bizarre and disturbing hallucinations. So intolerable was all this that despite receiving twice what they could normally earn, some of the subjects asked to leave before the end of the testing session.

Following this study other ways of producing sensory deprivation (e.g. having the subject, naked except for a pair of translucent goggles, suspended in a tank of water at body temperature) have been tried.[7] The results are always much the same. Experiences both during and after sensory deprivation are generally unpleasant. All the normal processes of perception, memory and thinking become progressively impaired. Sometimes the effects are nightmarish – 'The subject screams in pain – "there is an animal, having a long slender body with many legs. It's on the screen, crawling in the back of me!" ' The screen was examined by the observer and no animal was seen. The subject continued to be disturbed for five minutes. He insisted the animal was there and was an inch long.[8]

Since these first experiments on the dramatic effect of extreme sensory deprivation, it has become increasingly apparent that there are optimal levels of information flow for proper functioning of the human brain. With too little coming in – too little variety, change or novelty, people become bored, restless and anxious, and then hallucinate. With too much they become stressed, fatigued and, according to one authority, liable to coronary attack.[9]

Several other factors play their part in determining final outcomes. There appear to be constitutional differences between people in the amount of information underload and overload which they can take. Optimum levels are probably related to an individual's level of intelligence. People of very low intelligence may be quite happy carrying out simple tasks which would drive brighter individuals to distraction. And of course the effects of sensory deprivation are relative rather than absolute.[10] How extreme they are will depend upon what the subject is normally used to.

If he lives an exciting life with plenty of variety he may be worse afflicted than if he enjoys a more humdrum existence. This unsurprising conclusion is borne out by the history of boredom.[11] In days gone by boredom or, as it was sometimes called, 'gout in the head' was largely an affliction of the effete élite – the rich and highly born. On the one hand they rarely did anything of any lasting importance. On the other they had the wherewithal for greater variety in their lives. Not for them the daily moil and toil interspersed with a few simple pleasures, but a multitude of excitements – buying new things, visiting new places, having more sexual diversions and enjoying a greater variety of foods, drinks, clothes and pastimes.

At first sight this seems something of a paradox. With their richly variegated existence why should they have been bored? The answer is that what the French describe as *L'appétit vient en mangeant* applies much more to curiosity than it does to any of the other basic drives. Hunger, thirst, sex and sleep are all satiable. Once satisfied they cease for a time to be a problem. Unless suffering from bulimia, addicted to alcohol, a nymphomaniac or a narcoleptic, people can stop eating, drinking, sexual behaviour or sleeping for decent intervals of time – that is until the underlying need reasserts itself. If the appetite does increase with eating it is only briefly and to a very limited extent. It doesn't become ever more demanding. Natural selection has favoured such a state of affairs. Animals which grew hungrier or thirstier the more they ate or drank would certainly become so overweight, waterlogged and generally unhealthy as to be easy prey for their predators. Besides, their chances of reproduction would be seriously diminished. Quite apart from the sheer mechanical difficulties which confront the obese when attempting sexual intercourse, continuous eating, drinking and sleep would take up time that might otherwise be devoted to procreation.

For exploratory drive and curiosity it is quite another matter. Curiosity breeds curiosity. With every exploration comes the urge to explore further. Each new experience whets the appetite for newer ones. Unlike any other drive, curiosity terminates, once and for all, the usefulness of that on which it feeds. Each experience is novel only once. Habituation (the tendency not to respond to the same stimulus on subsequent occasions) makes the need for change increasingly insistent. One has only to witness the accelerating speed with which a spoilt child works through a pile of presents on Christmas Day, to realise that, with boredom forever lurking in the wings, the search for novelty becomes increasingly frenetic.

This is not an indictment of our inbuilt appetite for variety. The greater an animal's curiosity the more it learns about its habitat. The more it learns the better its chances of discovering food, water, and sexual partners and of avoiding what might harm it. By the same token the need for novelty is consistent with the tenets of 'selfish gene' theory.[12] For the male the more numerous his sexual conquests the greater his chances of siring a multitude of offspring, the wider the distribution of his genes and the less likely that major hazard to the species – excessive inbreeding.*

So boredom, like hunger, thirst and anxiety, has its uses. Without the need to escape its doleful grip there would be far less motive to explore, less impetus for scientific research, fewer great discoveries. But now, thanks to such baneful products of cultural evolution as mass unemployment and a plethora of man-made ephemeral distractions, there is less and less to keep boredom at bay. In Healy's opinion it is becoming an epidemic of pandemic proportions. One reason he suggests is that we don't take it seriously enough:

---

* The desire for variety would explain the fact that even the awful threat of AIDS does little to curb the urge for a succession of different sexual partners in a context which *precludes* procreation.

It is true of course, that 'boredom' is often used to refer to feelings that are superficial and fugitive, feelings so common and to so little effect that the state is thought to be too trivial and banal to warrant any sustained attention. This very fact may indeed explain why there has been so little recognition that boredom has far more profound and destructive forms: they have been concealed, or rendered invisible, by the apparently inoffensive, even childish, aura that has surrounded the word. This has provided a semantic smokescreen behind which has lurked, and continues to lurk, a grave sickness of the spirit, potentially destructive of the individual and possibly even of society as a whole.[13]

Another reason for not taking it seriously enough is typical of a general strategy for dealing with situations that are rather unpleasant but apparently inevitable: that of claiming for it some virtue or value which is both spurious and undeserved. This 'making the best of a bad job' strategy is exemplified by such inanities as 'It's a nice day for the ducks', or 'Suffering is good for the soul', or 'Homosexuality is the best form of birth control', or, as the world is about to be incinerated, 'It's better to be dead than Red.' In the case of boredom the trick has been to give it status value. Being bored, looking bored, and sounding bored have become signs of superiority. By responding to every situation with 'How boring!' the individual establishes himself as someone so totally sophisticated and worldly wise that nothing can surprise him. By making everyone else feel unutterably boring he is unassailably one up. Meanwhile those lesser creatures who can still find something of interest in this world, and who can still retain a naive capacity for enthusiasm, become awed by the languid exponents of this yawning, empty-headed affectation. Taken in, they may actually respect them and try to ape their unattractive ways. And so, instead of being pitied, the 'psychologically deceased' victims of hyperboredom, with their drooping eyelids and supercilious smiles become confirmed in their own conceit. But why should people get in such a state of almost permanent boredom that they have to assume these affectations? Since it seems inherently unlikely that babies are born bored (unless one assumes the very unlikely hypothesis that waiting around too long *in utero*, as a result of delayed delivery, induces some sort of pre-natal *ennui*) perhaps it is not so much genetically determined as due to something happening after birth.

There is considerable evidence to suggest that past experience plays a major role in other chronic, virtually irreversible states – anxiety, depression and hostility. The same may well be true of boredom. There has been plenty in the culture to implant and then reinforce this most widespread and destructive of emotions. Pride of place in this respect must be given to certain approaches to education. In the past anyway, many children found school excruciatingly boring. There were several reasons for keeping it that way – not the least being tradition. Given the natural curiosity of young children and their desire to explore the environment, it is an indictment of our educational system that knowledge of the world in which they live, descriptions and explanations of phenomena which, under happier circumstances, they may well wish to explore have been (and sometimes still are) presented in such a dreary, soulless and punitive way that it left them not just unmoved but 'bored out of their minds'.

Considering the number of hours children spent at their desks, during a time of life when their potential learning capacity was at its greatest, it is quite astonishing how little some of them absorbed. But there are two thing they did learn. The first was that everything from history to mathematics, and from biology to geography, could be rendered totally devoid of interest. They learned that all the phenomena of nature, of earth and sea and sky, and of how other people communicate with each other, really were exquisitely dull because their teachers evidently found them so. And the second thing they learned was the emotion of boredom.

Doubtless there have been exceptions to this gloomy picture, but this was certainly the pattern which prevailed in both schools I attended and in those to which many of my friends and colleagues (and my own children) had the misfortune to be sent. Such places of education appeared to operate on the principle that, if pupils enjoyed their lessons, there must be something wrong – that learning and indeed any other kind of work must be boring to be of any use.

One suspects several motives behind this principle. This is what the teachers had to endure when they were at school. *They* were bored so why shouldn't they pass it on? With some, a sadistic element might have been playing a part, with others it may have been the sincere belief, relic of the Protestant work ethic, that learning to carry out boring tasks strengthens and enriches the character. For the latter, school work could have been a coming to grips with reality. Most of life's tasks *are* boring and so the sooner one came to accept this fact the better. And of course, for many parents and teachers, children who didn't explore were much less trouble to look after. For many reasons, some noble, others less noble, society tends to inhibit curiosity in its offspring. But whatever the reasons, the outcomes include, for many people, a lifelong legacy of conditioned boredom – what Healy calls 'hyperborcdom'. It is through this underlying malaise that not only activities labelled 'work' but much else besides may evoke neurasthenic fatigue and that terrible slowing of time whereby the watched clock seems stricken with paralysis. However, whether or not traditional forms of education result in conditioned boredom probably depends upon earlier experiences. The prime candidate, one suspects, would be the child who was overly spoilt in pre-school years. The 'poor little rich girl' syndrome could well be the result of an over-whetted and then frustrated appetite.

Whatever its origins, the fact that even leisure, whether enforced or freely chosen, becomes tainted, spoilt, through boredom seems proof of the pervasive and incurable nature of the underlying disorder – a sort of smouldering psychic bilharzia which dulls the eye, saps the spirit and leadens the footsteps.

The contagion of malignant hyperboredom has also been encouraged in its spread by what should be the most intelligent and enlightened of people – society's intellectual élite. Few who have experienced the ethos of our great universities could deny that many academics bore their way to the top. To be considered 'sound' (necessary if not sufficient for promotion) they have to be boring. Any paper or book that is interesting to read runs the risk of being written off as 'lightweight'. Speculations that transcend or deviate from the establishment view tend to be treated with derision. And so people are trained to be as boring as they can be. If people have good ideas which are a bit unconventional they are usually encouraged to keep them to themselves.

One of the best antidotes to boredom is humour. Because it has to be novel, because it depends upon incongruity and making connections between ideas not hitherto related, because it works by releasing deep–seated emotions about such highly charged issues as those of sex, death and aggression, humour threatens boredom. Because it deflates pomposity, humour *can* be very salutary. But, because so rudely uncaring as it flips off the carefully positioned fig leaf, it is also a menace. And so not only is it excluded from much academic literature but also from the speeches and writing of Civil Servants, churchmen, doctors, judges and lawyers. Just one more reason why, to quote Healy – 'boredom continues to burrow deeply, a psychic black hole drawing man's energies, man's hopes, man's every sense of himself into an annihilating vortex, acting as an entropic force cooling and then freezing all aspiration, all ambitions, all sense of human being.'[14]

As if all this were not enough, the culture continues in various ways to further the contagion. Healy distinguishes several factors in contemporary society which reinforce the feeling that nothing is worthwhile, that life is weary, pointless and futile – the impermanence of objects in a throw-away economy, the relaxation of moral structures and the framework of manners, rising unemployment and overshadowing all, the ever-present threat of nuclear extinction.

An effect of unpleasant feelings is to motivate behaviour towards their alteration. Hyperboredom is no exception to this rule. But for the hyperbored the behaviour, which may range from general agitation to gambling, suicide or murder, can never succeed in anything other than the most temporary fashion. Burning through new experiences at an ever-increasing rate, the hyperbored may become increasingly outlandish and risky in their ventures.

For a telling illustration of what hyperboredom can do to people there is the story of what happened to Josslyn Hay, Earl of Erroll and his friends during the years between the wars.[15]

Having been 'asked to leave' Eton, Hay spent a brief spell in the Irish Guards. With his second wife Idena (following *her* brief spell in the divorce courts) he then decamped for Kenya. There they set up house in what became known as 'Happy Valley', a picturesque strip of country between the Aberdares and the Wanjiho river.

Quite soon, other expatriates, with their own reasons for leaving the home country, gathered around them. This brittle assembly of bright (and not so bright) young things included the drone-like younger sons of the aristocracy – victims of the English system of primogeniture, remittance men 'bribed' by their long-suffering and no doubt scandalised families to go (and stay) as far away as possible, female socialites with tarnished reputations, moneyed cads and penurious bounders.

Given their background and present circumstances, this Happy Valley set were ripe for hyperboredom. No doubt conditioned to the malaise by a spoilt early childhood and then the routine of an English upper-class system of education (six of them were Etonians), they had now placed themselves beyond the pale of British society. Many might regard this as a blessing, but for them it was probably quite burdensome. However beautiful the Kenyan landscape, however exhilarating the crystal air of the Aberdare uplands they were now marooned – 'prisoners' in a foreign land, isolated in an exotic garden of seemingly infinite magnitude and extraordinary dullness. Here was no Ascot, no popping into White's, no garden parties at the Palace, no long weekends in great country houses. Not for them the heady pleasures of a Scottish grouse moor or the English hunting scene. Theirs was a colony of social lepers in a gaol without bars (except those of an alcoholic kind). Of Happy Valley and its inhabitants it was said 'In this decor live a restless crowd of humans, hardly colonists – wanderers, perhaps, indefatigable amusement seekers weary or cast out from many climes, many countries. Misfits, neurasthenics, of great breeding and charm, who lacked the courage to grow old, the stamina to pull up and build anew in this land.'[16]

Attempts to cope with hyperboredom were manifested in two ways. First, notwithstanding the comment about 'not building anew', they did in fact (with the help of an army of black servants) try to anglicise their new abode, with tacky 'English' houses built by Indians; with trim lawns, and place mats of hunting scenes set amongst the Georgian silver. Stuck for something to hunt, they pretended jackasses were foxes.

But all this was not enough to ward off the plague of boredom, so they sought another remedy – oblivion through distraction – the distraction of continuous extravagant dissipation, of fornication on a heroic scale, of seduction, wife swapping and alcohol.

Alcohol! To say that alcohol played a major part in their coming to terms with Kenya would be an understatement. Champagne, scotch, gin, drink in all its different forms flowed through Happy Valley in a beguiling yet treacherous stream. It was their life blood, the great social lubricant, catalyst for all their pranks. Never was the old adage that the superego is that part of the mind soluble in alcohol more amply borne out. Such inhibitions as they might have had were quickly washed away. And if alcohol should fail there were always morphine and cocaine, flown in by private plane, to accelerate the downwards spiral towards total dissolution.

But then, quite suddenly in 1941, their lifestyle was brought to an abrupt and bloody stop by the murder of their ring-leader. In the early hours one morning Lord Erroll, with a bullet through his head, his golden hair streaked with gore, his noble features spattered with black powder from a shot at close range, was discovered sprawled across the footwell of his Buick.

The finger of suspicion pointed at Sir Jock Delves Broughton, the last of a long line of husbands whom Erroll had cuckolded. But he was never brought to book. As for the rest of Happy Valley, it was the end. The party was over. The reckoning was grim. Besides the murder, three had become hopeless alcoholics and two committed suicide.

The foregoing example is by no means unique in showing that the need to avoid boredom may take precedence over all other considerations. Rather than endure this enervating state, people were prepared to sacrifice health, social approval, achievement and even physical survival. Close parallels are to be found in the world of organised crime.

Doubtless, there are many reasons for becoming a criminal – poverty, the inability to earn a living by any other means, greed and the pressure to follow in father's footsteps. However reading between the lines of an autobiography by Vincent Teresa,[17] one of America's top criminals, one cannot help feeling that for men of his stamp, the avoidance of boredom is one of the strongest (if not *the* strongest) motives for devoting one's life to breaking the law.

According to Thomas Renner, who got to know him well, Teresa, Mafia's supergrass, 'enjoyed his life of crime, and the benefits he derived from it. Yet he possessed warmth, charm and a brilliant mind... had he turned his many talents to honest work he undoubtedly would have become a wealthy man legitimately. He possessed boundless energy and great imagination and he displayed innovative genius in every project he tackled.' Renner goes on, 'Teresa was one of the most proficient money-makers the mob had ever known. In a lifetime of crime he stole over $10 million for himself which he spent on horses, women and rich living; and he stole another $150 million for his bosses and confederates.' Now that he has turned informer the Mafia are offering $500,000 to anyone who kills him, which is why Teresa and his family live in hiding, guarded by the FBI. As a government witness, one of the most important informers the United States has ever had, he receives federal subsistence of $10,000 a month. By Teresa's standards this is a paltry income, but, as Renner comments, 'in the last three years his greatest enemy has been boredom, not penury'.[18] This should come as no surprise. Without recourse to the notion of boredom, as a driving force the behaviour of this master criminal is paradoxical.

Here is a man who could have become rich by going straight, who, with even half of what he earned for himself, could have retired years ago to a life of ease with his family; and yet he chose to risk imprisonment, even death, for the sake of excitement, of taking part in bank robberies, heists, loan sharking and an impressive variety of other dishonest ways of relieving 'suckers' of their money. Like many Mafiosi, Teresa is a great family man, deeply concerned about the welfare of his wife and children (it was because of them he turned informer) and yet he chose a lifestyle which entailed weeks away from his family, 'living on the street', creeping home for the occasional flying visit, putting (as subsequently occurred) his loved ones at risk from his personal enemies in the mob.

But most significant of all is how he *spent* his money. Here is a paradox within a paradox. Though contemptuous of mugs, though out to win every trick, and up to every sort of racket, Teresa let himself be fleeced time and again, as he freely admits, by those who prey on *gamblers*. Though himself an adept 'fixer' of horse races, a master in the art of 'loading' dice and 'rigging' roulette wheels, he squandered a fortune in bad bets at crooked race tracks and dubious casinos. Like any other 'junkie' Teresa *had* to steal in order to gratify his craving – in his case an addiction to uncertainty.

Great though the cost is to society of bored aristocrats, sensation-seeking criminals, and that section of the motoring public who use a combination of automobiles and alcohol to dispel *ennui*, it is slight compared to the havoc that has been, and could be, wrought by military and political leaders in the same pursuit. There are two grounds for this conclusion. First, there are reasons to believe that such people have an above average chance of being particularly prone to boredom. Second, they, and they alone, have the power and the means to reduce boredom in ways which make the antics of mad motorists and criminal tycoons hardly worth a second thought.

The argument hinges on a simple relationship between information, curiosity and unexpectedness. Because an unexpected event provides more knowledge (i.e. reduces more ignorance) than an expected event, it evokes more surprise, gratifies more curiosity and is therefore less boring than an expected event.[19] Hence, the more different things that might happen, the less boring when one of them does. This is one of the reasons why the weather is of such absorbing interest to the English. There are so many things it might do and we never quite know what it's going to do next. In England, planning a garden party or an outdoor concert is a gamble. Deciding every morning what to wear can be fraught with considerable uncertainty. However uncomfortable it may sometimes be the English climate is on the whole unboring which is more than can be said of, say, summer in South Australia, or winter at the Poles.

The other big source of the unexpected is, of course, people. Any one particular person may be a crashing bore, but generally people, because they can be unpredictable and can do a lot of different things in a great many different orders, are rich sources of information. They are full of surprises. It is hardly cause for amazement therefore that, to make a huge and mind-boggling generalisation, when society is not discussing the weather it is talking, thinking or reading about people. Take the matter of a newspaper which has the largest UK circulation of them all – the *News of the World*. Wherein lies its immense popularity? First, as a paper which appears on the Sabbath, it fits in very well with one of the classical descriptions of boredom as 'Sunday neurosis'.[20] Sunday is the one day of the week when most people have the time and some the inclination to do a whole lot of things, from fornication to murdering (when forced to visit) their in-laws which, for one reason or another, they are prevented from putting into effect. Sunday is the day of frustration. And so, according to this theory, people are reduced to vicarious gratification of their aggressive and libidinal fantasies by reading about the misdemeanours of others.

The trouble with this theory is that nowadays it only accounts for a relatively small readership of the paper in question. It does not explain those millions of readers who are neither sexually frustrated nor tormented by aggressive fantasies. It fails to explain the fact that the increasing liberalism of English Sundays has done nothing to reduce the paper's circulation. So what's the answer to this riddle? It surely lies in the second theory that by reputation (if not in fact) this paper is not only all about people, but, more important, about those people who are providing unusually large amounts of information. It is about ordinary people doing extraordinary things, like the man who lives on a diet of lawn clippings. It is about extraordinary people doing ordinary things – like royal Princesses having babies. And most newsworthy of all, it is about extraordinary people doing extraordinary things.* And if one doubts the validity of this theory about the *News of the World* consider the matter of fiction and the popularity of writers like Roald Dahl with his *Tales of the Unexpected.*

In itself this interest in people as boredom reducers, whether they be pop stars, record breakers, criminals or royalty is fairly harmless. There is, however, one way in which it threatens our survival as a species – the part which it plays in the emergence of leaders.

There are two sides to this coin. The first concerns the sort of people who aspire to become world leaders, and the second how the populace chooses between them. As to the latter, it is surely the case that, whether or not people get the sort of leaders (and governments) they deserve, they tend to be influenced in their choice not just by promises to fulfil their needs but also by characteristics which are not only irrelevant but may well turn out to be disastrous. Given minimal solid information to go on the electorate will be drawn to individuals who are different, who, in their behaviour, in what they do or say, and in their appearance are unboring. They will favour the candidate who commands attention, who stands out from the crowd, who is memorable. Even the most cursory glance at world leaders supports the view that being different, unusual, unexpected – in a word, unboring – is a factor of prime importance. Particularly is this so when the 'difference' is something which the media, advertising agencies, and cartoonists can amplify and build upon. Whatever else they might have been Churchill, Hitler, Stalin, Nixon, Kennedy, de Gaulle, Roosevelt, Idi Amin, Margaret Thatcher and Ronald Reagan were (or are) distinctive – in other words unboring. Whether they were (or are) good or bad, benign or malevolent, competent or incompetent, each had some unique quality which along with a host of other factors contributed to their emergence as leaders. As someone once said of a bad leader, 'His men follow him if only out of curiosity.' In comparison, people like Mondale and Hubert Humphrey, however worthy their aims and intelligent

---

* Unfortunately no example comes to mind which is not libellous.

their minds, remain, because really rather boring, only runners up. It is worth noting that this dichotomy between the ordinary and the extraordinary is compounded by another dichotomy – that between extreme and middle-of-the-road political ideologies. Obviously there are a lot of other important determinants at work, but it could be argued that the more hyperbored a society the readier it might be to opt for the *ends* rather than the middle-ground of the political spectrum. The far right (or the far left) may be ghastly, but it cannot be denied that their politics and their trappings have about them a certain novelty, trappings which, for example, helped the Nazis rise to power from the grey morass of the Weimar Republic. Obviously this secondary phenomenon would itself add lustre to the leaders of right- and left-wing parties as opposed to those of, say, liberals.

By itself, a predisposition for a bored populace to follow an unboring leader is only a recipe for disaster if the unboring candidates are of dubious worth. This might well be the case for, in general, the sort of unboring people who appeal to an electorate probably have an above-average chance of being some or all of these things – narcissistic, exhibitionistic, risk taking, talkative, theatrical and sentimental. That they might also be stupid, dishonest, ruthless, insincere, rigid, deluded and power hungry is immaterial because such characteristics are not only less immediately apparent, but can be easily ignored when people only see what they want to see.

But are those who aspire to be world leaders really likely to have undesirable traits? What makes someone wish to be a leader and, given the requisite motivation, what traits take them to the top? It would take too long, be very depressing and possibly libellous to try to answer these questions in any detail. Suffice it to say that some motives are noble, others are not. The former would include a sincere desire to improve the lot of one's fellow men, and to create a better, fairer, safer world. The good leader is one who puts the public interest before self-interest. There have been those – Gandhi, Golda Meir, Mao, Pitt, Keir Hardie, Lincoln, Washington, Carter and, of course, Christ, who to a greater or lesser extent appear to have been driven by such motives, and who, consistent with such motives, possessed such traits as those of modesty, honesty, compassion and moral courage.

Unfortunately, there is also a sizeable collection of less desirable motives. They have as their common denominator that self–interest is put before the common good. They include the need for adulation and approval, the urge to bolster self-esteem, the compulsion to act out some private prejudice or delusion, to avenge some personally experienced slight, to redress an ancient grievance, to dispel doubts about one's virility, and of course sheer unadulterated megalomania – the seeking of power over others. All this is bad enough, but there is one additional motive which may well play a significant part in advancing someone to a position of power and which, in a nuclear age, could prove more dangerous than all the others put together – our old friend boredom, or rather the pressing, growing, accelerating need to distance oneself from the stranglehold on mind and body of this ancient octopus.

Before considering this issue let's just recall for a moment how this state of affairs could have come about. It has been suggested that selective pressures favoured those animals which were best able to explore and therefore control or at least cope with their environment. With the evolution of conscious awareness, unexplored features of the habitat evoked a tension, the antecedent of what at a human level we call curiosity, which could only be discharged by exploring the unexplored. This subjective experience increased the motivation to investigate and investigation was the first essential step to controlling the environment. We cannot know whether lower animals experience feelings but there is, on the one hand, ample evidence[21] that monkeys, cats, and even rats will forgo the satisfaction of other needs for the sake of experiencing and exploring a novel stimulus, and on the other of special 'novelty detecting' cells in the mammalian brain.

At a human level dedication to research, embodied in the popular image of the scientist who, on the brink of discovery, is totally oblivious of the fact that he hasn't eaten a thing all day, the growing interest in so-called paranormal phenomena, space travel, even the compulsion to solve crossword or jigsaw puzzles; all suggest the evolution of a cerebral 'appetite' for solving the unknown that has acquired the stature of an autonomous need perpetually demanding satisfaction.

From the suggestion of a positive relationship between the amount of time spent passively watching television and progressive atrophy of the ageing brain, and the related finding[22] that the act of thinking actually increases cerebral blood flow, it seems that, to keep on functioning properly, the brain not only needs certain minimum levels of sensory inflow but also active cerebration. To keep fit, brains, like bodies, need exercise. The old precept, 'If you don't use it you'll lose it', is as true for brains as for most other parts of the human anatomy!

But what has all this to do with the motivation of leaders? Simply this: because people represent extremely high sources of information, controlling their activities constitutes a boredom-reducing goal of alluring proportions – irresistible grist to the cerebral mill.

The need to control others is also of course consistent with the paranoid fears and ego needs of at least some of those who strive to be world leaders.

However, when the man or woman whose urge to achieve political fame results from the need to reduce boredom reaches what may appear to be the summit of their political ambitions they will still not in fact have exhausted their appetite for excitement. On the contrary it will have been no more than whetted. For this is an appetite which is insatiable. And so leaders of this ilk cast around for yet further sources of boredom reduction. Traditionally this has taken one or more of three possible forms – amorous adventures, gambling and war. As to the first, it may well seem that many of these people are far too decrepit or insufficiently attractive to achieve variety through sex. There have, however, been others, such as Gladstone, who showed a compulsive concern with prostitutes, the philandering Lloyd George and several more recent examples who fit the theory rather well.

It is ironic that though sex as a boredom reducer is one of the least dangerous threats to survival of the species it is the one most frowned upon. Because of vestigial Victorian prudery (which makes us a laughing stock of other countries) society does its best to prevent our politicians from using this relatively harmless way of assuaging *ennui*. The consequences could hardly be worse. First, because of the shame of being found out, sexual activities provide a ready opportunity for blackmail. Second, some of those involved evidently felt compelled to resort to lying, bribery or other desperate measures to try to conceal their erotic diversions, and when such ploys failed otherwise competent politicians have been forced to resign. This is particularly unfortunate in view of a suggested relationship between competence and relative lack of sexual inhibitions, as exemplified by some of the world's greatest military leaders.[23] Through the sequence – dalliance → guilt → lying → exposure → resignation we may be depleting our stock of worthwhile political minds.

Finally, if bored politicians are scared of sexual adventures it will only increase their chances of indulging in other more dangerous patterns of behaviour.

As for gambling, this too has had its share of powerful leaders. The Emperors Augustus, Caligula, Claudius, Nero and Domitian 'were counted among the most passionate of gamblers'.[24] However, provided one does not get caught (or AIDS) in the case of sex, or bankrupt the State in the case of gambling, these two ways of reducing *ennui* are in themselves fairly harmless. The same cannot, unfortunately, be said of war. It has been pointed out that 'directing a war can be fun for a callous despot, Louis XIV – to mention one of innumerable possible examples – used to start a war whenever he was bored, without, of course, exposing himself to any dangers or privations'.[25]

Unfortunately, it is not only the callous and despotic leaders who become bored. In a nuclear age it would be prudent to take the view that those individuals who attain a position which enables them to start a nuclear war have an above average chance of forever seeking new excitements – for it was this among other factors which got them where they are. A second hypothesis, which follows from the first, is that for such people there are, apart from war, very few further excitements left with which to stave off boredom.

Critics of this thesis, who doubt that anything as mild and commonplace as boredom could possibly result in a holocaust, may well offer three objections. The first is that, however bored the leader, he or she is not going to start something which might rebound upon him or herself. Thanks to modern weaponry, so this argument goes, nobody is safe.

This belief, however, begins to look a little shaky when one considers that other likely characteristic of the excitement-seeking leader – a penchant for gambling. Not only are gamblers, by definition, risk takers, but they are possessed of an incurable optimism regarding their own ultimate invincibility.* It is a feature of such people that

* A striking feature of the 1987 General Election was that each party leader seemed certain of winning!

their subjective probabilities of winning are significantly larger than the mathematical probabilities of success. Gamblers tend to harbour a number of irrational beliefs such as that a run of bad luck must be followed by one of good luck. Gamblers are sustained by the delusion that they will always win in the end and that, so far as bad news is concerned, 'It can't happen to me.' Such biases towards optimism are reinforced by self-conceit. *If* they win it's through their cleverness. If they lose it's just bad luck.

It follows that those interested in the survival of the species should reckon with the possibility, indeed probability, that the leader who is prepared to risk a nuclear war partly out of boredom, will also be a person who likes gambling and possesses exaggerated ideas of his or her own cleverness and personal invulnerability.

For such a person, in his dotage and already threatened by the first symptoms of terminal disease, sabre rattling – a sort of pre-death rattle – is also a good way of warding off the anticipated hyperboredom of personal extinction.

The likelihood of such dangerous irrationality may well be increased by the high probability of what has been called 'brain failure' in ageing politicians. As one eminent neurologist remarked:

> Men and women become more powerful in human affairs as they grow older. Though they may grow wiser with experience up to a great age, power of intellect, and especially of insight, eventually fail. Then people are positively dangerous in proportion to the powers they wield and to the rate of progression and degree of damage before the problem is detected. The most frightening state occurs when brain failure is detected but concealed for reasons of policy and power.[26]

A second objection to the present theory is that risky leaders will always be held in check by their less sanguine followers. So far as war is concerned this seems not to be the case. History shows that hyperbored societies, particularly after a long outbreak of peace, welcome the possibility of an impending conflict. One has only to consider the enthusiasm which greeted the Falklands campaign or Reagan's bombing of Libya to realise that, far from inhibiting trigger-happy leaders, the general public gives them every encouragement. The same motivation which prompts an electorate to opt for exciting leaders makes it enthusiastic for the daring things which its choice gets up to. When boredom reigns, excitement is infectious, and of course everyone shares with their leader the comforting delusion that so far as nasty things are concerned, 'It can't happen to me.' This belief is encouraged by the fact that, whereas patriotic fervour is public, death, loss, grief and sorrow are private. And if the bodies must be brought home then the less said about their arrival the better.

Yet a third objection to the present thesis is that it is aggression rather than boredom which makes leaders bellicose. There need be no dispute about this. Of course they are aggressive. Were they not they would not be where they are. But boredom is one of the antecedents of aggression. Whether it's the cold-blooded murder of Bobby Franks by Messrs Leopold and Loeb, Roman Emperors watching Christians being torn apart by lions, or the unedifying sight of a bored schoolboy assiduously pulling the wings off flies, such acts have something in common with the behaviour of those who, in days gone by, brightened up their lives by watching people being hanged, drawn and quartered. After all, whether it's a watch, an insect, or a human body, taking it apart to see what makes it tick is as much a piece of exploration, prompted by curiosity, as it is an act of aggression. The very phrase 'I'll take you apart' might seem to suggest that boredom, curiosity, exploration and aggression are to say the least quite closely related.

But all this is perhaps something of a digression, for even without any manifestations of aggressive intent boredom can still be a killer. For an instance less ambiguous than the case of Leopold and Loeb or Louis XIV there is that of a DC10 which on November 2nd, 1973 was flying over New Mexico at a height of 39,000 feet. At this stage of the journey with direction, altitude and speed under autocontrol there was not a lot for the crew to do, which is presumably why, according to a subsequent replay of the cockpit voice recorder, the following conversation took place:

FLIGHT ENGINEER. I wonder, if you pull the number one tach [tachometer] will that . . . autothrottle respond to anything?
CAPTAIN. I don't know.
FLIGHT ENGINEER. You want to try and see?
CAPTAIN. Yeah, let's see.
FLIGHT ENGINEER. You're on speed right now though.

CAPTAIN. Well I haven't got it. There it is. I guess it does. Right on the nose.[27]

At this point conversation was interrupted by an explosion, clearly audible on the voice recorder. As a result of fiddling with the controls the Captain had so over-speeded the starboard engine that the vanes of its fan assembly struck the outer casing and the thing blew up. Fortunately (for most of those on board) a DC10 can lose an engine and still continue to fly* but for one of the passengers this was not the end of the story. A piece of disintegrating engine smashed the window just where he was sitting. At 39,000 feet such an eventuality produced catastrophic explosive decompression. With pressure inside the aircraft at 8 lbs per square inch and that on the outside at near zero, all the air on the inside suddenly does it best to reach the outside, carrying with it anything in its path. The man who had been sitting by the now broken window was in its path and so out he went, like a cork from a bottle. One can only hope that for most of his long tumbling fall to earth lack of oxygen and freezing cold rendered him unconscious. His body was never found.

It would be a pity if the full implications of this chapter have failed to make their mark. They are too important to miss and can be stated quite simply. Bored Presidents, risky Prime Ministers, hyperbored societies and those troglodytes who spend their days contemplating the 'autothrottles' of the world's missile systems have a potential for creating excitement on a scale never hitherto experienced. And after that there would be no more boredom for the simple reason that there would be no one left to experience this unpleasant emotion.

Just in case all this sounds unduly alarmist it should be pointed out that recent researches have shown significant relationships between susceptibility to boredom and impulsivity, extroversion (i.e. being more excitable, seeking more stimulation),[28] Type A behaviour[29] (i.e being ambitious, intolerant of frustration, with a keen sense of time urgency, and prone to heart attacks) and anti-social behaviour.

It is also worth bearing in mind that not only are sensation-seeking extroverts (when compared with introverts) more prone to boredom and less prone to see any situation as risky[30] but they are also more psychopathic and readier to indulge in acts of a criminal nature.[31]

---

* Provided it is not during take-off, as happened at Chicago airport.

They are also less likely to wear seat-belts[32] and more likely to have a car accident.[33]

One of the offshoots of boredom is what has been called the theory of risk homeostasis. It is based on evidence that people appear determined to maintain a desired level of risk.[34] As applied to behaviour on the roads (a well-known way of reducing boredom), well-intentioned safe-guards like better brakes are invariably compensated for by high speeds – i.e. any advance in accident prevention is invariably consumed in higher performance, thus ensuring that the risk factor remains constant.

Assuming, as argued in this chapter, that political leaders have an above average balance of being extrovert with a particularly pressing need to reduce boredom, the above miscellany of findings does not bode well for the future of mankind. But perhaps one could draw comfort from the fact that, with all their faults, sensation-seeking political leaders as they rush about getting things done bring to their various tasks some rather special intellectual characteristics. They probably do. According to Eysenck extroverts are in fact less good at learning and remembering than people who are not so extrovert.[35]

In principle, of course, highly extrovert political leaders have also an above-average chance of removing themselves once and for all from high office (or indeed any office) through coronary heart disease or driving too fast without wearing a seat-belt!

A popular way of describing boredom is in terms of mental occupation. Hence, 'He does this (usually something we would rather he didn't) because he's bored, which is because he hasn't enough to occupy his mind' is, after all, a common enough way of conceptualising the malaise. Now, assuming the brain is the organ of mind, what this might seem to suggest is that the brain's capacity for information has become too large. We can't ask them, but judging from the behaviour of lower animals, there does seem to be a relationship between cerebral capacity and boredom. Caged lions and tigers, apes and monkeys, dogs pleading to be taken for a walk, certainly *look* as if they are capable of experiencing boredom but it's hard to conceptualise a slug as suffering from *ennui*.

Now, if it's potentially boring to have too big a brain, one solution would be to neglect or at least deny some of its spare capacity, reserving conscious experience (which after all is where boredom is felt) for the immediate problems of living. That hymn, so favoured by those who organise school prayers which contains the fatuous precept, 'The trivial round, the common task, Would furnish all we ought to ask', and the cry, 'I'm far too busy to worry about this that and the other', certainly seem to suggest a sort of remedy for 'gout in the head'.

These speculations are a matter for debate, but nevertheless it is undoubtedly the case that many of us do neglect to use a large part of our cerebral equipment, the machinations of which should but don't feature in the decisions which we make. The possible costs of these cerebral arrangements which may be just as severe as that of boredom are considered in Chapter 14.

14

The Neglected Brain

Though the Life Force supplies us with its own purpose, it has no other brains to work with than those it has painfully and imperfectly evolved in our heads.

George Bernard Shaw, *The Irrational Knot*

It is highly likely that, if you had the opportunity to look inside someone else's head (or, with the help of mirrors, inside your own) you would discover not just one brain but what appear to be two, lying quietly side by side. The two cerebral hemispheres are, for want of a better term, semi-detached and connected by three bundles of nerves – the commissures, of which the largest, the corpus callosum, contains over a million individual fibres.

Judging from its ubiquity across species and the fact that it is found far down the animal scale, this division of the brain into two relatively separate halves conferred several advantages on the creatures so blessed. If one side got damaged or became diseased there was less chance of the trouble spreading to the other. There are plenty of people who, having had one side removed because of a malignancy, manage nevertheless to live relatively full and active lives. Function, it seems, can be transferred from one side to the other. There are other possible advantages. Temperature control, blood supply and neuro-electrical insulation are probably more efficient than they would be for one single monolithic cerebrum, and the likelihood of epilepsy and audiogenic seizures considerably reduced.

It has been suggested that there are also possible psychological advantages. Since the animal has two sides to its body receiving

221

and dealing respectively with the opposing two sides of the spatial envelope in which it stands, it does perhaps reduce the chance of confusion if the two sides of its environment are represented in opposite sides of the brain. The argument that a divided brain facilitates representations inside an animal's head of the external world,[1] appears to be based on the idea that the locations of the components of a system should be spatially related to the scene which the system is designed to store and display.

There are, however, four difficulties with this idea. First, provided the receptors, whether these be for light, sound, pressure or chemical stimuli, are oriented in different directions and internally labelled or 'tagged' as sources of information from these various locations, the relative positioning of their internal end stations hardly matters. The ability of devices like range-finders, electronic surveillance systems or computers to store and display spatial information in no way depends upon how their discs, tape decks, capacitors and chips are spatially positioned in relation to each other. Whether their bits and pieces are packed in one large box, or several small ones, and how the latter are disposed about the room, is of no relevance (apart from such considerations as those of thermal and electrical insulation) to their production of a spatial map of the scene which they are attempting to display. It's not *where* they are but how they are inter-connected that matters.

Second, if there *were* field forces in the brain which represented the external world there just might be a case for supposing that the relative locations inside someone's head of the visual, auditory and olfactory centres could facilitate the individual's subjective picture of his external environment. But the theory of field forces has been largely discredited. Imbedding artificial insulators or conductors in the brains of animals,[2] which should have disrupted distribution of an electrical field, had no discernible effect on their behaviour.

And if there were such field forces within a person's head, faithfully mimicking the outside world, the fact that the brain is divided into two asymmetrical structures would be something of a handicap – like those road atlases wherein adjoining regions of the real world are mapped on to different pages with white margins in between.

There is a third problem. One implication of the theory that the spatial location of brain processes is correlated with the spatial location of objects in the external world is that, assuming he knows the relationship between what's out there and the site of events within his head, the animal can, so to speak, read off the cerebral representation. Quite apart from the philosophical issue of who does the reading, there is the practical difficulty that since no lower animal (and comparatively few humans) know which side of the brain is concerned with representing what, and only a minority of humans know that visual information coming from the right ends up in the left side of the brain and vice versa, that sounds go from each ear to both sides of the brain yet are primarily dealt with by the contralateral hemisphere, and that smells go to the same side of the brain as the nostril by which they entered; since, as I say very few creatures know these vital, yet really rather unmemorable facts, it is difficult to believe that the relationship between the location of things out there and where they are represented inside the cranium has anything whatever to do with reducing confusion in the mind of some creature trying to find its way about. On the contrary, it might be even more confused.

In case this seems like a criticism of a favoured hypothesis, there are further considerations which militate against the idea that localisation of function in the brain helps the animal in any direct way to deal with its environment. How many animals or people know that their limbs on one side of the body are controlled by events on the opposite side of the brain? And how many know that instead of being dealt with just behind the eyes the visual world is represented upside down at the back of one's head? And if they did know these things would it help them? Manifestly not! Neurologists, neuro-psychologists and other sophisticates of that ilk are no better at turning to the right or turning to the left than is a rat in a maze. They may even be worse. And when you ask the way of one of these people and they answer take the second turning on the left, its just as likely they'll be as wrong as someone who has not the faintest idea of what's going on inside his head. And if you doubt the truth of these answers, consider the case of a great friend of the writer who is not only a competent psychologist who knows about the brain but was also a civil airlines pilot who, so he confided, had to wear a large ring on his right hand when flying because he was so prone to confuse right with left.

While it can hardly be disputed that there are obviously good biological reasons for the division of the brain into two and for localisation of particular functions in particular places it would seem equally indisputable that, except in the most general sense (i.e. that brains work better that way) this has little to do with an animal's ability to monitor the environment and find its way about.

So, for want of something better, we are left with the more modest and far more tenable hypothesis that in a highly compressed, enormously complex, poorly insulated electrical system it pays to separate, as widely as possible, those subsystems between which any leakage would cause maximum disruption to the workings of the whole. It perhaps matters less (from the point of view of survival) that the right side of the brain controls the left side of the body or that the visual areas are similarly disposed (for after all we can quickly adapt to those artificially contrived reversals of visual fields produced by 'reversing' spectacles)[3] than that the two hand areas on the somatosensory cortex are as far apart from each other as possible and, by the same token, that that region at the back of the brain which receives information from the right visual field should be well out of electrical reach from that which deals with projections from the left. All this smacks of good, commonsensical, biological engineering, but how did it start and what is its relevance to the theme of this book?

The short answer to the first question is that we simply do not know. There are several ingenious suggestions, such as that put forward by Dimond. 'If we think of the organism as moving head first and transferring food into its centrally placed mouth then much of the bilateral symmetry of its organization will follow as a consequence of this. Gravity will act on the organism to keep it flat on the surface and the natural tendency would be for the organs to spread bilaterally around the fixed position of the centrally placed mouth and gut.'[4]

As for the second question, the relevance of the dual brain to man's ultimate survival hinges upon the whole complex matter of the asymmetries which exist between the two hemispheres. Though at first sight identical, there are in fact important functional differences between the two sides of the brain. In particular that greatest cultural acquisition – language – has produced a psychological imbalance of far-reaching, and perhaps ultimately lethal, proportions.

This speculative argument can be explicated by the following analogy. Suppose a tidyminded householder decides to reduce chaos in his home by using one half of his house for all those aspects of his life which have to do with artistic, spiritual and musical activities, and the other half for everything that pertains to his day-to-day domestic needs. When wishing to relax with his tapes, pictures and *objets d'art* he goes to the right, but if he's hungry, needs to wash, or wants to visit the lavatory he goes to the left. For a time it all works very well. He doesn't get butter on his Rembrandt or find joss sticks in his soap dish. Leakage either way is reduced to a minimum.

Suppose he then buys a computer to assist him with his domestic administration – shopping lists, bills and PAYE deductions for his butler. Naturally, he makes a central place for this new toy in the left side of the house. Again it all works very well. Thanks to having acquired this new product of his culture he can pride himself on having become a more efficient householder.

So far, so good, but, as any computer buff knows, even the humblest microprocessor can become a tyrant of one's interests and time. What started as a useful gadget becomes an endearing toy, and then a mind-enslaving drug. It's so much more exciting writing programs for his responsive PET than, say, listening to Beethoven's Fifth or collecting water colours, that less and less often does he visit the other side of his house. Eventually, he may close it up for ever.

Like many analogies, this one is simplistic and inadequate,* but it does illustrate one of the serious consequences of what is undoubtedly the most important product of cultural evolution – language. Language enables us to communicate and store knowledge, to design and plan the other products of our culture, and to control those who execute these plans. Without it the social co-operation upon which survival depends would be impossible. But, in accordance with the law of side effects, a price is paid. Returning to the analogy of the divided house, the left side of the brain (in most people), perhaps because it controls the right hand, perhaps because it is larger as a consequence of a superior blood supply due to the heart being on the left side of the body, perhaps because during brain development the left hemisphere has, in comparison with the right hemisphere, an early growth advantage[5] – has, like the left side of the house, become the chief executive centre for daily living. For these reasons and because they were acquired for good practical domestic reasons,

---

* It is also, for purposes of exposition, a statement of the extreme case. Studies of split-brain patients (i.e. those who have undergone commissurectomy) suggest that division of function in the brain is rarely so complete.

language, numeracy, logic and ultimately the conscious domain of all rational decision-making have, with one accord (in most people), taken up residence in the left side of the brain. All this makes good practical sense – just as, in the case of the house for example, everything concerned with the preparation of food is gathered together in one place – so in the brain everything to do with what seemed to be the immediate practical problems (like social co-operation) of survival in a relatively hostile environment, is assembled in the left side of the brain. Once language had become predominantly a left hemisphere function this encouraged the proliferation of mechanisms underlying related skills in the same hemisphere. As a court moves with its monatch so that of conscious reasoning, with its messengers the right hand and the voice, became linked for all time to the left side of the head.

And so the right hemisphere – appositional, imaginative, emotional, artistic, repository of dreams and only such linguistic talents as those to do with verbal expression of the emotions – became, like the right side of the house, shut off and ignored by the busy consciousness of normal daily working life. It is possible, according to one ingenious theory,[6] that what has really amounted to a transition of executive power and conscious thought to the left hemisphere, with relative neglect of the right hemisphere may have been of fairly recent origin. Less than three thousand years ago, so it has been suggested, before the advent of mega-societies and the need for complex communication via the written word, people were ordered and directed by the voices of their gods. The latters' instructions, so the theory maintains, were literally hallucinated voices emanating from the right side of the brain. For bicameral man what we now call the minor hemisphere served two important and related functions. Having absorbed the multitudinous experiences of early man it then distilled from these such codes of behaviour and specific instruction as were necessary for survival and the regulation of society. Because they came across (literally) as hallucinatory voices from somewhere inside the individual's head and were taken as supernatural, they were obeyed without a murmur. But all good things come to an end and so it was with bicameral man. Under the impact of culture the now discredited voices of the gods gave way to those of earthly leaders. Irrational reasonableness gave way to rational unreasonableness.

But how *does* the possession of two asymmetrical cerebral hemi-spheres and resultant lateralisation fit the thesis that some of the consequences of genetic evolution which were once so useful may now play a part in threatening our continued existence?

There are two ways. The first concerns the simple matter of confusing left with right. The second concerns the consequences of neglecting that side of the brain on which survival must ultimately depend. Let's consider them in this order.

Confusions of left with right

A seemingly unavoidable feature of military life is what has come to be known as 'square bashing', a form of group activity in which one man (or woman) attempts to control the movements of others by shouting at them.

Along with such aims as those of inculcating smartness, conformity, docility and obedience, one of the main goals of Drill Sergeants is to so train their protégés that they can on the one hand stop and start, and on the other turn left or right whenever they receive the appropriate command. It is in following this course of instruction that they discover a curious fact. Whereas it is comparatively easy to start or stop (i.e. to 'quick march' or 'halt') the act of turning to the left or right presents enormous difficulties for some people.

Since, in contact with a hypothetical enemy, turning left or right at the appropriate moment may make all the difference between victory or defeat, getting it wrong could be very serious.

Closer analysis of this problem suggests that it's not that their arms, legs and bodies won't obey their wishes – after all it has never been noticed that these members of the awkward squad can't find their way to the canteen – but rather that they have difficulty in translating the order 'turn left' or 'turn right' into the appropriate direction of movement.

Why should they be afflicted in this way? One reason could be the potential for confusion which occurs through a combination of three factors – that those two parts of the body, the hands, which are the most visible expression of 'rightness' and leftness' are each controlled from opposite sides of the brain; that in most people the primary area for the reception of speech is located in the left hemisphere and that it is this same side of the brain which is con-cerned with conscious ideation. As if this were not enough, there is the added complication that, whereas unconscious reception and processing of information may take place in the right hemisphere, those conscious judgmental acts which initiate overt responses occur in the left hemisphere. This point has been exemplified by research on judgments as to whether or not stimuli arriving from different sides of the body are in fact simultaneous. It seems that such stimuli only appear to be simultaneous when that affecting the right hemisphere arrives *before* that affecting the left. Evidently information coming in to the right side of the brain has to cross over to the left before the two can be compared.

Given these asymmetries it is not perhaps so surprising that some people turn left when ordered to turn right. It is not perhaps so surprising that we get telephone numbers the wrong way round, or try to unscrew nuts by turning them clockwise, or confuse east with west. And, in case one doubts that all this has something to do with the lateralisation of the brain, it is noteworthy that no one stands up when asked to sit down or nods when they mean to shake their heads. It is from side to side not top to bottom that confusion occurs.

But are laterality confusions really so serious?

The following excerpts from Beaty[7] suggest that they can be: 'I remember flying a Botha in the early days of my flying training. We were to practise asymmetric flying, and the instructors cut the starboard engine on me. The aircraft swung to the right. I put on full starboard rudder and the Botha reeled over almost on its back.'[8]

Guy Gibson wrote in *Enemy Coast Ahead*, 'One day we flew down to an airfield in Cambridgeshire to collect Sir Archibald Sinclair, the Air Minister . . . We were carrying a brand new flight engineer. On the way home, the Air Minister jabbed a finger in my back and told me to feather* an engine. This was done and he seemed very pleased.' As to why Air Ministers should show such escalations of delight is a matter touched on elsewhere in this book. Gibson goes on: 'After we had flown along like this for a few minutes, one of the brass hats came forward and told me to unfeather as they were in a hurry. I gave the order, casually, to the flight engineer. Suddenly, to the horror of both myself and the man with goggles on, looking over my shoulder, the two other engines began to feather themselves. Our new flight engineer had pressed the wrong buttons. It was all

---

* So rotating propeller blades that they cease to obstruct air flow.

right though, because it didn't take him a second to get all four going again.'[9]

But there is not always such a happy ending. Consider what happened to a Constellation which on August 9th, 1984 took off from Lagens airport in the Azores. The runway at Lagens runs from south-east to north-west. Facing north-west to the right is a ridge. To the left is Monte de Pico. Dictated by these geographical factors normal procedure, after take-off on the north-west runway, is a *right* turn out over the sea.

During the war, a transport aircraft using this runway had turned *left* and crashed into the mountain, killing all on board. Ever afterwards special care was taken in briefing pilots for take-off. The Captain and navigator of the Constellation were told, 'Following take off, turn *right*, climb until 2,500 on heading 160 and proceed to Ponto Sul.'[10] These instructions were included in the first stage of the flight plan.

When the Captain subsequently asked for take-off clearance, the Tower repeated the earlier instructions to turn right and climb to 2,500 feet. After take off the Tower, ever conscious of its responsibilities, once again instructed the aircraft to turn right.

Shortly afterwards, since the Constellation had evidently *not* turned to the right, the controller asked the Captain to report his position. The latter replied that he was north-east of the airfield. He could in fact only have been north–east if he had turned right. He was in fact north-west.

Looking towards the north-east the controller could see no aircraft. He called up the Constellation but received no answer. The aircraft had already hit Monte de Pico killing all nine crew and twenty-one passengers.

With no evidence of mechanical failure the only explanation of this tragedy was that the pilot had turned left instead of right.

On June 22nd, 1955 the pilot of a Dove aircraft approaching London airport noticed that his airspeed had suddenly dropped from 128 knots to 110 knots. Having checked that there was no drag from drooping undercarriage or flaps he looked at the engine instruments. He remarked that the port engine gauges were registering high oil temperature and low oil pressure. But when he drew the attention of his companion to these signs of a failing engine he in fact pointed to the starboard engine gauges.

The pilot called up control. 'Tower, I'll do this run and then I'll have to land. I'm getting failing oil pressure on the *starboard* engine.'

Two minutes later he reported, 'I'm feathering.' London Tower informed him that he was three miles out on final approach and clear to land.

The pilot them moved the *port* pitch control back through the feathering gate. When the propeller stopped rotating, he switched off the *port* engine and according to him the rough running ceased. He then increased the power on the starboard engine, and lowered the undercarriage. Moments later a marked vibration developed. The plane crash-landed short of the runway – tearing off both wings.

Examination of the wreckage showed that the port engine was serviceable, but the starboard one, its cowling streaked with oil, had a broken crankshaft. The port throttle lever was fully closed. The starboard throttle was fully open, and the revolutions were at maximum. To recap – although he had stated that the port engine was failing he had pointed at the starboard gauges. He then, correctly, reported starboard engine failure to control, but in fact closed down the serviceable port engine and made his approach with the already faulty starboard engine at full revs.[11]

The evident discrepancies between what he heard, what he saw, what he said, and what he did suggest some confusion to say the least over the signals flashing backwards and forwards along those dense traffic lanes between his cerebral hemispheres.

But for those who dislike the implication that, by some monstrous anatomical transformation, a lateralised brain can become an Achilles heel there is comfort in another possibility. Maybe there's something funny about these aircraft beguilingly called Doves?

On July 23rd, 1955 another aircraft of that name was flying from Cardiff to Southampton. Once again severe vibration started and the pilot switched off the port engine. The plane rapidly lost height. At 200 feet, with the vibration still continuing, the port engine was re-started. The aircraft staggered over a ridge then descended into the New Forest. The crash killed the pilot and seriously injured his four passengers.

Subsequent examination on the test bed showed that whereas the port engine was in sound working order the starboard engine had a broken crankshaft. Though experienced, with 500 hours on Doves, the pilot not only shut down the wrong engine, but having realised his mistake failed to feather the right one, which was a pity for, provided the other has been feathered, a Dove can fly very well on one engine.

One might think that for a Dove the starboard engine crankshaft is not its strongest suit, but unfortunately for those who, seeking peace of mind, like to blame the tool rather than the man, Doves are not unique in causing laterality confusions.

In October 1959, a pilot with 23,563 hours' flying experience was under instruction in a Boeing 707. It was the first time he had ever sat in the left-hand seat of this particular class of aircraft. The flying instructor was concerned with teaching his student how to recover from a Dutch roll. Though this may sound like being restored to health after food poisoning in Holland, in fact it refers to stabilising a plane which has begun the wallowing from side to side which may occur with swept-wing aircraft.

Having initiated a number of Dutch rolls in the nose-left position, from each of which the student effected a recovery, the instructor suggested that a recovery should be made from the right. He initiated a roll in which the angle of bank was quite steep. Before attempting recovery the trainee allowed the aircraft to complete more oscillations with a roll-bank angle from 40° to 60°. Beaty's account of this tragedy goes on: 'Then he started to recover while the right bank was still increasing – by increasing it even further by full *right* aileron while the right wing was still moving. Immediately, the 707 yawed heavily to the right, well beyond a ninety-degree bank. The instructor took over, but it was too late . . .'[12]

Although 707s are big, strong aeroplanes, they were not designed for this sort of treatment. Three engines left the wing and fell to earth. Fire swept the aircraft. In the resultant crash four people lost their lives.

A common denominator of all these mishaps is a confusion between left and right. The same holds true for other accidents.

In 1963 a twin-engine plane approached to land with the port propeller feathered. At 600 feet, engine noise suddenly ceased. The pilot had switched off the other engine – the plane's only remaining source of power. Three were killed.

In 1965 the port engine of a DC3 was shut down because it seemed to be faulty. But after crashing the fault was traced to a cylinder head on the *starboard* engine.

While practising what to do during an emergency engine failure during take-off at Shannon, a trainee first officer crashed through applying the wrong rudder. At Nairobi in 1964 a pilot reversed the barometer figures which he had received from airport control. Instead of 839 millibars he set his altimeter at 938 millibars, thereby fooling himself that he was 3,000 feet higher than he really was. He hit the ground nine miles short of the runway.

Besides involving laterality confusion all these examples have one other common denominator. They all involve the making of a decision under some degree of stress. Sudden engine failure, being under the critical eye of an instructor and preparing to land at a strange airport of unusual altitude are all potentially stressful experiences. All these cases constitute specific examples of what can happen when the anachronistic stress response system exerts its influence on the delicate processes whereby we try to arrive at rational decisions.

So far as we know it hasn't happened yet but it would perhaps be wise to make the assumption that a pilot with laterality problems who is under some degree of stress, perhaps because his plane is carrying nuclear missiles, will get confused when trying to decide which lever he should pull or which button he should press.

Neglecting that Side of the Brain on which Survival must Depend
From pairs of electrodes on opposite sides of the head it is possible to find out which side of the brain is being used. The side used depends on what is being done. If, for example, a right-handed person speaks the words of a song, this produces electrical activity in his left cerebral hemisphere. If he merely hums the tune, only the right hemisphere becomes active. If he sings the song, both sides of his brain come into play.[13]

If you ask someone a question like, 'How many aunts do you have?' or 'What do the two words "extricate" and "intricate" have in common?' the chances are that while he is searching for an answer his eyes will swivel to the right, but if the question was, 'Would President Reagan (or Margaret Thatcher) look more convincing with a moustache?' his eyes would probably (having gone upwards) slope off to the left. In the first case, the individual is automatically activating that side of his brain, the left being best equipped to deal with questions involving numbers or words.[14] For problems involving spatial attributes or facial recognition, it is the right cerebral hemisphere which is pressed into service. In both cases, so it can be argued, he is not only activating the appropriate hemisphere, but also, through his direction of gaze, maximising the flow of information to the same side.

The plot thickens. But now a few more facts before we consider the fuller implications of all this.

If a Tom and Jerry cartoon is shown to the right cerebral hemisphere (i.e. projected in the left visual field) the emotions it produces are decidedly negative, quite the opposite of those experienced when it is digested by the left side of the brain. It's as if only the right hemisphere responds to the underlying aggressive symbolism of the film.[15]

Comparable results were obtained from the following experiment. Nearly a thousand people were asked which of the two mirror-image faces shown in Figure 14.1 (see page 234) looked happier. Eighty per cent of right-handed people opted for the lower one, presumably because it is those features which arrive in the right side of the brain that determine the emotional response.[16]

Clinical data support the conclusion from these studies that in right-handed people it is the right, so called minor, hemisphere which decides the way we feel about things. As a treatment for depression electro-convulsive shock is far more effective when applied to the right side of the head.[17] By the same token, temporary immobilisation of the right hemisphere by injecting an anaesthetic drug in the carotid artery makes the patient euphoric. Doing the same thing to the left hemisphere makes him depressed.[18]

What are the implications of all this for the thesis that some of the consequences of having two cerebral hemispheres may in the end be self-destructive? To summarise, evolution has provided us with what are in effect, two brains. Though they look very much alike and are richly interconnected they are, in fact, very different. They differ in what they do and how they do it – so much so that in people who have had them surgically disconnected from each other (usually as a treatment for epilepsy) one gets the impression of two sets of consciousness – in a sense two minds rubbing shoulders, but no more in the same head.

Originally, for primitive man – with each side of the brain contributing its quota to solving the problems of survival – the whole arrangement, as nature intended, probably worked extremely well.

For example, as Jaynes points out when discussing the differential responses to the two mirror-image faces in Figure 14.1, if someone saw an unrecognised man coming towards him, it would be of considerable value to decide if he was of friendly or unfriendly intent.[19]

But cultural evolution has upset this hitherto happy relationship between right brain and left brain and has done it in a way which poses a considerable threat to our future survival.

As an introduction to discussing how this may be, there are two further facts from recent research which need to be considered. The

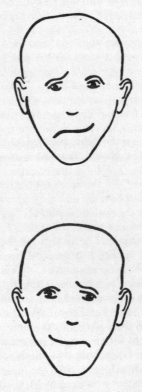

Figure 14.1   These faces are mirror images of each other. Stare at the nose of each. Which face is happier?

first is that individuals differ in what has been called their preferred hemisphere. There are some people who show a decided preference for using the right hemisphere. When asked a question they turn their eyes to the left. They seem readier to, happier to, activate and use the right side of the brain. Such people tend to be more imaginative, more creative, more emotionally sensitive, more intuitive and more hypnotisable[20] than those showing left hemisphericity. Not very surprisingly such people are also more affected by weak or subliminal stimuli.[21] Finally, such people in contrast to their counterparts are more global, less narrow, and less analytic in the way they perceive the world.

On the face of it there's nothing wrong with these individual differences. Both sides of the brain have their uses. Unfortunately, however, our cultural evolution has not only tended to reduce, even denigrate, evidence of right hemisphericity but actively encourages the incidence of left hemisphericity.

Should one doubt these admittedly tentative speculations regarding the pressure of cultural influences upon the relative contributions from the two hemispheres it is salutary to consider three small, but telling, examples. First, so-called Field Dependent people, a personality type associated with right hemisphericity, have been described in the academic literature as 'coming out on the pathological, more primitive, less desirable end of the continuum'.[22] One could hardly get more pejorative than that.

Second, the personality traits associated with right hemisphericity are also popularly asssociated with the female mind. In a culture which is dominated by males (notwithstanding Mrs Thatcher) this association does nothing for the trait of right hemisphericity.

Third, it says something about the way we educate our children that an excellent book comes to be written, which tries to compensate for the effect which a cultural bias towards left hemisphericity has upon creative art. Called *Drawing on the Right Side of the Brain*[23] it is largely concerned with methods, like that of trying to draw with the left hand or looking at things upside down while you sketch them, which help to free the right hemisphere from the dominating influence of language. Judging from the dramatic improvement in drawing which comes from overcoming this domination, it's much better to draw things as the right hemisphere sees them rather than as the left hemisphere labels them. As to the last point, the single biggest pressure towards left hemisphericity is, as we noted earlier, the fact that modern man conducts his affairs through words rather than pictures, and words – or rather the processes involving language – are largely resident in the left side of the brain.

Given these cultural pressures to develop and revere characteristics associated with the left side of the brain – largely because they *are* so suited to the practical problems of daily living – it is hardly surprising that those possessing them have the best chance of reaching positions of power. The goals of industry, government and the military are best achieved by those whose talents for verbiage, arithmetic and logical thinking exceed their capacities for intuition, feeling and creative imagination.

We can, it seems, do without art, but not without the ability to balance budgets, design sewage farms and develop superior missile systems.

It can be argued that, in days gone by, such a one-sided emphasis on the talents of the left hemisphere was no bad thing. The more delicate sensibilities of the right hemisphere could have been a positive handicap. The Industrial Revolution which, for a time, made Britain top nation would have been severely hampered if society had been 'illogically' squeamish about employing women and children for long hours in the mines and textile mills. The huge fortunes made from sugar, cotton and tobacco might have been much smaller if people had worried about importing slaves from Africa, and that magnificent creation, an empire on which the sun never set might never have happened if governments, traders and missionaries had been overly concerned about what they were doing to the natives in these lands.

Unfortunately, however, for devotees of left hemisphericity those days are over. The world has a new problem for which characteristics of the other, neglected, side of the brian are urgently required.

Let's go back for a moment and consider again the thesis put forward by Ronald Higgins.[24] Higgins, it will be recalled from Chapter 1, has pointed out that those six threats to our survival – the population explosion, maldistribution of food, the using up of vital resources, degradation of the environment, misuse of nuclear power, and the growing tendency of science and technology to escape human control are converging with increasing acceleration towards a state of world chaos from which there will be few survivors.

Although he considers it is probably already too late to avert the coming disaster, Higgins does allow that there is just one thing which could delay the awful day – ourselves.

If now, at two minutes to midnight, we could feel sufficiently concerned about the plight of those millions (at least one-third of the world's population) who live in degrading poverty, sufficiently fearful of the anarchy, suffering and ultimately oblivion so swiftly coming towards us, and sufficiently able to *imagine* what that cataclysmic era would be like, then it is just conceivably possible that we might be sufficiently jerked out of our present ostrich-like complacency to postpone if not avert the terminal stages of man's existence.

I see no reason to disagree with this view of our present dilemma, nor with the steps that could be taken to extend our time, but would point out that though Higgins makes no mention of these matters the origins and remedies sound suspiciously like emanations from the two sides of the brain.

Two quotations from *The Seventh Enemy* sum it up. Of the optimistic highly defended left hemisphere it might be said: 'We have a profound psychic investment in not taking the crisis on board.'[25] And of the pessimistic right hemisphere it might be said; 'We have to resist every expression of the icy calculus that puts abstract "efficiency" before personal intimacy.'[26] Sadly, judging from a study by Maccoby,[27] the latter recommendation has very little chance of being implemented.

As a result of extensive interviews with 250 business managers from twelve major American companies, Maccoby distinguished four types of executive – jungle fighters, craftsmen, company men and gamesmen. From his descriptions the first three of these types, from the primitive hunter/killer to the over-socialised organisation man, show a remarkable resemblance to stages in the cultural evolution of man.

Jungle fighters, epitomised by men like Carnegie and Ford, tyrants driven by the desire to dominate others, are, fortunately, on the way out. Evidently, they are more trouble than they're worth. The craftsmen, manifesting more in the way of ego rather than purely id motives can be identified with a later stage in socialisation, that at which people turned their attention from destructive to constructive pursuits.

Third, there is the oversocialised company man, depressive, anxious, conforming, authoritarian and totally dependent on the organisation, which he serves with courtly deference to his superiors. In Freudian parlance the company man might be described as having a weak ego and repressed id held down by a punitive superego – in common parlance, something of a creep!

There is nothing so unusual about these three personality types. But the fourth type, the gamesman, is something new and not so easily positioned on any simple continuum of socialisation.

As their name suggests the most striking characteristic of gamesmen is that they see life, and in particular their careers, as a game. Outwardly detached and playful, they are in fact compulsively driven to succeed and gain victories. For them other people are either pawns to be used or competitors to be vanquished.

For them the game is everything and the prize is fame and glory. For them, 'Tis all a Chequer board of Nights and Days Where Destiny [or rather they] with Men for Pieces plays, Hither and thither moves and mates, and slays, and one by one, back in the closet lays.'[28]

Their own career, other people, and human relations are seen in terms of options and possibilities. They are insensitive to the feelings of others, not because they are basically hostile or lacking in compassion, but simply because other people's feelings are irrelevant. For at the end of the day all the players are only either winners or losers. The gamesman has only one concern – to win. His greatest fear is to lose. All else is irrelevant.

On the face of it the concept of a gamesman is by no means unattractive. Against a background of heavy-handed jungle fighters, unspeakably diligent craftsmen and sycophantic company men, he scintillates in an otherwise gloomy (if not naughty) world. Captivated by his adolescent charm, society looks kindly on the gamesman if only as a welcome antidote to boring bureaucracy.

So what's the snag? And what might all this have to do with the two halves of the brain?

The short answer to the first question is that since, however much he might like to, the gamesman cannot go on being an adolescent for ever and all games come to an end, he will eventually overplay his hand. If and when he is in a position of political power, this could be very dangerous.

For many gamesmen, according to Maccoby, these unavoidable truths manifest themselves in a mid-life crisis:

> The fatal danger for gamesmen is to be trapped in permanent adolescence, never outgrowing the self-centred compulsion to score, never confronting their deep boredom with life when it is not a game, never developing a sense of meaning that requires more of them and allows others to trust them . . . at their worst moments gamesmen are unrealistic, manipulative, and compulsive workaholics. Their hyped up activity hides doubts about who they are and where they are going. Their ability to escape allows them to avoid unpleasant realities. When they are let down they are faced with feelings that make them feel powerless . . . deprived of challenge at work, they are bored and slightly depressed. Life is meaningless outside the game, and they tend to sit around watching TV or drinking too much . . . An old and tiring gamesman is a pathetic figure.[29]

But what has all this to do with the two sides of the brain and the risk to humanity of gamesmen, ageing or otherwise?

Since Maccoby did not subject them to any test of hemisphericity we cannot know in any anatomical sense whether gamesmen favour using the left side of the brain while almost totally neglecting contributions from the right, but they certainly behave as if they do. For them it *is* a case of the 'icy' calculus that puts efficiency before personal intimacy. Secondly, because virtually shut off from the nagging pessimistic voice of the right side of the brain, they are impervious to those issues which threaten the continued existence, not only of gamesmen, but of everyone else besides.

Again, we do not know in any anatomical sense if there are many left hemisphere gamesmen in the higher reaches of the White House, the Pentagon, the Politburo and the British Government but, judging from the conduct of many political and military leaders, this seems highly likely. Their apparent lack of any real motivation to halt, let alone reverse, the arms race, their quite extraordinary absence of any imagination as to what will happen if they don't, and the fact that scoring points in the game of nuclear threat and counter threat is evidently more important than making the world a safer place, support this contention.

It would be wise, therefore, to assume that the fate of mankind could well be decided by people who might think nothing of unleashing a world conflict provided their side wins. In the event, for all its playful machinations, the left side of the brain could, if neglectful of emanations from the right, have quite a lot to answer for. An old and tiring gamesman may be a pathetic figure, but if he is a world leader he is a terrifying liability.

As we saw earlier, the task of making rational decisions is extraordinarily difficult. The factors of boredom and of an imbalance between the two sides of the brain make it doubly so. Maybe one solution would be to take decision-making out of the hands of one fallible human being?

Chapter 15 looks at this possibility.

15

Are Two Heads Better Than One?

A little group of wilful men reflecting no opinion but their own have rendered the Great Government of the United States helpless and contemptible.

Woodrow Wilson, March 4th, 1917

Given the hazards which attend attempts to make a rational decision, it might be thought that decisions arrived at jointly, by two or more people, would have rather more chance of being sound.

Strictly speaking, a group decision implies a unanimous or majority vote for a particular course of action. Sometimes, however, what passes for a group decision is merely what one person chooses to do on the basis of information provided by a number of others. A variant of this is mere concurrence by a group with what their leader wishes. He decides. They agree, or at least pretend to agree. Finally, there is the case of groups which lean on their leader to make a decision of their choosing.

Presumably, all four sorts of group decision-making – the 'Multiple input single decider' model, the 'I decide you must all agree' model, the 'Let's work on him until he concurs with our wishes' model, and that very rare species the 'unanimous, after careful weighing of the odds' model, originated way back when early man was driven towards the necessity of social co-operation. In principle, all four models are useful if not essential to a proper solving of life's problems. It is good to have as much information as possible from many different

241

sources. Since the group will have to implement the decision, it is important that everyone is of a like mind. Since people are not too good at thinking statistically, there's less chance of error if a number of individuals are making the same calculation.

Why then is it that group decisions are often the most inept? Why is it that most of the worst decisions in the history of man, such as that which resulted in a wooden horse being admitted to the city of Troy, or those which cost us the American colonies, or that which resulted in the Bay of Pigs fiasco, or that which allowed General MacArthur to invade North Korea, or that which resulted in the Aswan dam, have all been products of people putting their heads together?

There are two main reasons. First, groups encourage diffusion of responsibility. Second, the pressure to conform, experienced by members of a group, not only vitiates the advantages of contributions from theoretically independent minds, but fails to provide a safeguard against irrational and sometimes fatal wish-fulfilment fantasies.

There is no shortage of examples to illustrate just how fatal these effects can be. According to Janis,[1] the four worst decisions in American history – decisions which cost thousands of lives and millions of dollars – may be laid at their door. Typical of such monumental blunders was that which resulted in the Bay of Pigs disaster – subsequently described as 'among the worst fiascos ever perpetrated by a responsible government.'[2]

So inept was the decision to try and overthrow Castro by an invasion of Cuban exiles that it seriously shakes any faith one might have had in the rationality of high-ranking government officials. Planned by the CIA, based on six assumptions each one of which proved wrong, the enterprise was doomed before it even started. Within forty-eight hours the entire invasion force was either dead or behind bars. The survivors of this 'perfect failure' were eventually ransomed back to the United States for fifty-three million dollars.

How was it that some of the most intelligent men ever to participate in the government of a great and ordinarily rational nation could behave in such a way as to make their administration the laughing stock of an incredulous world? And how could it happen that Kennedy, one of the more astute of American Presidents, came to approve a scheme so hare-brained that, within days, he was saying, 'How could I have been so stupid to let them go ahead?'

The answer has to do with the ramifications of human needs. Needs provoke feelings, which, in turn, impel towards behaviour. If the behaviour is blocked, the unrequited wish provokes fantasy fulfilments. So far, so good. Whether they are to do with food, sex, aggression or anything else that happens to be occupying the mind, fantasies are nature's way of exploring possibilities and finding a solution to what had seemed a pressing, but insuperable problem.

And if they should fail to solve the problem then at least it could be said of them that in the mind, if not the body, they provide a useful second best – a sort of psychic safety valve. And there, for most of our imaginings, the matter rests. But once in a while the curbs on acting out a fantasy that should on no account be translated into a reality become so diminished that the individual begins to embark on behaviour which he may subsequently, bitterly, regret. Since it is usually fear or guilt that holds a person in check, anything which reduces or overrides these emotions could turn an all-consuming wish into what may turn out to be a terrifying reality. Alcohol fulfils this function, so do sudden rage or jealousy. But another, no less common factor, is other people. And it is the latter (possibly in conjunction with the others) which resulted in the Bay of Pigs. For obvious reasons – national pride, fear of communism, the need to present an image of strong leadership – Kennedy and his aides wished to rid Cuba and themselves of Fidel Castro. Given the underlying wish, they were more than receptive to the CIA plan.

But the plan was faulty in every detail. Founded on ignorance, steeped in prejudice, it had as much chance of success as a wart hog in a beauty contest! So how did it get by a group of men who individually and independently would in all probability have rejected it out of hand?

The answer resides in a phenomenon, long known to psychologists as the shift to risk, which may afflict a close-knit group of people when they become victims of what Janis calls groupthink. The eight symptoms of this malaise include:

1   An illusion of invulnerability, shared by most or all the members, which creates excessive optimism and encourages taking extreme risks;
2   collective efforts to rationalize in order to discount warnings which might lead the members to reconsider their assumptions before they recommit themselves to their past policy decisions;

3 an unquestioned belief in the group's inherent morality, inclining the members to ignore the ethical or moral consequences of their decisions;

4 stereotyped views of enemy leaders as too evil to warrant genuine attempts to negotiate, or as too weak and stupid to counter whatever risky attempts are made to defeat their purposes;

5 direct pressure on any member who expresses strong arguments against any of the group's stereotypes, illusions, or commitments, making clear that this type of dissent is contrary to what is expected of all loyal members;

6 self-censorship of deviations from the apparent group consensus, reflecting each member's inclination to minimize to himself the importance of his doubts and counterarguments;

7 a shared illusion of unanimity concerning judgments conforming to the majority view (partly resulting from self-censorship of deviations, augmented by the false assumption that silence means consent);

8 the emergence of self-appointed mindguards – members who protect the group from adverse information that might shatter their shared complacency about the effectiveness and morality of their decisions.[3]

Most of these 'symptoms' were common not only to the groups which made Janis's 'four worst decisions' but to many others as well. They result from an interaction between the needs of individuals – to aggress, to conform, to maintain self-esteem, and to please 'father' – and the condoning, facilitating influences of mutual reassurance by other people.

If the group which is making the decision happens to be highly cohesive, amiable and led by someone all are trying hard to please, such symptoms are particularly likely to occur. However, as shown by Kennedy's adroit handling of the Cuban missile crisis, the dangers of groupthink are by no means inevitable. There *are* other factors, such as a recent past experience. Confronted with the problem of Soviet missiles in Cuba, Kennedy was perhaps influenced by his inept handling of the previous crisis. The conclusion, that for the world to remain a relatively safe place, every major international crisis facing an administration should be preceded by a minor one is, however, somewhat depressing.

The effects of groupthink are not only the hazards of group decision-making. There are at least two others which can cause trouble. Take those which may beset the British legal system.

Whatever else it may be, a court of law is a group of people whose goal it is to arrive at fair and rational decisions. It is, in fact, made up of three subgroups – the prosecution, the defence and the jury – all operating under the direction of a judge.

Ideally, and in principle, the final decision – guilty or not guilty – which emerges from a court is arrived at by careful consideration of facts and arguments provided by these various subgroups.

Since this final decision may be, literally, a matter of life or death to the accused, it might be expected that every effort would be made to exclude from the proceedings any possibility of irrationality, prejudice or unfairness. After all, since the purpose of a court is to mete out justice it would be ridiculous for it to behave in any other way than justly.

Ridiculous it may be, but one has only to consider the long history of groups of people sitting in judgment on their fellow men – the Bloody Assizes, kangaroo courts, or those military tribunals which, as recently as the First World War, had men shot for cowardice – to realise that the decision-making of so-called courts of justice can be just as inept as that of any other decision-making body.

There are few better (though there are many other) illustrations of this point than the case of Oscar Slater, who was sentenced to death for a murder which he did not commit, reprieved at the eleventh hour, and then imprisoned for nineteen years.[4]

On the evening of January 21st, 1909, an old lady was beaten to death in her flat at Queen's Terrace, Glasgow.

Between this murder and the date on which Slater was committed to Peterhead prison for life, there unfolded a sequence of events so extraordinary, so squalid and distasteful, that credulity is stretched to breaking point. Of the Glasgow police, the prosecution witnesses, the Lord Advocate (leading Counsel for the prosecution), the presiding judge and the Secretary of State for Scotland, it might well be asked how *could* they behave with such inhumanity, such meanness of spirit and such palpable dishonesty. When one considers this collection of individuals alongside such people as Sir Arthur Conan Doyle, who worked to obtain Slater's release, it is hard to believe they belonged to the same species.

Slater was arrested as a result of a tip-off from a cycle dealer that he (Slater) had been trying to sell a pawn ticket for a brooch which, it was believed, had been stolen from the murdered woman. From that moment on, saved from further cerebration by arrival of this clue, the witnesses and the judge did everything within their power to ensure a conviction, and this despite the fact that quite early on the court was confronted with evidence which might well have deterred a less resolute prosecution. For example, it was soon discovered that not only did the incriminating brooch not belong to the deceased; it had actually been in pawn for some time before the murder occurred. As for Slater, not only had he been seen elsewhere at the time of the crime, but descriptions by independent witnesses of a man seen leaving the house in which the murder was committed in no way fitted him. These tiresome discoveries, however, were not allowed to interfere with the court's intention of finding the accused guilty. So great was the prejudice against Slater, so single-minded the judge, and so unencumbered by moral scruples the police and prosecution that there was no hesitation about:

1 Suppressing evidence favourable to the defence;
2 not calling key witnesses who might have exposed the weaknesses in the prosecution case;
3 accepting the evidence from an identification parade even though the witnesses had been 'accidentally' allowed to see the accused before the parade began;
4 coaching two of the prosecution witnesses as to what they should say in court so that their evidence tallied with what the prosecution wanted;
5 deliberately introducing into the Lord Advocate's speech for the prosecution, and the judge's summing up, such inaccuracies in the first place, and defamatory remarks about the accused's character in the second place, as would guarantee misdirection of the jury towards finding Slater guilty.

It says something for the fair-mindedness of ordinary people that, despite all the efforts of judge and prosecution, it was only by a slender majority of three that the jury returned a verdict of guilty. The court thereupon sentenced Slater to death.

This was not the end of the matter. So uneasy was the public mind about this outcome that the death sentence was commuted to one of life imprisonment. However, some people (fortunately) are never satisfied. Since it seemed illogical, if not morally wrong, that a man reprieved from death because of faulty evidence should then be gaoled for life, repeated attempts were made to get the Secretary of State for Scotland to reopen the case. This he equally repeatedly refused to do.

When, in the light of further evidence supporting Slater's alibi, and after two doctors had dismissed as absurd the theory that a small tack hammer belonging to Slater had been the murder weapon, the Secretary for State was at last compelled, very much against his will, to hold an inquiry. Since the only people allowed to participate in this secret conclave were those who had helped to get Slater convicted in the first place, and since crucial sections of the reported proceedings of the inquiry were carefully deleted before the latter was made public, the inquiry did not result in a release of the prisoner, let alone an admission that he had been wrongly convicted.

In outlining the details of this case, we must not lose sight of its implications for the pathology of group decision-making. Here was a group of individuals interacting with each other in such a way that, when eventually making a life or death decision, the latter lacked all reason, truth and compassion. In condemning Oscar Slater to death this Scottish court, aided and abetted by the police, was behaving in some ways no better, and in others much worse and with less excuse, than an ordinary lynch mob. At least a lynch mob is impelled by passionate emotion, at least it does not get paid for what it does, and at least it is open about its intentions and does not need to hide behind a hypocritical allegiance to authority and the so-called majesty of the law.

And there is another factor – whether it is the local assizes, a Stalinesque court trying Soviet dissidents, the Star Chamber or even magistrates sitting close for comfort on the local bench – those who gather together for the express purpose of passing judgment on another human being are, like those who dispatched Mr Slater, further handicapped in their quest for justice by being in a sense prisoners of the group. People don't have to join a lynch mob, but for members of an official body it is so difficult to rebel against authority, so painful to be expelled from the group, so frightening to imagine those fateful words 'Those who are not with us are against us' that any doubts about the rightness of their cause is, if not actually quelled, certainly concealed. And if they had any doubt about the wisdom of remaining silent, there are always examples like the following to make them think twice.

Among those who believed in the innocence of Oscar Slater was a certain Inspector Trench of the Glasgow police. Unable to live with his conscience, he eventually published evidence that had not come out at the trial. The response of authority was swift and unequivocal. Trench was sacked from the police with ignominy. He and a colleague enlisted in the Royal Fusiliers. But, for the Secretary of State for Scotland, it was not enough to ruin a man's career. The vindictiveness of authoritarian groups towards dissenters is not so easily assuaged. Within a few weeks of joining the army, Trench and his friend were arrested and imprisoned for receiving stolen goods. Their 'crime' related to an event some five years earlier in which they had succeeded in recovering items stolen in a robbery. So pleased was an insurance company involved in the case that they had rewarded Trench and his colleague for their excellent police work. Only when all this became known at the trial were both men exonerated.

Such retaliation on the part of the authorities illustrates the lengths to which a group will go to defend its position. So powerful are the needs to justify an unjustifiable decision, so acute the mental dissonance evoked by facts which conflict with what has been decided, and so sensitive to criticism those concerned, that no act is too bizarre, no plot too ridiculous, and no outcome too malicious provided it will serve the needs of vengeance. In a welter of irrationality, with all caution thrown to the winds, the threatened authorities in a situation of this kind may become prone to behaviour far beyond the conscience of most ordinary citizens.

One particularly worrisome feature of this syndrome is the likelihood that the more powerful, prestigious and self important the personages concerned, the more ruthlessly psychopathic their behaviour may become. As exemplified by the hounding to his death of Stephen Ward following the Profumo/Keeler scandal, by the behaviour of Nixon and his cronies after Watergate, and by the alleged murder of Pope John Paul I by dignitaries of the Vatican,[5] there are at least two reasons for this resort to bloody-mindedness by people in high places. First, the character traits which take some people to the top of their profession are likely to include extremes of narcissism, the urge to dominate others and depths of dishonesty rarely encountered outside the criminal fraternity. Second, the higher one has got the further there is to fall. Just as the delusions of grandeur experienced by the Secretary of State for Scotland in the

Slater case would make it virtually impossible for him ever to admit he might have been wrong, so we should expect the worst excesses of retaliatory rage and defensive postures from people with the most to lose.

This certainly happened in the case of Oscar Slater. During the nineteen years Slater spent in gaol successive Secretaries of State for Scotland resisted all attempts to have the case re-opened. When eventually, in the light of yet more evidence proving Slater's innocence, they had to capitulate, an appeal court involving five English judges was set up. In due course the prisoner was acquitted. After his release, Slater received £6,000 compensation. But even this 'generous' gesture was somewhat marred by the fact that out of this sum he was required to pay back no less than £1,500 to cover the cost of his defence.

Those who, for reasons of their own, like to defend official groups and their leaders against the faintest breath of criticism may well object that no importance should be attached to the Slater case because it is unique. This is not so. One has only to consider those miscarriages of justice recently brought to public notice by the now disbanded BBC *Rough Justice* team, to realise it is not unique.

Before enlarging on this topic, it should be made clear that what follows is in no way intended as a criticism of either the police or our courts of justice, both of which groups are having to contend with an immense and growing problem of lawlessness; rather it is meant to show how certain psychological factors inherent in group decision-making may result in outcomes which turn out to be utterly wrong. If the activities of the police and the courts result in miscarriages of justice it is because they themselves are victims of sometimes extreme and often insidious group pressures.

For example, because it is their business to apprehend villains the police are under pressure from the public, especially relatives of the victim, from the Home Office, from the Press and from their own organisation to solve crimes as quickly as possible.

Given these very real pressures to do something and do it fast, it is understandable that once they have found a suspect every effort will be made to confirm their suspicion.

With attention narrowed on this task there is an increasing tendency to look for evidence which will support the favoured hypothesis, and to ignore facts which conflict with the hypothesis.

In the course of time, under mounting pressure from outside, belief hardens into certainty; from then on even glaring discrepancies between existing 'certainties' and new-found facts become discounted if not totally ignored.

There follow some examples from the files of *Rough Justice*.

A man was sentenced to life imprisonment for the murder of a young girl. She was clutching a handful of hair, yet the convicted man's hair did not match the sample . . .

A father and son were convicted of murder during a fight in a Manchester house, despite the fact that no weapon was ever found. Yet independent witnesses say that another man confessed to the crime, a man who habitually carried a knife . . .

A young man was sentenced to four years for sexual assault. Three independent witnesses and the girl herself testified that the assailant was around five feet seven to nine inches tall, slimly built, and wearing blue denims. The man sent to jail is six feet tall, weighed fourteen and a half stones at the time of the crime and did not own any blue denim clothes. Today he has served almost nine years and is in Broadmoor Mental Hospital, detained partly because he will not confess that he was guilty of the original crime![6]

Throughout history, survival of the individual has depended upon his membership of a protective group, so it should occasion no surprise that maintaining the solidarity of a group may on occasion take precedence over the calls of justice and rationality. The above cases, like others investigated by *Rough Justice*, bear out this supposition. They illustrate how decisions emanating from a group may, for the reasons given by Janis (see page 243), be even less reliable than those coming from someone operating on his own.

Any residual doubts about this matter should be reduced by considering the response of official bodies upon receiving evidence that their earlier decisions may have been at fault. Are they ready to admit miscarriages of justice and put matters right? Not if they can help it.

In days gone by, after someone had been hanged for a murder which he did not commit, very little by way of redress could be done for the deceased. However, those responsible for irreversible miscarriages of justice could at least admit their mistake, pardon the victim of their incompetence and compensate the dead person's relatives. One would have thought that in such groups as those of the Home Office, the police and the judiciary some prickings of conscience would have resulted quickly in such simple acts of reparation. Yet it took years before poor half-witted Timothy Evans, wrongly executed for murders committed by the necrophile John Christie, was granted a pardon. If there is such a thing as group conscience these particular groups seem well able to live with theirs. Presumably it is part of the philosophy of the group mind of official bodies that since one cannot resurrect the dead there is absolutely no point in resurrecting those issues which sent a man to the grave.

With the abolition of capital punishment, however, the whole situation changed. The impossibility of resurrecting a corpse is no longer a problem. Verdicts of 'guilty' and consequent life sentences are not irrevocable. This, after all, was one of the main reasons for abolition. At long last a change in the law made it possible to rectify errors of judgment. Given these new and felicitous conditions (were it not for what we know about the dynamics of group behaviour) the following facts may seem quite extraordinary:

1 Jock Russell, the man whose hair did not match that clutched in the hand of a dead girl, remained in prison for three years *after* it had become perfectly clear that he was innocent.

2 Michael and Patrick McDonagh, a father and son, went on serving life sentence for two years *after* the Home Office knew that another man had confessed to the murder for which they had been sentenced.

3 In at least four other cases investigated by *Rough Justice* the victims of wrongful arrest continued (or continue) to remain in gaol long after their innocence was proved beyond any reasonable doubt.

In the circumstances one would have thought that the authorities concerned would have done their utmost to atone for the blunders which put innocent people in prison and, as part of this atonement, would have congratulated the *Rough Justice* investigators for saving these victims from many more years of wrongful imprisonment. But this was not to be. The *Rough Justice* team was disbanded, thus ending one of the few mechanisms which British society had for rectifying the tragic consequences of rough justice. So sacrosanct are the decisions of official groups that woe betide anyone who can prove they were mistaken.

Before leaving this worrisome matter there is a further hazard which needs to be considered. It concerns the fact that people who make decisions at the apex of a hierarchy are so far removed from those who will have to implement their decisions, so out of touch with those who will be affected by their decisions, and so abysmally ignorant of the real issues involved in what they are deciding to do, that even with the best will in the world the consequences of their deliberations may turn out to be quite the opposite of what they intended.

In his book *The IRG Solution*, which concentrates on the incompetence of hierarchies, David Andrews gives several illustrations of this point. Here is just one.[7]

Obviously the advisability of a major project like that of damming one of the world's largest rivers hinges on a great many factors – its cost, the time it will take, the availability of labour and materials, transportation, housing and health of workers (in the building of the Panama Canal thousands died of malaria and yellow fever) and political implications. It depends upon the likely benefits – how many megawatts of electricity will it generate, to what extent will it reduce flooding and the effects of drought? What will be the benefits to industry and to the image of the State as an industrial power; to what extent will it subdue social unrest by reducing unemployment and improving the fertility of the land?

The advisability of a major project like the Aswan dam would also depend on the risks involved – the likelihood and consequences of structural failure; the agricultural, scenic and archaeological losses from inundating a large area of land. It would depend on the negative effects of reducing a river hitherto rich in alluvial silt and plankton.

All in all, the building of the Aswan dam would, like many other major projects, depend upon a cost/benefit analysis of almost infinite complexity. It would depend upon collating the advice of many experts and in particular the views of those most likely to be directly affected by the dam. It would (or should) depend upon input from surveyors, agriculturalists, water engineers, health officials, marine biologists, archaeologists, lawyers and politicians. Ideally, information from all these and more should be heeded before ever construction starts.

Judging from the consequences of building the Aswan dam it was not. Those ultimately responsible for its construction either did not know or did not heed what they should have known and heeded.

Completed in 1970 at a cost of £2,000 million the dam, 360 feet high, retains a lake (named after President Nasser) of 164,000 million cubic metres of water. In theory the annual hydro-electric output from all this water – some ten million megawatts of electricity – would not only meet Egypt's domestic needs but provide a valuable surplus for export.

In practice it did not. There were three main reasons. First, it has proved impossible to synchronise the flow of water for the varying needs of irrigation with that for maximum electricity generation, while at the same time maintaining sufficient spare capacity in the lake for flood-control purposes. Second, the amount of electricity that can be utilised is so restricted by limited transmission capacity that only about half of Egypt's electricity needs are met by the dam. Finally, part of the electricity generated is used in the manufacture of fertilisers to replace the alluvial silt which the Nile no longer deposits on the previously fertile flood plain.[8]

The last problem has its own adverse side-effect. Instead of settling where it's needed, the alluvial silt is now filling up Lake Nasser, thus reducing the latter's capacity for storing water, and shortening its life.

There are further problems. Because it no longer delivers a rich alluvial soup of aquatic micro-organisms to the Mediterranean, the previous nourishment of anchovies and sardines living in this sea has come to an untimely end. The effects on those who used to fish for these delicacies are little short of catastrophic.

One of the purposes of the Aswan dam was to substitute year-round constant irrigation for the previous excessive irrigation that occurred when the Nile was in flood. But even this has backfired. By producing salination of soil which no longer benefits from being leached by periodic flooding, the land is *less* fertile than it was before.

A second adverse consequence of the new inadequate irrigation policy bears out the old adage that it's an ill wind which blows nobody any good. Unfortunately the creatures, perhaps the only creatures, to benefit from the Aswan dam are snails and the tiny parasitic liver flukes which they carry. It is infestation with these pests from the snail-ridden waters of the new irrigation system that has produced a dramatic rise in the incidence of bilharzia. According to present estimates at least one-third of the Egyptian population is now afflicted with this debilitating disease.

So much for the sad tale of the Aswan dam. But how could they get it so wrong?

The answer is to be found in two characteristics of hierarchical groups. First, the people at the top who make the ultimate decisions are simply too far removed from those on the ground who really know what's what.

Second, because those at the apex of a hierarchy tend to be preoccupied with political or economic issues as a result of necessary interactions with outside bodies, they may well have neither the time nor the wish to consider, let alone accept, advice from lower down. Particularly is this so when the 'advice' conflicts with what those at the top desire. As the following lines suggest, such factors certainly seem relevant to the case of the dam at Aswan; 'The policy errors that have studded the High Dam's history are rooted in the highly political atmosphere in which the project has been appraised. Quiet and serious technical debate and analysis became impossible because the analyst's motives were suspect.'[9]

The evidence and arguments presented in this chapter compel a less than sanguine view of group decision-making. People operating as part of a group may be less stressed than someone working on his or her own, but only because they have forfeited that safeguard against irrational behaviour, the feeling of personal responsibility.

Long ago those of our early ancestors who banded together for mutual protection and support probably felt safer and certainly were much safer than those who lived in lonely isolation. From these primitive groupings, be they extended families, tribes, or merely a bunch of hunters, there has evolved a variety of modern decision-making groups – committees, cabals, juntas, cabinets. Like their forebears, the members of such councils probably draw comfort from each other, their sense of responsibility is diffused and if the worst should happen they can all, metaphorically speaking, hide behind each other. But when the guardians of Singapore and the defenders of Pearl Harbor luxuriated too long in the false security of *their* respective groups they brought down upon their hitherto untroubled heads two of the worst disasters in British and American history. And when the Argentinian junta connived to invade the Falklands it was a decision so foolhardy that it cost their country very dear. And so we might ask if a group of intelligent politicians encouraged by their military advisers can set in motion an enterprise like the Bay of Pigs how easy might it be for a comparable group to initiate the Third World War?

16

Wars to End Wars

The easier it seems by means of technology to destroy human life with the touch of a button, the more important it is for the public to understand how it can be possible for someone to want to extinguish the lives of millions of human beings.

Alice Miller[1]

This book has considered several characteristics of mankind with two common denominators. All were, once upon a time, useful products of learning or genetic evolution. Without them, without the capacity for conscious representation of a very limited part of the external environment, or the ability to acquire egos and superegos, or the potential for feeling bored, for coping with stressors, or for practising social co-operation, we would probably not be here.

The other common denominator of these characteristics is that they, or their side effects, are so ill-tuned to the products of cultural evolution that they now threaten our survival. They do so because of what Higgins[2] referred to as 'galloping technology' – that sorcerer's apprentice which through a combination of laziness, greed, ingenuity and misguided good intentions has turned against its master. The ultimate threat is of fairly recent origin. Without his ability to split the atom, man's other dubious characteristics would not matter too much. People might destroy themselves, and others, in large numbers, but they could not extinguish once and for all every trace of what could, for all we know, be the sum total of life within the universe. Now it is not only possible that they can but probable that they will.

Now, the proposition, technology plus man gives extinction of the species, is a reality. So what can be done about this worrisome equation? Since it is not possible to disinvent modern technology, our only hope is to alter man or rather his approach to the fruits of his ingenuity.

Let's go back a bit.

Mincing machines of the sort made by Mr Spong have for many years constituted a significant if humble component of Western culture. Whether as a substitute for teeth or as a means of disguising unpalatable meat they may well seem a relatively harmless artefact – not the sort of thing Mr Higgins had in mind when citing technology as one of the great threats to survival. As an early step in the growth of technology Mr Spong's contribution was more of a slow walk than a gallop.

And yet in 1926 a Purley housewife, though not actually killed, was savaged by one of his machines.

As anyone who has ever tried to eat a hot potato while delivering an after-dinner speech must know, there are some activities best not combined with others. One such is to mince up the remains of Sunday's joint while chatting to the milkman through the kitchen window. Had she thought about it while unwinding her hand from the mincer, the lady in question might have seen her painful experience as prototypical of all those situations wherein technology turns (literally) against the hand which feeds it.

Whatever its ultimate purpose human life involves carrying out a succession of tasks all of which have three characteristics in common. They all resist solution. They do so because they require information and energy, and because they require information and energy they deplete the operator. This argument holds true for all tasks, whether as simple as peeling a potato, as difficult as peeling a grape, as waging a war or extricating a budgerigar from a treacle tart.

Technology is fashioned to meet these characteristics of tasks. It is an extension of the operator – an aid to the basic activities of eating, drinking, fighting, sex and even sleeping. No one could deny that whether it is in the shape of ships, aircraft, telephones, kidney machines, life-size inflatable dolls or mincing machines, technology has done much to enrich the quality of life.

The reason it now threatens our survival is not just because of its destructive potential but because of our attitudes towards it. Take what is probably a widespread view, that 'Technology will answer all our problems'. In fact there is very little sign of this ever being true. There are, for example, at least three devastating natural hazards, drought, hurricanes and earthquakes, which technology has scarcely dented.

As for social ills, some of the worst – drug addiction, unemployment and war have been made worse rather than diminished by technology. Food supplies and the quantity and distribution of drinkable water have been impaired rather than improved. In many parts of the world arable land, forests, lakes and rivers are being destroyed or rendered unproductive by such side-effects of technology as dust-bowl farming, acid rain and over-use of herbicides. And now this belief in technology as a cure-all has given rise to what could be its most dangerous application – star wars.

Another belief with dubious consequences is that 'Modern technology is virtually foolproof – we can trust it.' As Peter Walker, who, one month before Chernobyl, said; 'Nuclear power is the safest form of energy known to man,'[3] now knows, this also is simply not true. Ships still capsize through carelessness, planes crash because of cracks in their combustion chambers, bridges collapse, tower blocks fall down. Here again the problem is not the technology, but in this case, how we use it, in particular the effect on technological applications of unnecessary risk-taking, greed, corner-cutting, and sheer blind faith in the gadget's infallibility.

The catastrophic misuse of available technology is not a new phenomenon. In the early days of steam railways it was the custom of impatient but unimaginative engine drivers to extract more power from their locomotives by screwing down the safety valve – a practice which produced some spectacular explosions and killed quite a lot of people. Nowadays a richer yield of misapplied technology is to be found in the field of aeronautics. In this case cost cutting seems to be a prime factor in the untoward killing of people. For example, many lives are lost because airlines refuse to incur the extra expense of installing non-inflammable seats.

Others have died because airlines seem to have a blind spot about tyres. Norris is explicit on this issue.[4] Since most aircraft accidents occur on landing or take-off, everything possible should be done to reduce risks at these critical times. One obvious precaution would be to prevent any possibility of tyre failure. Considering that, on landing, the tyres of a Boeing 747 have to sustain an impact load of around 300 tons, are required to accelerate from 0 to 120 m.p.h. in a fraction of a second, and have to bring the aircraft to rest within the braking distance of the runway, it would be absurd to think that airlines might ever fit different sorts of tyre on the same axle. Even the average motorist would think twice about such a practice. Since, on take-off, each ounce of rubber on the tread of a 747 tyre increases, through centrifugal force, to an equivalent of 331 pounds; and while taxiing and during take-off that same tread may increase in heat to temperatures which weaken the structure of the tyre; and since 87 per cent of all aborted take-offs occur through failure of tyres, wheels or brakes, it is unthinkable that airlines would ever fit retreaded tyres to any of their aircraft. Few owners of high performance sports cars would favour such economies.

But on March 1st, 1978 a fully laden DC10 during its take-off from Los Angeles airport suffered a succession of three burst tyres. The first was a retread with patches inside its cover. The second was already weakened by being mismatched with the first. The third tyre disintegrated through being hit by the debris of its neighbours. As a result of this domino effect in which the reliability of a system is determined by that of its weakest part, the DC10 ended up as a blazing hulk on the grass beside the runway.

Why do airlines take such risks with the lives of their passengers? Presumably because new tyres cost nearly four times as much as retreads.

But it is in the area of defence that our use of and attitudes to technology constitute the greatest risk. There was a time when it centred round the old problem of weighing safety against efficiency. This appears to have been a factor in the choice of bomb fuses used in the Second World War. Whether or not they intended to, the Germans opted for safety by using highly sophisticated, relatively expensive electrical fuses wherein the firing condenser only became charged sometime *after* the bomb had left the plane. If someone was careless enough to drop a bomb before or during the time it was being loaded up, or the plane crashed with its bombs still unreleased, the trembler switches inside the fuse might close but there would be no electricity within the fuse to detonate the bomb. As a consequence they probably suffered few serious accidents but their air raids left behind many unexploded bombs. The British, on the other hand, went for much simpler mechanical fuses, which depended on strikers hitting percussion caps. They cost less, but the bombs to which they were fitted were more likely to go off *wherever* they were dropped.

Nowadays attitudes to the technology of defence are of a rather different and far more dangerous kind. Old worries as to its limitations, which gave rise to agonising about the right compromise between safety and performance, have been largely replaced by what appears to be an unjustified confidence in its reliability. A major source of this unquestioning belief could be the sheer lack of comprehension by many people, including most politicians, of 'how the damn thing works'. There are everyday examples of this phenomenon. In the old days most shoppers would watch critically while their grocer totted up the bill with a pencil still warm from behind his ear. How many of them today question the accuracy of those supermarket check-out systems which involve passing everything from beans to toothpaste across a dimly illuminated grill? In fact supermarkets are probably less accurate than the grocer with his pencil but, thanks to the sheer incomprehensibility of the bar-code ritual, the customers are content to put their trust in the wonders of modern technology.

Undue faith in the accuracy of supermarket check-out systems is not going to wreck this planet, but what if the same trusting attitudes were extended to machines which do more than price a tin of beans?

At 23 minutes 40 seconds past 1 a.m. on April 26th, 1986 there occurred what is to date the worst accident this world has ever known. Within ten seconds a massive surge of power in Chernobyl's No. 4 reactor initiated a terrifying sequence of events.

With its protective cover blown open by the blast of exploding hydrogen the reactor, now a blazing inferno, began shooting dense plumes of radioactive particles high into the sky. Within days the fallout from the resulting cloud was contaminating virtually every Eastern and Western European country. A few people, those nearest the disaster, died instantly. In the weeks that followed many more died from radiation sickness. During the next thirty years or so thousands more will die from the long-term cancerous effects of Chernobyl.

This accident exemplifies most of the worst features of man's relationship with his technology. First, the destructive potential of this technology is now *so* great that, until something actually does go wrong, nobody seems to appreciate just *how* great. By which time it is too late.

Second, despite the enormous forces involved, forces which, in the Chernobyl case, could suddenly accelerate the reactor's energy output by a factor of seven (approaching a hundred million watts), they are still left to the tender care of a few fallible operators.

Because the individuals concerned are now dead, we may never know for certain how it started, but the most likely cause of the disaster appears to have been 'a simple human error'. The evidence suggests that, as a result of unauthorised experimenting with the control rods, the man in charge brought about a critical change in the core of the reactor, which he was then unable to control.

Third, there is the factor of a fatal interaction between commercial interests, enthusiasm for a major project, risk-taking and a failure to take account of possible contingencies. There are precedents for such an interaction.

Years earlier competition between two railway companies resulted in enthusiasm for the building of a bridge. Despite warnings by an Inspector of Railways – which related to the limitations of cast iron as a building material, the effect of strong winds upon long lattice-girder spans, and the strains imposed by passage of a train – risks were taken and construction went ahead. The result was that on the night of December 28th, 1876 a combination of faulty workmanship, storm-force winds, and passage of a train above its recommended speed, caused the Tay Bridge to collapse with the loss of many lives.[5]

In the case of Chernobyl similar factors were at work but with outcomes that were immeasurably worse. One of the reasons was the total failure of the emergency systems to cope with both the speed and nature of the disaster. Attention had been so narrowed upon the possibility of a failure of the coolant system at the base of the core that the design of the emergency systems did not cater for the remoter possibility of damage at the *top* of the core. This occurred when a 200 ton crane came crashing through the roof.

As Hawkes and his colleagues remark in their account of *The Worst Accident in the World*, 'It is a frightening illustration of psychological limitations which prevent proper consideration of all accident possibilities. Rightly, anti-nuclear campaigners, and suspicious members of the public, must now ask if other countries' nuclear planners have been similarly misguided.'[6]

The most serious and certainly most pathetic aspect of our attitude towards technology became apparent during the aftermath of Chernobyl. Instead of admitting that it was a major blunder which must never be allowed to happen again, three things happened. While the Soviets dragged their feet in publicising the disaster, the USA tried to make political capital out of the Russians' misfortune, and those with a vested interest in nuclear power did their best to convince themselves and everybody else that nuclear power is safe, that a similar disaster could not happen here.

Had Chernobyl been the first accident to a nuclear reactor there would have been some excuse for this ostrich-like behaviour. But it was not the first. Between the disastrous Windscale fire in 1957 and the near melt-down at Three Mile Island there have been many occasions when less dramatic accidents have resulted in the carcinogenic products of nuclear fission reaching the world which the rest of us inhabit. As Hawkes et al. remark, 'In reality, of course, nuclear engineers know very well that sub-systems within their plants will fail. But they behave as if this knowledge were too dangerous for the public to be told.'[7]

In the past such single-minded enthusiasm for what appears to be a major breakthrough on the technology front has been of enormous value to the march of progress. Without such dedication we would still be crouching in dark caves, wearing out our teeth on indigestible hunks of raw meat. But the advent of nuclear power, the single biggest impact of cultural 'progress' upon our genetic make-up, has turned single-minded persistence into an obstinate self-destructive vice.

Manifestations of this 'vice' were seen most clearly during the 1976 Salzburg Conference for a Non-Nuclear Future. When Amory Lovins, a young American energy expert working for the British branch of Friends of the Earth, delivered a cogent refutation of the claim that there were no viable alternatives to nuclear power as a source of energy, he was vigorously attacked by the nuclear advocates. Having dismissed his case for such alternatives as geothermal, wind, wave, and solar energy, many of which (unlike coal, oil or uranium) are renewable sources of power and none of which contaminate the world, Lovins was criticised for ignoring the adverse side-effects of these alternatives. As Pringle and Spigelman put it, 'Lovins and his supporters were attacked for all the things that had characterised the nuclear community for decades.' They added, 'The irony passed unnoticed.'[8]

What, in addition to the ego motive of not being able to admit one was wrong, could explain such short-sighted and palpable dishonesty? There are two incentives which would seem of particular importance – nuclear reactors are a source of plutonium, a prime ingredient of atomic bombs; and secondly the nuclear barons' legacy of genetic damage and death through cancer will only become fully apparent long after they and their political masters are safely dead.

As for further nuclear disasters, one cannot help wondering how many more 'Chernobyls' there have to be before the enthusiasts relinquish their enthusiasm.

To return to defence, within the last few years alone there have been at least three false alarms which resulted in American nuclear forces being placed on the early stages of alert.[9] On two occasions the false alarms resulted from faulty 'chips' in computers of the Air Defence Command, on another, from inadvertently inserting into the system a test tape depicting a missile attack.

Over-reliance on the 'chips' of early warning systems appears to be matched by abounding faith in the reliability of delivery systems. Such faith is belied by the succession of 'broken spears' (accidental dropping of nuclear bombs, etc.) which included depositing four hydrogen bombs on Spain in January, 1966. This accident, in which three twenty-foot-long hydrogen bombs fell in the vicinity of the village of Palomares, and a fourth into the sea nearby, resulted from a mid-air collision between a B52 bomber and the air tanker from which it was attempting to refuel. Fortunately the bomber did not explode, but three of the bombs split open, releasing radioactive uranium and plutonium into the Spanish countryside. Nothing if not possessive about their belongings, the American authorities announced (what was obvious) that one of their aircraft had crashed, but failed to inform the local peasantry of what it had been carrying. They spent nearly three months, using a bathyscaphe, 2 miniature submarines, 20 ships, 125 frogmen and 2,000 seamen, finding and recovering the bomb which had fallen into the sea.[10] At least it can be said of the Americans that they bothered to clear up their mess, unlike the Russians who, like psychopathic picnickers, left the Atlantic contaminated with an entire submarine of fissile garbage.

So far the world has survived this chapter of accidents but, given the manifestly far from foolproof nature of defence technology, it is inevitable that sooner or later a malfunction of some component in a nuclear defence system will trigger off the first stages of a global war.

Schell has outlined a likely course of events:

> The greatest danger in computer-generated misinformation and other mechanical errors may be that one error might start a chain reaction of escalating responses between command centers, leading, eventually, to an attack. If in the midst of a crisis Country A was misled by its computers into thinking that Country B was getting ready to attack, and went on alert, Country B might notice this and go on alert in response. Then Country A, observing the now indubitably real alert of Country B, might conclude that its computers had been right after all, and increase its alert. This move would then be noticed by country B which would, in turn, increase its alert, and so on, until either the mistake was straightened out or an attack was launched. A holocaust might also be touched off by conventional or nuclear hostilities between smaller powers, which could draw in the superpowers. Another possibility would be a deliberate unprovoked preemptive strike by one side against the other.[11]

But there is another less specific, albeit more certain way in which attitudes towards defence technology may contribute to a global disaster – the reverential but unwarranted belief that the very existence of the technology of mutually assured destruction will continue to ensure that mutually assured destruction never occurs. This is like saying that, since it is so dangerous to fall off a high cliff, high cliffs are necessary to deter people from falling off them. It is a supreme example of the observation that in our desire to trade survival for peace of mind even the silliest rationalisations may play a useful role.

Applied to the possibility of a nuclear exchange it would surely be more prudent to take the view that '. . . If we are honest with ourselves we have to admit that unless we rid ourselves of our nuclear arsenals a holocaust not only *might* occur but *will* occur – if not today, then tomorrow; if not this year, then the next. We have come to live on borrowed time . . .'[12]

A belief in the peace-keeping properties of nuclear technology has the additional disadvantage of providing a heaven- (or hell-) sent excuse to remain complacent and do nothing towards finding political solutions to the world's problems.

Having surveyed the hazards of our attitudes towards technology the notion of political solutions to the ideological differences which divide the world sounds attractive, indeed absolutely necessary. The trouble with political solutions is that they are the province of politicians and, from what we have seen of some of these people, the chances of them doing something other than merely threaten their opposite number on the other side with yet more weapons, is remote to say the least.

The problem may be stated in the form of three truisms. The first is that the fate of the world resides in the hands of a few people who control the so-called 'levers of power' (the very use from time to time by politicians of this awful cliché would seem to signify a large part of their underlying motivation). It follows that the fate of the world is being decided by a handful of people with an above-average chance of being more ambitious, ruthless, exhibitionistic, insincere, Machiavellian and more easily bored than their fellow men (of course, there are some statesmen, as opposed to politicians, who are noble, altruistic and not self-seeking, but I am speaking statistically).

The second truism, a corollary of the first, is that the fate of the world is not really being decided by governments or even ideologies but by the psychopathologies of a few particular individuals. This is probably hard to accept for those who prefer to believe that the angry exchanges mislabelled 'peace talks' are conducted by a sort of posse of wise parents who know what is best for all of us. The comforting thought that they know best and will save us from harm is almost certainly delusional. So is the belief that the political leaders will surround themselves with great minds – rational, disinterested, far seeing and altruistic.

As exemplified by the following report in *The Times* on November 12th, 1986, these beliefs do not accord with reality: '

Serious arms control negotiations between the United States and the Soviet Union seem to be over at least until the spring after top-level talks in Vienna last week apparently degenerated into an extraordinary slanging match.

Administration officials who accompanied Mr George Shultz, the Secretary of State, to the talks with Mr Eduard Shevardnadze, the Soviet Foreign Minister, said that both sides screamed at each other 'like children'.

At one point, Mr Paul Nitze, the senior arms adviser to Mr Shultz, allegedly called Mr Viktor Karpov, the Soviet chief negotiator at the Geneva talks, 'a liar'. Mr Karpov threw back the insult.

Outcomes of 'peace talks' and similar gatherings are more likely to depend on the pride, hurt feelings, prejudices and egotism of people who would probably have made pretty indifferent parents. Such individuals may well believe that what they are doing is best for everyone, but in reality it is more likely to be what is best for them, and even in this they may ultimately be wrong.

As for the notion of wise and disinterested advisers, we know from studies of group decision-making that this too is an unrealistic fantasy. The sort of people who become top leaders are in fact more likely to surround themselves with aides who think as they do, and are poor replicas of themselves. Far from exercising restraint and discouraging irrationality, such acolytes will help to propel their leaders even further along the path of self-destructive lunacy. This state of affairs is made worse by the fact that the more neurotic, insecure and generally incompetent a leader the greater the chance that he will choose counsellors even less able than himself. It is worth noting in this connection that since anyone groomed by a leader to succeed him will tend to come from his own group of aides, the protégé will probably be even more incompetent than his predecessor. Were it not for other factors this could, over the years, produce such a decline in political competence that the world would end up being ruled by morons, then imbeciles, and eventually idiots. Fortunately there *are* other factors. We should be grateful for small mercies.

Anyway, whether or not the fate of the world will eventually be decided by idiots (using the word in its technical sense), the plain fact remains that in the past it has often been in the hands of a few individuals who may well have become leaders for the wrong reasons and who, by reason of their mental make-up, were ill-equipped to carry out what appears to be the most difficult of jobs, that of making it a fairer, safer place for the rest of us.

So what can be done about this alarming state of affairs? Before suggesting a remedy let's consider what we could be up against.

Take first a few prototypical political leaders. At the worst they might bring to their high office the following characteristics – a tendency towards absent-mindedness (through information overload) and risk-taking (through a predisposition towards boredom); residues of early traumatic experiences such as those of threatened castration and the Phaeton complex; a plethora of ego motives such as those to please, to keep up with the Joneses, and to boost self-esteem. Concerned about approaching senility and declining virility, they may well waste energy on sprightly behaviour in the mistaken belief that this gives them a macho image. They will probably be plagued by chronic conflicts between what they would like to do, what they ought to do, and what they can get away with. Subject to such conflicts they might either solidify into rigid closed-minded authoritarians with generous reserves of repressed hostility, or emerge as guilt-free psychopaths eager to see how far they can push their luck. They have an above-average chance of manifesting left hemisphericity and a penchant for shedding any feelings of responsibility by hiding behind the dubious machinery of what purports to be group decision-making. And of course, like most of us, they are only too ready to trade survival (particularly other people's) for peace of mind (particularly their own).

So much for some of the likely characteristics of a top political leader.

Now imagine such a person in the seat of power during a period of international crisis. Subject to information overload and deprived of sleep, the demands made of him may soon exceed his resources. He will become stressed. Unable to cope he may become physically ill and/or show an exacerbation of all his least desirable personality characteristics. Under stress he will suffer impairment of every stage in the processing of information. He will show narrowed attention, perceptual distortion, blocking of recall and every conceivable disruption of the means whereby the human brain arrives at rational decisions. At this stage on the downward path the severely stressed leader has become a liability. He should be replaced. But this is unlikely to happen. In collusion with his doctors, strenuous attempts will be made to conceal his physical and psychological deterioration. Regrettably he will be protected. Regrettably because, in point of fact, as Arthur Schlesinger remarked in *The Times* on January 2nd, 1987, 'Presidents need our protection less than the rest of us need protection from Presidents.'

An obvious solution to this problem is that nobody who betrays the slightest evidence of these traits should ever be allowed to become a leader. Otherwise there could be literally millions of people whose lives were in jeopardy for no other reason than that a potential for destruction on a scale hitherto undreamt of lay in the hands of a few ageing individuals who, in terms of personality, motivation, state of stress and cerebral efficiency, should hardly be trusted with the weekend shopping.

It is a curious reflection on society that, though we would think twice about entrusting our mouths to the attention of a toothless dentist and our scalps to the care of bald trichologists, our feet to lame chiropodists and our airlines to blind pilots, we happily entrust our lives to the care of people whose qualifications for their particular tasks may be even less convincing.

Of course there have been and there may be great leaders and wise statesmen, but there have also been others for whose egomania, neuroses, brain damage and general shortcomings the world has already paid a terrible price.[13]

Before leaving this issue there is one final point. It concerns the role of lethal technology in the decision-making of those who have it in their power to unleash a nuclear holocaust. Perhaps the knowledge that they possess the wherewithal to exterminate mankind would incline them towards a less aggressive stance. Maybe it would, but such evidence as we have points in quite the opposite direction.

According to several researches,[14] far from reducing aggression the mere presence (let alone ownership) of weapons makes people behave *more* rather than less belligerently, and this even when the individuals concerned were neither angry nor afraid. A weapon is, it seems, a stimulus to violence.

Discovery of this so-called 'weapons effect' is, to say the least, disquieting. If the mere sight of a gun can bias decision-making towards aggressive options, what about the knowledge that one possesses not just a gun but a whole arsenal of nuclear weapons?

The 'weapons effect' demonstrates, so it has been said, that 'the trigger pulls the finger'. So what of the political leader, already stressed, angry and frustrated whose 'trigger' is a telephone connected to Air Force Strike Command or a Trident submarine?

So much for problem number one – that of cataclysmic decisions being made by people ill-equipped to make them. The obvious answer is to make sure the world chooses its political leaders with a little more care than hitherto. They should, if possible, meet the following criteria – be relatively unbored, have strong egos and a high stress threshold. They should also be tested for psychopathy, neurosis, brain damage and psychosis. To the writer, if we value survival of mankind, the case for these proposals is *so* obvious that it hardly needs spelling out. And yet the chances of even the slightest move towards adopting them are, to say the least, miniscule.

Why should this be? Some of the answers are to be found in the chapters of this book, but there is one not yet touched upon – what has come to be called 'Learned Helplessness'.[15]

For a simple example of this unhappy state consider the following experiment. Two white rats are so wired up that every time a switch is closed both receive an electric shock to their tails. The shocks arrive at random intervals. Placed in this unenviable situation one of the rats is the helpless recipient of unpleasant surprises – powerless to predict the time of their occurrence and unable to avoid their effects. For the other rat, however, the situation is rather different. Not only can he see a light which signals advance warning of each shock, but soon he learns that if he pushes a lever every time the light comes on he can prevent the shock from occurring. Once he has mastered these contingencies both animals remain safe from any further shocks to their tails. Provided the second rat watches the light and pushes the lever all is well for both of them. But rats are like people. If they can get away with it they prefer to conserve their energy. Lulled into a false sense of security by experiencing no more shocks the 'leader' rat grows careless. Maybe he ceases to watch the light or is just too lazy to press the lever. The apparatus, however, is unremittingly efficient, and so every time he fails to respond both animals receive an unpleasant reminder.

After it has been running for some time the experiment is stopped, the animals are killed, then subjected to post mortem examination. This reveals a significant state of affairs. Upon opening him up, the rat which had control of the situation is found to be in no way harmed by the experiment. He is in perfect shape (apart from the fact that he's dead). For his companion, however, it is a very different story. The lesions inside his body show that he has been stressed so severely that had he not been killed he would probably have died anyway. The conclusion to be drawn from this and similar studies is that since both animals had the same number of electric shocks, it is not pain but helplessness – the inability to predict and control – which constitutes the major stressor in situations of this sort.

In humans, the consequences of prolonged learned helplessness include increasing despair and depression possibly terminating in death by suicide. As in lower animals they may also include such a state of passive resignation that even when the organism can, to some extent, control its destiny it fails to do so. Its attitude of mind may be summed up by, 'I'm powerless. I've learned that I cannot influence the course of events. This being so there's no point in trying. I may as well give up.'[16]

It is surely no exaggeration to say that large numbers of people, whole societies, are in a state of learned helplessness. The best they they can hope for is that their leader 'rats' continue (if indeed they ever started) to have their interests at heart, that they remain awake and competent and don't suffer from narrowed attention or absent-mindedness, that they are vigilant for crucial signs and don't push the wrong lever at the right time or press the right button at the wrong time. And of course because they, the helpless passenger 'rats', *are* so helpless, it is useless for them to try to interfere with what their leaders are about.

It is likely that many people living under the shadow of the bomb and an ever-present threat of extinction, whose actual time of occurrence they cannot predict, are suffering from a chronic state of stress. And, as for anticipating extinction, their present state of apathy makes this a self-fulfilling prophecy.

But that is not the end of the story. Why *should* people get themselves into such a position of learned helplessness? After all, at least in the democracies, it is a self-inflicted misery. Since, unlike the rats in the experiment, humans are free to choose their leaders, why do they elect someone who will, in all probability, lead them to destruction? In Chapter 13 we examined one reason – to escape from boredom. But there is another which, curiously enough, has once again to do with that double-edged sword – man's moral sense.

An early lesson of life is that bad behaviour tends to evoke retaliation from irate parents. Hence transgressions give rise to fear of punishment. If not immediately forthcoming the anticipated punishment may produce a sense of guilt. Particularly is this so when the transgression conflicts with the individual's conscience (i.e. they are transgressions against introjected parental authority). By itself, of course, this is no bad thing. As a determinant of good behaviour a capacity for guilt is an essential part of being socialised.

But it can be overdone. For people with an overpunitive superego the feeling that they are not measuring up to their own internalised moral standards can be so burdensome that they may try to reduce it in a number of ways – through alcohol, by confession, by reparation or by inviting punishment. It is the last of these, a manifestation of the so-called Polycrates Complex, which, ironically, poses the greatest threat to the survival of mankind.

The story goes that the tyrant Polycrates, who ruled Samos between 540 and 522 BC was one of those tiresome individuals for whom nothing ever goes wrong. So successful was he that his friends, including the King of Egypt, became worried. 'We'll pay for this,' they said. There was only one thing to do, Polycrates must make a sacrifice. So they persuaded him to part with his most valued possession, a ring, by throwing it into the sea. But the gods were not so easily placated. A thoughtless fish swallowed the ring, got itself caught, and being a fine specimen was served at the tyrant's table. Needless to say this return of the sacrificial object was greeted with consternation. Nothing it seemed could avert the catastrophes which lay ahead.

Now, obviously, throwing rings into the sea is no great threat to anyone (other than greedy and myopic fishes), but the tendency of societies which have enjoyed a run of unprecedented good fortune to choose a leader who will reduce their guilt by making sacrifices could be. The point is made most convincingly by Lloyd de Mause in his month-by-month history of Reagan's presidency.

Conditions in the United States in the early 1980s were ideal for activating a 'We've never had it so good – things are too good to last, we'll pay for this later' feeling. America was not at war. The Iranian hostages were safely home. There were no major strikes or episodes of domestic violence to worry about. Economically and militarily the United States was the strongest nation in the world with the highest Gross National Product. The previous decade had seen the creation of twenty million new jobs, a higher level of personal income than ever before, and major advances in caring for the poor and the sick. And all this was achieved without internal strife, repressive governmental control or war.

As de Mause remarks, 'We had every reason to be proud of what we had accomplished in the 1970s and secure in the knowledge of our ability to achieve further economic and social progress.'[17]

And yet, he goes on, 'Our success in the previous decade made us feel just terrible. Never before in history had a nation so strong and wealthy felt so weak and impoverished.' These conclusions were based on three sorts of evidence. First, there were polls, which indicated that 75 per cent of people believed that 'the United States had gone off on the wrong track', 60 per cent that the United States needed a new leader who would 'bend the rules a bit' and 40 per cent that force should be used to restore 'the American way of life'. A second source of evidence for what looked uncommonly like a severe case of national Polycrates complex were the cartoons, speeches and newspaper headlines of that troubled era. These reflected a number of grim and largely unrealistic beliefs, such as, for example, that the economy was in a precarious condition with a 'soaring Federal debt, low corporate investment and out of control inflation'.[18]

The third sort of evidence that the ghost of Polycrates was stalking the land came from the election, antics and widespread adulation of a not terribly bright, third-rate ex-film actor, Ronald Reagan. In electing him to the presidency the United States was choosing someone who would gratify its need for punishment. Reagan did not disappoint them. Combining the duties of hangman, pest control officer and moral cleanser, the new President set about reversing America's hitherto good, easy, affluent way of life. As the great guilt reducer, wielder of the sacrificial axe he introduced economic policies (Reaganomics) which resulted in two orders of punishment. First, by drastic cuts in social welfare programmes (including such masterly economies as the stopping of free school lunches) and by increasing unemployment, it is estimated that he accounted for well over 150,000 lives.[19] But these were paltry sacrifices and by themselves insufficient to assuage the guilt, and discharge the pent-up rage of those puritanical American superegos which had been handed down since the time of the Pilgrim Fathers. So Reagan turned his attention to two other ways of inflicting pain – excessive military spending and an approach to international affairs which elicited such responses in the American Press as the following.

The *New York Times Magazine* featured an article on 'Thinking the Unthinkable': 'After more than a decade during which the idea was all but dismissed, the possibility of nuclear war is again on many people's minds. Some strategists believe it's an option that must not be ruled out – indeed that such a war can be won. Others fear the entire world will lose.' As de Mause remarks, none of the articles tried to show that the new interest in winning a nuclear war was brought about by any real change in world conditions. Like the *New York Times* they just noticed that inexplicably 'nuclear war is again on many people's minds'.

The *New Republic* captured the mood perfectly in its article on 'The New Brinkmanship':

> For the first time since the 1950s, the possibility of nuclear war with the Soviet Union appears to be seriously accepted by key figures inside and outside the US government. What long have been unthinkable thoughts now are entertained by influential men and women in Washington . . . A senior White House foreign policy specialist says, 'In 30 years, I never thought war was really possible: now I think it *is* possible.'[20]

It was left to the women's section of the *New York Times* to express directly our deepest feelings about 'thinking the unthinkable' once again. Maggie Scarf, reviewing the literature on the 'increasingly threatening reality' of engaging in atomic war, said simply, 'I'm getting scared again'.[21]

Thus Reagan's own severely damaged personality was turned to good account in the service of his country.

The belief that the United States might be compelled to fight a limited nuclear war in Europe, and such exploits as the invasion of Grenada, the fomenting of war in Central America, the provocative over-flying of Soviet territory (which has already cost some hundreds of American lives, pp.142-3), the baiting and bombing of Libya, and the setting up of events in Lebanon which resulted in the killing of 241 unarmed Marines fulfilled, according to de Mause, two pressing needs of the American psyche – an expiation of guilt through sacrifice and the discharge of hatred on to enemy outgroups. Now, whether or not one subscribes to these psychoanalytic interpretations three things are indisputable. Reagan *was* elected at a time of peace and plenty. Once in power he probably inflicted more misery upon his fellow Americans than had any other President at any other time. And yet, despite all this suffering and all his errors of judgement, Reagan remained a hero simply because he did what he was elected to do.

If de Mause *is* correct in his analysis, and the old saying 'Societies get the governments they deserve' (i.e. which will inflict punishment when they feel they deserve punishment) is generally true, and the wherewithal for punishment is so available, so unstoppable once it's started, and so ultimately self-destructive then, even without all the other factors which hazard our survival, this one is a killer.

So, is the outlook totally bleak? Not necessarily. Take the last threat – that of the relationship between guilt expiation and choice of a leader. The syndrome is in fact symptomatic of an older psychic class, people who suffered an upbringing soured by the sort of child-rearing practices discussed in Chapter 9. For such people, weaned on guilt, imbued with authoritarian attitudes towards sex and aggression, the idea that all pleasures must be paid for by sacrifice and suffering is an inevitable consequence of parental methods that hopefully have been laid to rest. With any luck future generations will find more rational ways of dealing with the problems of affluence than that of hiring a neurotic leader to make and execute their enemies.

But these are hopes for a dangerously distant future. In the meantime is there nothing else we could do at least to postpone the final day?

Of course there is. But, if so, why is it that a creature clever enough to unravel the mysteries of the 'double helix', compose a symphony, or build a machine which in the twinkling of an eye can immolate a population – why has such a creature failed so abjectly in the task of trying to prevent his own imminent demise? Part of the answer is to be found in a recent book by the British philosopher Nicholas Maxwell.[22] Maxwell's thesis is that the evident failure of science to free society from poverty, hunger and the threat of extinction results from a 'fatal flaw in the accepted aim of scientific endeavour',[23]

– the pursuit of knowledge purely for its own sake. It is precisely because of 'the accepted aim' that acquisition of knowledge, which presumably originated as an essential strategy for survival, has given rise to the relentless pursuit of new and better ways of achieving the exact opposite.

This situation is analogous to that which plagues another field of human endeavour – fighting. Just as the professionalising of violence could not occur without taking on board the hindering rules and regulations of militarism,[24] so science, the systematic acquisition of knowledge, has to adopt rules of procedure which negate *its* own original purpose – survival.

In accordance with the philosophy of knowledge, science has to be single-minded in its search for truth, objective and impartial, but only achieves these ends by ignoring the distraction of moral issues and value judgments. In the pursuit of knowledge for its own sake, the philosophy of wisdom, that is to say organised inquiry towards developing 'A moral, just, humane, co-operative – and even loving – world',[25] had to take a back seat.

For Maxwell, the solution is obvious – a radically new approach to the whole business of intellectual inquiry: '. . . I am advocating nothing less than that the basic aims and methods, the whole character of the academic enterprise, be changed.'[26]

It is hard to argue with these aims, but any hope of realising them is confronted by one huge and seemingly implacable obstacle – human feelings. Throughout this book we have seen many examples of how feelings, emotions, affects, call them what you will, the very springs of human action, have become not only increasingly inappropriate to the products of cultural progress but actually militate against any rational coping with this progress. If we could only change the way people *feel*, Maxwell's solution would be easier, if not easy.

What follows are some suggestions regarding steps that might be taken to this end. They start from the premise that resolving a conflict of interests by force of arms is no longer a rational option (if it ever was).

The major problem of government is that of reconciling the biological characteristics of mankind with the demands of civilised society. Solutions range from imposing constraints, with consequent loss of personal freedom, to encouraging survival of the fittest. The first involves control through the apparatus of a police state.

The second relies upon a combination of market forces and the talents of individual citizens to determine where power ultimately resides.

Whereas the first attempts to deny, suppress or punish some features of our biological make-up which evolved over millions of years to ensure our survival, the second tries to make the 'laws of the jungle' compatible with the demands, products and moral standards acquired in the course of cultural evolution.

It must be obvious by now that both forms of government, when carried to extremes, are psychologically inept. By itself each form of government has some very unpleasant side effects, but when they co-exist the resulting conflict of interests hazards us all.

For most people who become involved in a disagreement, whether they be neighbours, strangers, or husbands and wives, the usual solution is some sort of compromise. Very few end up by killing each other, and, if they should resort to physical violence, the State intervenes. Fratricide, patricide, matricide, infanticide, indeed any form of homicide, are, to say the least, frowned upon.

But when a conflict of interests exists between large groups of people, the preferred solution has often been for one side to try to destroy the other.

The killing of lots of people by lots of people differs from that of one person by another in several ways. First, very few of the individuals concerned are particularly motivated to slay each other. When they are, it is usually because compelled by social pressure exerted through the government of the country or group to which they belong. Whereas the individual murderer is driven by such primitive emotions as rage, fear, greed and jealousy, the state-controlled warrior may be driven by no more than the need to earn a living and avoid social disapproval. The second big difference between private and public killers is that since, in the latter case, little or no risk attaches to the man or woman who plans and incites the killing, he or she has few incentives to reach a bloodless compromise.

Any agreeable solution, therefore, to those conflicts of interest which now threaten our survival must involve changing the attitudes of political leaders and those who elect them. So far, the favourite form of this remedy has not been terribly successful. The history of bloody wars, vendettas, terrorism and such continuing obscenities as apartheid suggests that it is virtually impossible to make people change their minds by physical force. At the best they smoulder on until given a chance to continue killing each other with renewed ferocity.

An alternative strategy which aims to deter people from doing things one doesn't wish them to do is that embodied in the arms race. This is preferable to an all-out war, but in either case the irrationality of the means precludes the desired end of achieving a stable peace. If it could be arranged that the first victims of a nuclear war were the political leaders who started it, then, of course, the existing policy of deterrence would be far more reliable than it is at present.

There are, however, two other ways of replacing irrational with rational attitudes. The first involves trying to alter the underlying psychopathology of that relatively small collection of individuals who, at the moment, have it in their power to initiate a global catastrophe. The second is to replace them with other people who are less likely to destroy the world.

While neither of these remedies is easy to bring about, they are not impossible. Both involve substituting rationality for irrationality. Already there are small moves in this direction. It is just a question of time as to whether either or both will have advanced far enough before it is too late. One approach to the first is outlined in the following response to an early draft of this book:

It seems to me that many of the problems you describe are due to unhelpful ways of handling emotion. People do not know what to do with their emotions, particularly negative ones, and so they build elaborate devices to protect themselves from facing them. As you so rightly say, this locked-in emotion jams the processes of rational thought, causes narrowing of attention, inability to think flexibly, etc. (and arguably encourages cancer and other illness).

It seems to me that the quickest way to eliminate the harmful effects of emotion is to discharge them. Children show the way here. If a child is hurt, s/he seeks the attention of someone around and just howls for 10 or 15 minutes, and then just walks away from the hurt, completely on top of things again. What seems to happen for most of us is that this natural process of regaining equilibrium through discharge is interrupted and discouraged (e.g. 'there, there, don't cry', or 'Be a big boy'.) If the process is interrupted enough (and I think you will see that societal pressures against discharge are immense) then eventually the inability to think and discharge becomes chronic. When this happens, not only do people stop thinking, but they internalise what has been done to them and actually begin to defend the system, and pass on the same prohibitions to their children (disguised as 'teaching them how to behave' or whatever). The English Public School system can be seen as one particularly horrendous and brutal method of perpetuating people's inability to recover from hurt.[27]

These views are consistent with many of the topics discussed in earlier chapters. Those psychological defences which enable us to trade survival for peace of mind did not come about by chance but reflect the suppression of painful feelings which occurred in the sometimes far distant past of the individual. In some people the undischarged emotion attaching to these ancient hurts becomes added to by subsequent experiences which in some way resemble the original event. The process is cumulative and malignant. Each new trauma which has something in common with the original rejection or frustration adds its quota to the existing scar. An increasingly wide range of situations acquires the capacity to reactivate the old hurt. As a result the individual's ability to think, let alone act, rationally becomes increasingly diminished. One of the consequences of this disability is to discover 'legitimate enemies' on to whom he can now deflect his pent-up rage. As a world leader such a person is an extremely dangerous liability.

According to the logic of this argument the cure is simple. If undischarged emotions are a prime cause of irrationality then the obvious way of recovering rationality would be to allow, indeed encourage, people to discharge their bad feelings.

At first sight this technique, known as re-evaluative counselling,[28] sounds naive in the extreme – on a par with such other long-haired cure-alls as encounter groups, dianetics, gestalt therapy and listening to primal screams. But it is not. For a start it requires no lengthy training or gimmicky procedures. Secondly, it has already been used with considerable success upon thousands of people all over the world. If more people, particularly our political leaders, could be persuaded, cajoled or compelled to undergo this treatment the world might become a safer, happier place.

As applied to some contemporary world leaders this idea is of course a non-starter. Trying to get them to straighten out the mess inside their own heads would be like trying to converse with a Trappist monk. But inasmuch as the neuroses of leaders reflect those of the people who elect them, a therapeutic transformation of public attitudes might, given enough time, achieve the desired end. Unfortunately, not only is there not much time left, but how are people to know who is a safe bet when it comes to choosing leaders?

The short answer to this question is obvious if not banal – confine political leadership to that half of the human race who are less likely to indulge in mass genocide – women. Of course there are exceptions to this rule of thumb, but *generally* women are preferable to men for three reasons – they are less aggressive and sadistically destructive, and are more concerned with preserving than destroying life. They tend to be less competitive in any struggle for power, and they are possibly less easily bored, hence less likely to take risks.

Of course women can be irritating, cruel, vicious, vindictive and malicious, but when it comes to sanctioning mass murder their record is startlingly different from that of men.

In case this seems unfair, consider the following summary[29] of male leadership over the years:

Between AD 444 and 453 the ruthlessly aggressive leader Attila the Hun accounted for well over 100,000 lives.

Of a similar ilk was Genghis Khan. In the early part of the thirteenth century this bloodthirsty warrior wiped out hundreds of thousands of his fellow men. He was especially fond of submitting his enemies to painful executions (such as pouring molten metal into their ears and eyes). Nothing if not dutiful, his son and grandsons carried on the tradition of killing everyone who stood in their way. Still in the family business, a great-great-grandson of Genghis Khan, appropriately called Tamerlane the Great (1336–1405) slew over a quarter of a million people. With a fine reputation for sadism, this gentle creature had vast pyramids of skulls constructed at his pleasure. When not contemplating these structures he assuaged boredom either by tossing people over cliffs, or by having thousands bricked up alive to die slowly from suffocation.

Tamerlane was followed in due course by another forceful character, Ivan the Terrible (1530–84). A religious fanatic and sexual athlete, Ivan was probably Tsarist Russia's most bloodthirsty tyrant (which is saying quite a lot). Ivan the Terrible exterminated some hundreds of thousands of people in a number of imaginative ways. One of his less endearing habits was to roast women alive on revolving spears.

These Mongol leaders were by no means unique exemplars of male savagery. For three centuries up to 1915 the rulers of the Ottoman Empire maintained a tradition of sadistic cruelty well in keeping with the times. They, the Sultans, included Suleiman the Magnificent, who killed 200,000 people. He is noteworthy for having hundreds of unwanted peasants thrown on to a gigantic fire. Not to be outdone his son, Selim, massacred 30,000 people in Nicosia and had their leader flayed alive.

Then there was Osman II, a sporting Sultan, who whiled away his time in archery practice using page boys and prisoners-of-war as targets.

Rather less sporting was Mahomet III. Having murdered nineteen of his brothers, all under the age of eleven, this not very lovable monarch went on to put seven pregnant concubines into sacks which were then heaved into the Bosphorus. His particular delight was to watch women's breasts being scorched off with hot irons.

Of the same genre was Murad IV, a savage dark-eyed giant who is credited with having executed 25,000 people (many personally) in the name of 'justice' – that is to say anyone who opposed him. His son, taking a leaf from Mahomet III's book, had 280 girls tied in sacks, which were then committed to the Bosphorus. Originality was not his strongest suit.

Of apparently more moderate aspirations, Abdul Aziz killed a mere 12,000 men, women and children. He was replaced by Abdul Hamid II, a paranoid Turk who survived to celebrate his Silver Jubilee in 1908. To fill in time while waiting for the day he slaughtered 100,000 Armenians, 3,000 of whom were roasted alive.

Finally there was Enver Bey who, in 1915 rounded up the inhabitants of eighty villages and then shot the lot. Of Turkey's two million Armenians, one-third died and one-third fled to Russia.

Other murderous leaders of bygone days included Roderigo Borgia (who became Pope Alexander VI), his son and their successor, the bellicose Julius II. It was about such people that Tuchman said, 'The process of gaining power employs means that degrade or brutalize the seeker, who wakes one day to find that power has been bought at the price of virtue'.[30] This seems something of an understatement.

Then there was Francisco Pizarro, leader of the Conquistadores, who ended the lives of 7,000 Incas, and Salamon Reinach, who set a record for the Crusades by killing 70,000 people in one week. This was apparently a noble gesture to attest the superior morality of the Christian faith.

If one picks one's way delicately forward in history it is to discover that bloodlust and sadism are by no means confined to Mongols, Russians, Italians and Turks. During the five years of the French Revolution two men – a doctor called Jean-Paul Marat (whose father came from Sardinia and whose mother was Swiss), and that Himmler of the Revolution, Maximilien Robespierre, a cold, humourless barrister from Arras – directed a mounting tide of carnage which consumed many thousands of French lives. At the beginning of this holocaust Marat wrote, 'In order to ensure public tranquillity, 200,000 heads must be cut off.' Thenceforth, until stabbed in his bath, he did his best to achieve tranquillity by these means.

When Robespierre, who carried on the good work, was himself eventually guillotined a woman screamed at him before he died, 'You monster spewed out of hell, go down to the grave burdened with the curses of the wives and mothers of France.' It was a fitting epitaph for a man whose sadistic hatred for his fellow citizens seemed inexhaustible. Apologists for male savagery may be tempted to say, 'Yes, but that's all ancient history, we've come a long way since then.' To which there is one brief answer: 'Some of us have.'

In the first half of this century Hitler and Stalin, ably assisted by such male henchmen as Himmler and Beria, outdid all their predecessors. Between them they accounted for over fifty million lives. But we must be fair. Partly because he had more time, Stalin's total was even greater than Hitler's. In thirty years he killed more people than the Tsars had done in four centuries.

When faced with disagreeable statistics there is a tendency to cast around for some comfortable excuse or explanatory factor. In this case, judging from the list so far, it could be colour – after all they were all white (or at least off-white) men. Perhaps people with skins of a completely different colour don't behave so badly? This is not strictly true. In just four years, between 1975 and 1979, that chubby faced, tyrannical fanatic Pol Pot, one-time boss of Kampuchea, set (in terms of ratios) an all-time record. Out of a total population of eight million he killed three million. Not devoid of imagination, one of his 'methods' was to bury people up to their heads and leave them to die.

No less interesting amongst despots of a different skin colour was the self-styled 'Emperor' of the Central African Republic, Jean Bedell Bokassa. This unprepossessing little man specialised in having children clubbed to death. Having had them expertly butchered, they were then served up as delicacies at palace banquets.

Last, but by no means least in this galaxy of bloodthirsty leaders is our old friend Idi Amin. Once described by his British Commanding Officer as 'a tremendous chap to have around', this overgrown, slow-witted, semi-literate village bully killed 500,000 of his fellow Ugandans. He could be equally unpleasant to his young ex-wives. 'Kay Amin's mutilated torso lay on the operating table. Her head and all her limbs had been amputated. Now her head had been reversed and sewn back face down on her torso. Her legs had been neatly sutured on to her shoulders and her arms attached firmly to her blood-stained pelvis.'[31]

There are several points worth noting about this list of undesirables. First, it is by no means exhaustive. From the mad Roman Emperor Caligula to the loathsome Duvaliers of Haiti there have been many others who qualify for inclusion. Secondly, though differing in race, colour and creed, there *are* common denominators. All were brutal, vicious and bloodthirsty. All enjoyed the mental and physical suffering of their victims. All sought absolute power over their fellow men. All support the proposition that power corrupts.

Another feature of this unsavoury band is that many of them betrayed signs of ego weakness and/or feelings of inferiority. From the crippled Tamerlane to the pock-marked Stalin; from Marat with his painful skin disease to the Kaiser with his withered arm; from monorchic Hitler and the pasty-faced, myopic, narrow-chested Himmler to the squat and ugly Bokassa, the history of what Fromm calls 'malignant aggression'[32] in bloodthirsty leaders is littered with individuals who not only showed signs of severe ego damage but were not without reasons (often of a physical nature) for such deformation of character.

All this makes good sense in the light of topics discussed in previous chapters. Early hurts, such as losing a parent in childhood (see p. 98), infantile experiences of fear and humiliation due to particular sorts of child-rearing practices, feelings of inferiority which result from physical imperfections may, together or apart, produce, under certain conditions, three lasting manifestations. The first is an overwhelming ambition to achieve power over others; the second is to discharge previously suppressed hostility on to suitable outgroups; and the third is to suffer such a pathological 'touchiness' that the slightest hint of insult or criticism unleashes extreme vindictiveness towards the perpetrator. One further characteristic of these damaged individuals is a predisposition towards becoming what Hoffer calls a 'True Believer',[33] that is to say someone who espouses some creed or set of political beliefs with such fanatical zeal that the 'end' always justifies the means however brutal and obscene the latter may be.

This method of dealing with feelings of inadequacy, inferiority and shame by submerging oneself in a cause greater than oneself is typified by such self-righteous leaders as Hitler, Pol Pot and, in the field of religion, by the equally self-righteous Reverend Jim Jones who, in the name of the People's Temple cult, murdered his entire flock in the Jonestown settlement massacre.

There is one last and most important common denominator amongst the people we've been discussing. They were all, without exception, males. It is hard to imagine, let alone compile, a comparable list of murderous females. Why should the incidence of malignant aggression be so much more common amongst men? Why are the excesses of criminal murderers, mobsters, the Mafia, the Al Capones, the Krays and the Nicholson torture gang unrivalled by any female equivalents? Endocrinological differences between male and female, and cultural pressures towards masculine patterns of behaviour, may be enough to explain benign aggression – fighting for one's rights and in self-defence – but cannot account for the sadistic and wanton savagery of so many of those who ardently sought and ultimately achieved political or criminal power.

One possible explanation, in line with the general thesis of this book, is that male savagery derives from an interaction between, on the one hand, innate characteristics of the male – his physical strength, his natural aggressiveness and his role in sexual behaviour – and, on the other, the constraints on free expression of these characteristics.

Ironically, such constraints are partly necessitated by the nature of many male pursuits. Such predominantly male occupations as medicine, the law, banking, the manufacture and use of complex technology, and that second oldest profession – the carrying of arms – would be impossible were they not strictly ordered and controlled.[34]

The related fact that more men than women belong to hierarchical organisations, the very existence of which means maintaining a strict pecking order, means that, starting in childhood, there has had to be more taming of the male than of the female. But, as we have seen (pp. 137–40), one by-product of authoritarian constraint is a residue of suppressed hostility which under certain conditions may eventuate in malignant aggression towards some convenient outgroup.

This is just one reason why men tend to be far more dangerous candidates for political leadership. But there are other reasons. All relate in one way or another to what has been called the 'longest war'[35] – that between the sexes. In recent years overt signs of this conflict have become increasingly apparent. Votes for women, laws against sexual discrimination, even such linguistic phenomena as the substitution of 'Chairperson' for 'Chairman' and 'access chamber' for 'manhole' (deplored by one observer as unfair to Barclaycards) and a spate of books by feminists testify to the fact that, far from being over, the longest war is gathering momentum. More and more battles, some minor, others of great moment, are being won by beleaguered women.

For many years the struggle has provided little more than a topic for discussion over suburban dinner tables. But now, suddenly it has become a matter of central importance to human survival. It is also germane to the central thesis of this book that many of the outcomes of genetic evolution are inappropriate (to say the least) to the products of cultural evolution.

In the past, biological differences between male and female not only determined but were compatible with the roles of the two sexes. If you were soft, broody, warm, loving and milk-producing, it was appropriate to stay at home looking after the children. If you were strong, hard and aggressive, with zero mammary output, it was appropriate that you went out hunting to provide a back-up for domestic activities at home. For a long time it all worked very well. Indeed, so suited were the biological characteristics of the two sexes to their roles and so strong the opinion that 'If something works, let's keep it that way', that cultural patterns evolved to maintain the status quo. For many years this too worked very well but in the end gave way to some curious, one might say bizarre, anomalies.

Because men tend to be taller, heavier, stronger, more aggressive and more flat-chested than women, they seem to consider themselves better equipped to be bank managers, brain surgeons, barristers, bus drivers, popes, priests, pilots and politicians. However, since in reality none of these callings requires height, strength or flat chests, there must be some other reason for these phenomena. One such is that these predominantly male reservations are sanctuaries, safe hidey holes from the awful threat of maternal domination. Since the most difficult task facing many small boys is freeing themselves from mother, it is hardly surprising that, having achieved this end, many of them devote a lifetime to finding and then defending niches from which women are excluded.

Needless to say these hypotheses will be most vigorously resisted in those very circles where it is most likely to be true. To admit to the threat is to admit that it is threatening, which admits that one is still not free. From the burning of witches to the recent suspension and 'trial' of obstetrician Wendy Savage,[36] there is no shortage of historical data to support these hypotheses.

Why should some men develop such fear of maternal domination that they become rooted in their antipathy towards the opposite sex, and why should this render them unfit for political leadership? The short answer is that through a succession of traumatic events which began in early childhood they become necrophilous characters, that is to say people who believe that most social problems can be solved by force and destruction. Whether or not one subscribes to Freud's theory of incestuous stirrings during the Oedipal period, there can surely be little doubt that for many men the transition from having a warm, physical, loving relationship with mother to being suddenly told 'That's enough of that . . . Be a man . . . Men don't cry . . . Do as mother says, but not as mother does', then forced into trousers, given toy guns, packed off to boarding school where they encounter a fresh crop of icy mother figures is extremely traumatic. Feminists like Marilyn French[37] quite rightly portray women as victims of a patriarchal society. But there is also a case for supposing that patriarchal societies are themselves products of far greater matriarchal power – that is women who, through their sons, create and reinforce what 'appears' to be a patriarchy. It is true that in many families father 'appears' to be the boss, but is in reality an extension of the mother's power, the ultimate deterrent used by mother to threaten and control their sons. At school the headmaster or housemaster is used in just this way by his wife or such lesser henchwomen as the 'hags' (matrons) who report back the misdemeanours of their charges.

This state of affairs is no reflection on the shortcomings of mothers, women, or indeed men, but rather an inevitable consequence of a mismatch between evolutionary and cultural processes. To feed and protect their young, females have to put pressure on the male to fulfil his role as hunter and defender. Their practice, in the First World War, of handing out white feathers to men who did not appear to be 'doing their bit' is one of the more bizarre manifestations of this biologically determined role. The enormous genetic loss through male casualties during the same conflict is just one of its sad side effects.

The fact that women are biophilous, that is to say interested in and concerned with preserving life while men are necrophilous, more concerned with the inanimate and destroying life, gains support from a number of other common observations. For example, favourite books, magazines, topics of conversation, leisure activities and types of work appear to differentiate quite clearly between the biophilous interests of women and the necrophilous ones of men. Generally speaking, women are concerned with people, men with things. As Fromm points out, many men devote far more attention and loving care to their cars than to their wives.

Though fully aware of the many ways in which the goal of amassing material wealth is polluting every aspect of his environment, the necrophilous male, provided such degradation is not reducing profit margins, remains unmoved. It has been said and with good reason that 'severely necrophilous characters are very dangerous. They are the haters, the racists, those in favour of war, bloodshed and destruction.'[38]

Of course women can have necrophilous tendencies, but it is perhaps significant that the perversion of necrophilia is predominantly male.

One obvious and anticipated objection to the present thesis is that the sort of woman who seeks and achieves political power does so by aping, even outdoing men. If they are tough, she has to be tougher. If they are ruthless, she has to be more so. Judging from characters like Boadicea, Elizabeth I and our present Prime

Minister, there would seem to be more than a grain of truth in this proposition. A woman who has set her heart on Trident missiles, who could order the sinking of the *Belgrano*, and allow the United States to bomb Libya from airfields in Britain is surely, according to this argument, just as dangerous as any man. Doesn't this make nonsense of the suggestion that the world would be a safer place if political leadership were confined to women?

Not really – in my opinion such a conclusion is not only mistaken, but actually misses the point. Take the specific case of Margaret Thatcher. On statistical, let alone theoretical, grounds it is highly unlikely that Mrs Thatcher is a necrophilous character. She may not be everyone's ideal woman let alone political leader. She may be obstinate, opinionated, strident, narrow and a rigid pursuer of policies with which others disagree, but this does not make her a bloodthirsty neurotic. She does not manifest those signs of malignant aggression which were so apparent in the long list of necrophilous leaders we considered earlier. To lump her in with despots like Tamerlane the Great, Hitler and Idi Amin is patently absurd. Pouring molten words into the ears of Mr Healey in response to his describing of her as 'The Pasionaria (passion flower) of privilege' should not be confused with Genghis Khan's pouring of molten metal into the ears of *his* adversary.

So how are we to regard our first woman Prime Minister? Does she in any way constitute an argument against the view that since women are (for a number of obvious reasons) less likely than men to be necrophilous they are safer for political leadership?

First, there is nothing in her policies, however short-sighted, ill advised, unkind or disastrous some might regard these to be, nor indeed in her speeches or behaviour, to suggest an undercurrent of malevolent genocidal sadism. Why *should* there be? She does not appear to be suffering from any crippling physical infirmity nor did she experience any of those tribulations of early childhood – loss of a parent, cold, rejecting mother or drunken, brutal father – which might have sown the seeds of a malignant complex. On the contrary she has emerged from her supportive, close-knit family background led by a Methodist teetotal father, with palpable self-confidence.

But what about her being described as Attila the Hen, implying total indifference to the suffering of others – another mark of the necrophilous character?

As jealous rivals for mother's affection, elder sisters have a reputation for not enlarging upon the virtues of any younger female siblings. Hence it is of some significance that the Prime Minister's older sister Muriel, angered at the suggestion that Margaret was cold and aloof, should have told a *Daily Telegraph* reporter that her sister was 'a warm and very generous person and someone who is very interested in other people'.[39] Is this a conscious reaction against underlying feelings of a quite opposite kind? Perhaps, but according to one of her biographers, an old friend of Mrs Thatcher, Margaret Goodrich (now Mrs Wickstead), has said, 'She had, and still has, a very soft and generous side to her nature. When she came to tea at the Vicarage at Corby, she never forgot to bring some butter'.[40] Such sentiments may not bring tears to the eyes of Britain's unemployed, but it is highly unlikely that anyone ever said anything like that about Attila the Hun.

Even Mrs Thatcher's detractors at their most detracting do not reveal a monster. Take these comments on her mishandling of the Parkinson affair:

> This famous image has always suggested a woman of firm moral principles who believed in marriage, repudiated divorce, indiscretion and domestic instability in those in public life, and chose members of her team with those standards clearly in mind. Yet she abandoned them in the case of Parkinson.
>
> The image suggested, furthermore, that she believed in resolution, firmness and consistency. Yet she supported a man who could not make up his mind, and repeatedly betrayed first his wife, then his mistress and his wife, finally dragging in his party and his leader.[41]

None of this reflects well on Mrs Thatcher, but of prime importance in the present context are not the woman's failings – her double standards, hypocrisy, inability to deal firmly with even a minor domestic crisis and, perhaps most serious of all in a Prime Minister, her lack of judgment in whom she selects and whom she wishes to retain as members of the government, but the fact that when faced with a situation that threatens her image, a wave of tenderness, a sort of natural female compassion got the better of her. For a leader of such consuming ambition driven by enormous self-interest, this softness when she needed to be ruthless suggests an underlying character quite unlike that of the genocidal necrophile.

Critics of this view may well retort, 'But what about the *Belgrano*? What about Libya? Surely these were the acts of a callous, trigger-happy politician?' Two points – few would deny that Margaret Thatcher is a tough, aggressive, combative lady, but there is a world of difference between defensive aggression in a potentially threatening situation, however inappropriate this may turn out to be, and the cold-blooded calculating savagery of those male necrophilous hawks on both sides of the Iron Curtain who calmly estimate the odds of winning (preferably on somebody else's territory) a global war in terms of permissible megadeaths. It would be extremely surprising if Margaret Thatcher, or indeed any other female, thought along comparable lines.

But if she is not a necrophilous character, why *did* she sanction the unnecessary killing of Argentinian sailors and become a party to the bombing of Libyan civilians? Two reasons suggest themselves. First, as a defender of British interests, she probably felt it her duty to heed the advice of her male military advisers. In the case of the *Belgrano* she was evidently persuaded by Admiral Sir Terence Lewin – who, rightly or wrongly, considered the *Belgrano* to be a threat to ships of the Royal Navy in the vicinity of the Falklands.[42] In offering this advice, no doubt in the strongest possible terms, he was doing what he felt to be his duty. In accepting his advice she was merely acknowledging his expertise. As things turned out, it may well be that both were wrong in what they said and what they did, but this is a question beyond the confines of this book and quite irrelevant to the point at issue.

In the case of Libya, we find much the same pattern of events – an apparently strong, self-opinionated woman suddenly yielding to the pressure of a male, and this despite the fact that she must have known there would be adverse political repercussions.

Why should this otherwise 'iron' lady give in so readily to male pressure?

There is, for what it's worth, a psychoanalytic explanation of this paradox. Inside the well-groomed head of our Prime Minister dwell two very different sorts of people – the ambitious, power-seeking, outspoken, down-putting rebel who is not above using her tongue to lacerate such gadflies as unappreciative schoolmistresses, TV interviewers and members of the Opposition, and the dutiful daughter, obediently fetching books from Grantham library for that pillar of rectitude, her much-respected father. Given these two sides of her nature, it is not surprising that she dichotomises her world into the weak and the strong, the wets and the non-wets; into wayward sons and powerful fathers. Nor is it so surprising that having once decided in which category anyone belongs she behaves towards them accordingly. The weak get moved around, admonished, sometimes discarded, sometimes, in the case of Parkinson, favoured with tolerant, maternal compassion. The strong are listened to and on occasions obeyed. But what constitutes 'strong' in Mrs Thatcher's mind? Why should she listen to Sir Terence Lewin and Ronald Reagan? Perhaps, who knows, she listens to the first simply because he is an expert in a field about which she knows absolutely nothing, and to the second simply because he is the head of the world's largest grocery store? Or is it just because she is a very female female when dealing with the opposite sex and knows it is policy and rather more fun sometimes to say 'yes'.

If, of course, a female 'leader' is no more than a decorative mouthpiece for hawkish males, the greater safety of having women at the top disappears. But this is probably a needless worry. The sort of woman who fights her way to the top is unlikely to let herself be forever pushed around by men. On the contrary it is rather more likely that men will play into her hands. As noted earlier a major factor in the 'longest war' is the male's fear of, and need to escape from, maternal domination. There is however another side to this particular coin, namely that if once again back under her domination, having submitted, so to speak, to the incestuous bond, there may well be an enormous sense of relief. Judging from the history of courtiers and consorts – not to mention Mrs Thatcher's favourite Ministers – it is no great hardship being tethered once more to mother's apron. For now there is no shame in being mother's boy. At last they're back where they have always wanted to be. Like Harlow's baby monkeys they sense perhaps that safety and survival depend ultimately upon being subject to the protection of the biophilous sex. The resulting contentment and stability of women-dominated governments is yet another argument in their favour. Of course there will be tiffs and sulks, but mother usually comes out on top. By way of illustration, consider some prototypical relationships between powerful women and the menfolk in their lives – those involving Catherine the Great, Cleopatra, Elizabeth I, Victoria,

Indira Gandhi, Golda Meir and, let's face it, Mrs Wallis Simpson. The common feature of these ladies is that they manipulated men rather than the other way about. Moreover, their influence upon the course of history was largely through the biophilous arts of sex and maternal domination rather than by slaughtering millions of their fellow men. Even Catherine the Great is remembered more for being a libertine than a killer. And can one imagine a Mrs Teller being described as Mother of the H Bomb – surely not?

Any comparisons between this list of famous women and that of the male leaders which was considered earlier must surely lead to one inescapable conclusion. Purely in terms of one single (and fairly important) criterion – that of maximising our chance of survival as a species – women are a far better proposition than men.

Why then is it so difficult to take the obvious step of ensuring that women rule the world? There are three by no means insurmountable reasons. Men are loath to relinquish the power and financial control which they now exercise; women are resistant to usurping male power; and this state of affairs is perpetuated not just by the individuals themselves but by public attitudes, which have been shaped over millions of years of our biological history.

We are talking about a sex-role bias in society which, having its origins in physical differences between men and women which used to determine their respective roles in an eminently sensible way, is now no longer appropriate.

How inappropriate can be gauged from the following research:[43] essays that were believed to have been written by men were consistently judged superior to those thought to have been written by women – *even when the essays were identical*. If merely altering apparent authorship at the top of the page from John Smith to Jane Smith can so bias estimates of excellence, we are in the presence of a prejudice so bizarre as to be almost unbelievable, so ridiculous that it would be amusing, were it not so alarming in its implications.

Take another example. Clinically trained psychologists, psychiatrists and social workers of both sexes were asked to say what constituted a mature, healthy, socially competent adult a) if they were male, b) if they were female, and c) if their sex was unspecified. For the male and for the individual or unspecified sex the desirable traits were identical. Being mature, healthy and socially competent were associated with being dominant, independent, adventurous, aggressive and competitive.

In contrast, to qualify as a 'mature etc.' female, a woman should be less independent, less adventurous, less aggressive, less competent, more easily influenced, more excitable in minor crises and more concerned regarding her appearance.

It follows that, whereas in general, health, maturity and social competence of an adult human are associated with possession of male traits, a woman who is assertive, aggressive, competitive and independent must have something wrong with her. This conclusion is consistent with an additional finding. When asked to cite the most desirable human traits, people of both sexes suggested characteristics belonging to the male stereotype. These traits – such as being logical, aggressive and worldly – were given twice as often as any of those belonging to the female stereotype. The very few traits of the female stereotype which were considered desirable included being talkative, tactful and gentle. If these stereotypes are so deeply embedded in the minds of even sophisticated professional men and women one cannot help but wonder at their strength in the general mass of society.

Such findings need occasion no surprise. The stereotypes reflect exactly what was appropriate for the early settlers in North America. To 'win the West' frontiersmen had to be tough, aggressive and competitive. It was, had to be, a man's world with women relegated to a back place, back at the ranch, and in between times back on their backs.

The sad paradox is that in a nuclear age persistence of the old sex-role bias is as inappropriate as continuing to wear boxing gloves and oversize gumboots while perched on a high wire carrying out brain surgery – ridiculous and dangerous.

The relevance of all this to the case for female leadership is twofold. A relaxation of the sex-role biases which have characterised Western society for so long would increase the chances of political leadership passing into female hands; moreover, women who aspire to political leadership would no longer feel obliged to act like quick-on-the-draw cowgirls. And if the supply of suitable female applicants is insufficient then at least the general public might be more inclined to elect androgynous males rather than the highly aggressive gun-toting machos who at present threaten our survival.

Let's hope those changes in attitudes towards the two sexes which are already under way will have progressed far enough before it is too late.

There are precedents for this thesis. Sabine women brought war to an end by positioning themselves between the opposing armies. Those ladies of Greenham Common who lie down in front of Cruise missiles appear to be following the same tactic. Another possible approach is embodied in *Lysistrata*, a Greek comedy by Aristophanes. In this play, which provided the central idea for Eric Linklater's novel *The Impregnable Women*, an Athenian woman managed to stop the Second Peloponnesian War by persuading all Greek women to deny their husbands sexual relations for as long as the war continued. There could hardly be a more fitting victory for biophilia over the necrophilous horde.

One final word – for readers who cannot see any sense, virtue or hope in these suggested 'remedies' – this may not seem a very cheerful book. But take heart, do not despair, and remember Chapter 1. The world was in existence for millions of years before man, let alone you, appeared on the scene. And nobody minds about missing out on all that. Whether or not it goes on for millions of years after you are dead is also of absolutely no consequence because you won't be there to know it. Remember too that it may well be better to be dead than living under an intolerable system (red or any other colour). It may well be better to be dead than confronted with the daily toll of man's irrationality. It may well be better to be dead than starving or brain-damaged through chronic malnutrition. It may well be better to be dead than anxious, tortured, frightened or depressed. It may well be better to be dead than have to go on contemplating the fearful shortcomings of a creature which built himself a world that he is quite unfitted to inhabit.

POSTSCRIPT

At the time of going to press there appears to have been a sudden lightening of the international scene. Hopefully this will prove to be the start of a new, more rational approach to the problem of human survival. Whether or not this turns out to be the case, it is perhaps worth noting two facts, consistent with arguments in this book, which have contributed to more cordial relations between Britain and Russia:

1 There has evidently been a relative decline in the power of rigid hardline Soviet authoritarian conservatives.

2 The recent 'Summit' meetings between Mr Gorbachev and Mrs Thatcher constitute prolonged 'co-counselling' sessions between a man with a *strong ego* and, for the first time in living memory, a British *female* political leader.

References

NOTE: Full bibliographic details for books and articles cited in the References are given in the Bibliography.

1 Our Own Worst Enemy

1 See M. Ryle, *Towards the Nuclear Holocaust*.
2 See T. Malthus, *An Essay on Population*.
3 See R. J. Barnet, *The Lean Years*.
4 See J. Schell, *The Fate of the Earth*; see also J. A. Verdoorn, *Doctors and Prevention of War*, pp. 13–29.
5 See R. H. Moody, *Life after Life*.
6 See I. Stevenson, *Twenty Cases Suggestive of Reincarnation*; see also his *Xenoglossy: a Review und Report of a Case*.
7 J.A. Verdoorn, *Doctors and Prevention of War*, p. 22.
8 L. F. Richardson, *Statistics of Deadly Quarrels*, p. 153. Cited by D. Freeman 'Human Aggression', p. 110.
9 J. Whitton, *Disasters*, pp. 347–70.
10 See N.F. Dixon, *On the Psychology of Military Incompetence*.
11 See N. Tinbergen, Functional Ethology and the Human Sciences.
12 See R. Higgins, *The Seventh Enemy*.

2 Accidents Are Rarely Accidental

1 L.T.C. Rolt, *Red for Danger*, pp. 166–7.
2 Ibid., p. 168.
3 Ibid., p. 170.
4 Ibid., p. 171.
5 Ibid., p. 123.

6 D. H. Hubel, 'The Brain . . .', Foreword and pp. 2-11, *Scientific American*.

7 *The Spectator*, (1711). Cited by J.T. Reason and K. Mycielska, *Absent Minded?*, p. 180.

8 Ibid.

9 Rolt, *Red for Danger*, p. 286.

10 Ibid.

11 J. T. Reason and K. Mycielska, *Absent Minded?*

12 J. S. Antrobus, 'Information Theory and Stimulus Independent Thought'.

3   The Need for Peace of Mind

1 See J. L. Katz et al., 'Stress, Distress and Ego Defenses'.

2 See D. P. Spence et al., 'Lexical Correlates of Cervical Cancer'. See also D. P. Spence, 'Lawfulness in Lexical Choice – a Natural Experiment'.

3 See M. Wirsching et al., 'Psychological Identification of Breast-cancer Patients before Biopsy'.

4 G. H. Bower, 'Mood and Memory', pp. 60–9.

4   The Fall of France, 1940

1 See J. Benoist–Mechin, *Sixty Days that Shook the West*.

2 See E. Spears, *Assignment to Catastrophe*.

3 See A. Horne, *To Lose a Battle*.

4 B. Bond, *France and Belgium, 1939–1940*, p. 105.

5 See G. Chapman, *Why France Collapsed*.

6 Bond, *France and Belgium*, p. 79.

7 Ibid., p. 101. A metaphor which, according to Bond, was used by one of Gamelin's own staff officers.

8 Ibid.

9 Viscount Montgomery, *Memoirs*, pp. 56–7.

10 Bond, *France and Belgium*, p. 111.

11 Spears, *Assignment to Catastrophe*, p. 200.

12 Chapman, *Why France Collapsed*, pp. 203–5.

13 Walt Patterson, 'Why a Kind of Hush Fell Over the Chernobyl Conference', *Guardian* (October 4th, 1986), p. 9.

5   The Dark Cellar

1 D. Bannister, 'Psychology as an Exercise in Paradox', p. 21.

2 R. Brown, *Social Psychology*, p. 503.

3 C. S. Bluemel, *War, Politics and Insanity*, pp. 78–82.

4   S. Beer, ... *Designing Freedom*, p.22.
5   See L. Rangell, *The Mind of Watergate*.
6   Ibid., p. 246.
7   D. R. Hamachek, *Encounters with the Self*, pp. 112–29.
8   Rangell, *The Mind of Watergate*, p.121. Quote taken from M. Miller, *Plain Speaking*.

6   The Exorbitant Ego

1   G. R. Taylor, *The Natural History of the Mind*, pp. 112–15.
2   Ibid., p. 113.
3   See A. H. Maslow, 'A Theory of Human Motivation'.
4   See R. Dawkins, *The Selfish Gene*.
5   D. Beaty, *Strange Encounters*, p.23.
6   D. Beaty, *The Human Factor in Aircraft Accidents*, pp. 142-5.
7   N. Blundell (ed.), *The World's Greatest Mistakes*, pp. 101–17.
8   Bromberg and Small, *Hitler's Psychopathology*, p.20.
9   Ibid., p. 266.
10 Ibid., p.136.
11 See A. Hitler, *Mein Kampf*.
12 Leader in the *Guardian* (November 27th, 1986).

7   'Secret Agent'

1   See E. R. Hilgard, *Divided Consciousness*.
2   See U. Kragh, 'Precognitive Defense Organisation with Threatening and Non–Threatening Peripheral Stimuli'.
3   Personal communications from soldiers who fought in the Falklands campaign. Received during the Staff College course on battle stress, 1983.
4   See P. Kline, *Fact and Fantasy in Freudian Theory*, pp. 130–68.
5   See S. M. Friedman, 'An Empirical Study of the Castration and Oedipus Complexes'.
6   See B. Schwartz, 'An Empirical Test of Two Freudian Hypotheses Concerning Castration Anxiety'.
7   See J. L. Lasky and L. Berger, 'Blacky Test Scores before and after Genito–urinary Surgery'.
8   See E. F. Hammer, 'An Investigation of Sexual Symbolism'.
9   See I. Sarnoff and S. M. Corwin, 'Castration Anxiety and the Fear of Death'.

10 See W. N. Stephens, 'A Cross–Cultural Study of Menstrual Taboos'.

11 See L. de Mause, *Reagan's America*. See also R. Reagan, *Where's the Rest of Me?* and D. Cohen, 'My Fellow Americans This Is a Real Bomber'.

12 See S. Freud, *New Introductory Lectures in Psychoanalysis*. See also Kline, *Fact and Fantasy in Freudian Theory*, p.146; J. C. Touhey, 'Penis Envy and Attitudes towards Castration'; L. S. Kubie, 'Communication between Sane and Insane', p. 97, describes young girl's use of phallic adornment as penis substitute.

13 See M. Choisy, 'Le Complexe de Phaeton'.

14 See H. F. Harlow, *Learning to Love*; also, with M. K. Harlow, 'Social Deprivation in Monkeys'.

15 See Iremonger, *The Fiery Chariot*, pp. 17–21.

16 See R. A. Spitz, 'Hospitalism'. See also J. Bowlby, *Maternal Care and Mental Health*, and *Attachment and Loss*.

17 S. Wolff, *Children under Stress*, cited by Iremonger, *The Fiery Chariot*, p. 27. For a brief summary of researches on effects of maternal deprivation see J. C. Coleman, *Abnormal Psychology and Modern Life*, pp. 152–5.

18 See D. Black, 'The Bereaved Child'.

19 See M. Rutter, *Maternal Deprivation Reassessed*, also, *Children of Sick Parents*.

20 See D. P. Spence and C. M. Gordon, 'Activation and Measurement of an Early Oral Fantasy'.

21 L. H. Silverman et al., 'Effects of Subliminal Stimulation of Symbiotic Fantasies on Behaviour Modification Treatment of Obesity'. See also N. F. Dixon, *Preconscious Processing*, pp. 173–5.

22 See F. R. Schreiber, *The Shoemaker: Anatomy of a Psychotic*.

23 See B. Masters, *Killing for Company*.

24 Ibid., pp. 300–1.

25 Ibid., p. 298.

26 Iremonger, *The Fiery Chariot*, p.50.

27 Ibid., p. 302.

28 Crazet et al., 'Survey of Treatment of Primary Breast Cancer in Great Britain', pp. 1793–5. See also A. Ferriman, 'Health Correspondent'.

8   *Murderous Morality*

1 F. T. Jesse, 'Rattenbury and Stoner', p. 49.

2 Ibid., p. 30.

3 See D. Yallop, *In God's Name*.

4 See N. F. Dixon, *On the Psychology of Military Incompetence*.

5   See G. Turner, 'What England Still Expects'.
6   S. Milgram, *Obedience to Authority*, p.188.
7   D. Beaty, *The Human Factor in Aircraft Accidents*, p.148.
8   Milgram, *Obedience to Authority*, pp. 52–4.
9   Ibid., pp. 49–50.
10 Ibid., pp. 45–7.
11 See J. M. Carlsmith and A. E. Gross, 'Some Effects of Guilt on Compliance'.
12 See D. Baumrind, 'Some Thoughts on Ethics of Research'.
13 Milgram, *Obedience to Authority*, pp. 196–200.
14 See C. L. Sheridan and R. G. King, 'Obedience to Authority with an Authentic Victim'.
15 Milgram, *Obedience to Authority*, pp. 201–2.
16 See A. H. Hastorff, 'The "Reinforcement" of Individual Actions in a Group Situation'.
17 See R. Hough, *Admirals in Collision*; also Dixon, *On the Psychology of Military Incompetence*, pp. 112, 245–69.
18 *New York Times* (November 25th, 1969). See S. Milgram, *Obedience to Authority*, pp. 183–6.

9 ' ... Cometh Forth Hatred'

1   See A. Miller, *For Your Own Good*, pp. 3–91.
2   J. K. Jerome, *Three Men in a Boat*, pp. 116–17.
3   Miller, *For Your Own Good*, pp. 31–42.
4   Ibid., p. 18.
5   Christoph Meckel, cited ibid., p.3.
6   See T. W. Adorno et al., *The Authoritarian Personality*.
7   For the role of authoritarianism in military incompetence, see N. F. Dixon, *On the Psychology of Military Incompetence*.
8   *Diplock Report*.
9   Ruth Rehman, *The Man in the Pulpit*; see Miller, *For Your Own Good*.
10 S. Hersh, *The Target Is Destroyed*, p.182.
11 Ibid., p. 208.
12 Ibid., p. 74.

10 Options

1   See C. E. Osgood, 'Towards International Behaviour Appropriate to a Nuclear Age'.
2   H. L'Etang, 'Official Secrets Syndrome', p.258.

11 Stress

1 See T. Cox, *Stress*; V. Hamilton and M. Warburton (eds.), *Human Stress*; R. S. Lazarus, *Psychological Stress and the Coping Process*; H. Selye, *The Stress of Life*.
2 See Selye, *The Stress of Life*; also Cox, *Stress*, pp. 24–6.
3 D. Beaty, *The Human Factor in Aircraft Accidents*, pp. 124-5.
4 R. Hurst (ed.), *Pilot Error*, pp. 60–3.
5 See R. Totman, *Social Causes of Illness*.
6 See H. Krystal (ed.), *Massive Psychic Trauma*.
7 See H. L'Etang, *The Pathology of Leadership*; and *Fit to Lead?*
8 L'Etang, *Fit to Lead?*, pp. 86–7.
9 Ibid., p. 89.
10 Ibid., p. 96.
11 L'Etang, *The Pathology of Leadership*, pp. 187–8.
12 Ibid.
13 Beaty, *The Human Factor in Aircraft Accidents*, pp. 125–7.
14 Hurst (ed.), *Pilot Error*, pp. 33–4.
15 See C. Ryan, *A Bridge too Far*; also N. F. Dixon, *On the Psychology of Military Incompetence*, pp. 145–8.
16 W. Norris, *The Unsafe Sky*, p.61.
17 J. Whitton, *Disasters*, pp. 33–57.
18 L. T. C. Rolt, *Red for Danger*, pp. 207–13.
19 Norris, *The Unsafe Sky*, pp. 70–2.
20 See A. Tversky and D. Kahneman, 'Judgement under Uncertainty'.
21 Norris, *The Unsafe Sky*, pp. 73–4.
22 Ibid., pp. 81–2.

12 Verdun

1 See A. Horne, *The Price of Glory*, p.32.
2 Ibid., pp. 25–6.
3 Ibid., p. 51.
4 Ibid., p. 52.
5 Ibid., p. 53.
6 Ibid.
7 Ibid., pp. 175–6.
8 From the diary of Second Lieutenant Alfred Joubaine, cited in ibid., p. 240.
9 Ibid.

10   Ibid., p. 294.
11   Ibid., pp. 301–2.

13   Boredom

1   F. Dostoevsky, *Notes from the Underground*, p. 145.
2   See R. S. Woodworth, *Experimental Psychology*, pp. 137–9, for description and investigations of 'latent learning'.
3   R. A. Butler, 'Incentive Conditions which Influence Visual Exploration', pp. 19–23.
4   G. P. Sackett et al., 'Food Versus Perceptual Complexity', pp. 518–20; see also R. N. Haber (ed.), *Current Research in Motivation*, pp. 304–22, for researches on exploratory behaviour and sensory deprivation.
5   O. Fenichel, 'On the Psychology of Boredom', pp. 349–61.
6   W. A. Bexton et al., 'Effects of Decreased Variation in the Sensory Environment', pp. 70–6.
7   J. F. Corso, *The Experimental Psychology of Sensory Behaviour*, pp. 550–89.
8   P. Solomon and J. Mendelsohn, 'Hallucinations in Sensory Deprivation', p. 137.
9   Z. J. Lipowski, 'Sensory Overloads', pp. 204–71.
10   O. J. Harvey, 'Cognitive Aspects of Affective Arousal', pp. 242–62.
11   See Healy, *Boredom, Self and Culture*.
12   See R. Dawkins, *The Selfish Gene*.
13   Healy, *Boredom, Self and Culture*, p. 16.
14   Ibid., p. 35. See also Fenichel, 'On the Psychology of Boredom'; H. R. Pollio and J. W. Edgerly, 'Comedians and Comic Style'; and N. F. Dixon, 'Humor: a Cognitive Alternative to Stress'.
15   J. Fox, *White Mischief*.
16   Ibid., p. 33.
17   V. Teresa, *My Life in the Mafia*.
18   Ibid., p. 9.
19   See C. E. Shannon and W. Weaver, *The Mathematical Theory of Communication*.
20   See Fenichel, 'On the Psychology of Boredom'.
21   See D. E. Berlyne, *Conflict, Arousal and Curiosity*.
22   See D. H. Ingvar and N. A. Lassen (eds.), *Brainwork: the Coupling of Function, Metabolism and Blood Flow in the Brain*.
23   See N. F. Dixon, *On the Psychology of Military Incompetence*.
24   See J. Cohen and M. Hansel, *Risk and Gambling*.

302   REFERENCES TO PAGES 215-33

25 S. Andreski, 'Origins of War', p. 132.
26 W. Gooddy, 'Brain Failure in Private and Public Life', p. 391.
27 W. Norris, *The Unsafe Sky*, p. 660.
28 See M. Zuckerman, *Sensation Seeking*.
29 See A. Furnham, 'Extraversion, Sensation–seeking, Stimulus Screen-ing – Type A Behaviour Pattern'.
30 See R. Jamison, 'Personality, Anti–social Behaviour and Risk Perception in Adolescents'.
31 C. H. M. Stewart and D. R. Hemsley, 'Personality Factors in the Taking of Criminal Risks'.
32 R. Clement and B. A. Jonah, 'Field Dependence, Sensation-seeking and Driving Behaviour'.
33 R. Loo, 'Role of Primary Personality Factors in the Perception of Traffic Signs and Driver Violations and Accidents'.
34 See J. G. U. Adams, *Risk and Freedom*.
35 H. J. Eysenck, *The Biological Basis of Personality*.

14   The Neglected Brain

1 See J. Z. Young, 'Why Do We Have Two Brains?' and S. J. Dimond, 'Symmetry and Asymmetry in the Vertebrate Brain'.
2 K. S. Lashley et al., 'An Examination of the Electrical Field Theory of Cerebral Integration'.
3 See G. M. Stratton, 'Vision without Inversion of the Retinal Image', and I. Kohler, 'Experiments with Goggles'.
4 Dimond, 'Symmetry and Asymmetry', p. 195.
5 See M. C. Corballis and M. S. Morgan, 'On the Biological Basis of Human Laterality'.
6 See J. Jaynes, *The Origin of Consciousness in the Breakdown of the Bicameral Mind*.
7 See D. Beaty, *The Human Factor in Aircraft Accidents*.
8 Ibid., p. 154.
9 Ibid., pp. 154–5.
10 Ibid., pp. 157–9.
11 Ibid., p. 159.
12 Ibid., p. 159.
13 See G. E. Schwartz et al., 'Patterns of Hemispheric Dominance'; also E. R. Hilgard, *Divided Consciousness*, p. 110.
14 See M. Kinsbourne, 'Eye and Head Turning'.
15 See S. J. Dimond and L. Farrington, 'Emotional Response to Films Shown to the Right or Left Hemisphere'.
16 Jaynes, *The Origin of Consciousness*, p. 120.

17 See D. Galin, 'Implications for Psychiatry of Left and Right Cerebral Specialisation'.

18 H. Terizian, 'Behavioural and EEG Effects of Intercarotid Sodium Amytal Injection'. See also Galin, 'Implications for Psychiatry'.

19 Jaynes, *The Origin of Consciousness*, p. 120.

20 See Hilgard, *Divided Consciousness*, p. 111.

21 See H. Sackeim et al., 'Hemisphericity, Cognitive Set and Susceptibility to Subliminal Perception'.

22 Galin, 'Implications for Psychiatry', p. 580.

23 See B. Edwards, *Drawing on the Right Side of the Brain*.

24 See R. Higgins, *The Seventh Enemy*.

25 Ibid., p. 178.

26 Ibid., p. 218.

27 See M. Maccoby, *The Gamesman*.

28 E. Fitzgerald, *Omar Khayyam*, p. 206 (28).

29 Maccoby, *The Gamesman*, p.107.

15   Are Two Heads Better Than One?

1 See I. L. Janis, *Victims of Group Think*. See also B. Tuchman, *The March of Folly*.

2 Ibid., p. 14.

3 Ibid., pp. 197–80.

4 See W. N. Roughead, *Classic Crimes*, II; See also J. Mortimer, *Famous Trials*.

5 See D. Yallop, *In God's Name*.

6 M. Young and P. Hill. *Rough Justice*, p. 7; see also P. Hill and M. Young with Tom Sargant, *More Rough Justice*.

7 See D. Andrews, *The IRG Solution*; see also R. W. Rycroft and J. S. Szyliowics, *Decision–making in a Technological Environment*.

8 R. E. Benedick, 'The High Dam and the Transformation of the Nile', p.129.

9 J. Waterbury, 'The Nile Stops at Aswan', p. 26.

16   Wars to End Wars

1 A. Miller, *For Your Own Good*, p.17.

2 See R. Higgins, *The Seventh Enemy*.

3 Peter Walker, cited by N. Hawkes et al., *The Worst Accident in the World*, p.41.

4 W. Norris, *The Unsafe Sky*, pp. 97–105.

5 L. T. C. Rolt, *Red for Danger*, pp. 95–104.

6   Hawkes et al., *The Worst Accident in the World*, p. 110.
7   Ibid., p. 223.
8   P. Pringle and J. Spigelman, *The Nuclear Barons*, p. 419.
9   J. Schell, *The Fate of the Earth*, p. 26.
10 N. Blundell (ed.), *The World's Greatest Mistakes*, pp. 108-12.
11 Schell, *The Fate of the Earth*, p. 27.
12 Ibid., p. 183.
13 See H. L'Etang, *The Pathology of Leadership* and *Fit to Lead?*
14 L. Berkowitz and A. Le Page, 'Weapons as Aggression–eliciting Stimuli'. See also L. Berkowitz, *How Guns Control Us*.
15 See M. E. P. Seligman, *Helplessness*.
16 See C. B. Wortman and J. W. Brehm, 'Response to Uncontrolled Outcomes'.
17 L. de Mause, *Reagan's America*, p. 1.
18 Ibid., p. 6.
19 Ibid., p. 58.
20 *New Republic* (November 8th, 1980), p.18.
21 *New York Times* (January 5th, 1981), p.C2.
22 See N. Maxwell, *From Knowledge to Wisdom*.
23 See C. Longuet–Higgins, 'For Goodness' Sake'.
24 See N. F. Dixon, *On the Psychology of Military Incompetence*.
25 Maxwell, *From Knowledge to Wisdom*, p. 152.
26 Ibid., p. 153.
27 J. Sloboda, personal communication from University of Keele.
28 See H. Jacklins, *The Human Side of Human Beings*.
29 See N. Blandford and B. Jones, *The World's Most Evil Men*. Also relevant are M. French, *Beyond Power* and B. W. Tuchman, *The March of Folly*.
30 Tuchman, *The March of Folly*, p. 103.
31 Blandford and Jones, *The World's Most Evil Men*, p. 17.
32 E. Fromm, *The Anatomy of Human destructiveness*, pp. 294-574.
33 See E. Hoffer, *The True Believer*.
34 See Dixon, *On the Psychology of Military Incompetence*.
35 See C. Travis and C. Offir, *The Longest War*.
36 See W. Savage, *A Savage Enquiry*.
37 See French, *Beyond Power*.
38 Fromm, *The Anatomy of Human Destructiveness*, p. 488.
39 R. Lewis, *Margaret Thatcher*, p. 14.
40 Ibid., p. 14.
41 B. Arnold, *Margaret Thatcher: a Study in Power*, p. 250.
42 D. Rice and A. Gavshon, *The Sinking of the Belgrano*, p. 100.
43 See I. K. D. Broverman et al., 'Sex–role Stereotypes'.

Bibliography

Adams, J. G. U., *Risk and Freedom: the Record of Road Safety Regulation* (Cardiff: Transport Publishing Projects, 1985).

Adorno, T. W., Frenkel-Brunswick, E., Levinson, D. J., and Sanford, R. N., *The Authoritarian Personality* (New York: Harper, 1950).

Andreski, S., 'Origins of War', in J. D. Carthy and F. J. Ebling (eds.), *The Natural History of Aggression* (London: Academic Press, 1964), pp. 129-360.

Andrews, D., *The IRG Solution* (London: Souvenir Press, 1984).

Antrobus, J. S., 'Information Theory and Stimulus – Independent Thought', *Brit. J. Psychol.*, (1968), pp. 423-300.

Arnold, B., *Margaret Thatcher: a Study in Power* (London: Hamish Hamilton, 1984).

Bannister, D., 'Psychology as an Exercise in Paradox', *Bull. Brit. Psychol. Soc.*, 19 (1966) pp. 21-70.

Barnet, R. J., *The Lean Years* (London: Sphere, 1981).

Baumrind, D., 'Some Thoughts on Ethics of Research: after Reading Milgram's Behavioural Study of Obedience', *Amer. Psychol.*, 19 (1964), pp. 421-30.

Beaty, D., *The Human Factor in Aircraft Accidents* (New York: Stein & Day, 1969).

—— *Strange Encounters* (London: Methuen, 1982).

Beer, S., ... *Designing Freedom* (New York: Wiley, 1974).

Benedick, R. E., 'The High Dam and the Transformation of the Nile', *Middle East Journal*, 129(Spring, 1979).

Benoist-Mechin, J., *Sixty Days that Shook the West* (London: Jonathan Cape, 1963).

Berkowitz, L., 'How Guns Control Us', *Psychology Today*, 15 (6) (1981), pp. 11-12, and Le Page, A., 'Weapons as Aggression-Eliciting Stimuli', *J. Personality and Social Psychol.*, 7 (1967), pp. 202-7.

Berlyne, D. E., *Conflict, Arousal and Curiosity* (New York: McGraw-Hill, 1960).

Bexton, W.A., Heron, W., and Scott, T.H., 'Effects of Decreased Variation in the Sensory Environment', *Canadian Journal of Psychology*, 8 (1954), pp. 70-6.

Bettinger, L. A., Davies, J., Meikle, M., Birch, H., Kopp, R., Smith, H. E., and Thompson, R. F., 'Novelty Cells in Association Cortex of Cat', *Psychonomic Science*, 9 (7B) (1967), pp. 421-2.

Black D., 'The Bereaved Child', *J. Child Psychiat.*, 19 (1978), pp. 287-92; 'Mourning and the Family', in S. Walrone Skinner (ed.), *Developments in Family Therapy* (London: Routledge, Kegan Paul, 1981), pp. 189-210.

Blandford, N., and Jones, B., *The World's Most Evil Men* (London: Octopus Books, 1985).

Bluemel, C. S., *War, Politics and Insanity* (Denver: World Press, 1948).

Blundell, N. (ed.), *The World's Greatest Mistakes* (London: Octopus, 1984), pp. 101-7.

Bond, B., *France & Belgium, 1939-1940* (London: Davis-Poynter, 1975).

Bower, G.H., 'Mood and Memory', *Psychology Today*, 15 (6) (1981), pp. 60-9.

Bowlby, J., *Maternal Care and Mental Health* (Geneva: World Health Organisation, 1952).

—— *Attachment and Loss,* vols 1 and 2 (London: Hogarth Press, and Harmondsworth: Penguin, 1969 and 1973).

Bromberg, N., and Small, V. V., *Hitler's Psychopathology* (New York: International University Press, 1984).

Broverman, I. K. D., Broverman, D. M., Clarkson, F. E., Rosenkrantz, P. S. and Vogel, S. R., 'Sex-Role Stereotypes and Clinical Judgments of Mental Health', *Journal of Consultant and Clinical Psychology*, 34 (1) (1970), pp. 1-7.

Brown, R., *Social Psychology* (New York: Macmillan, 1965).

Butler, R. A., 'Incentive Conditions which Influence Visual Exploration', *J. Exp. Psychol.*, 48 (1954).

Carlsmith, J. M., and Gross, A. E., 'Some Effects of Guilt on Compliance', *J. Personality and Social Psychology*, 11 (1969), pp. 232-9.

Chapman, A., and Foot, H. (eds.), *Humour and Laughter: Theory, Research and Applications* (London: Wiley, 1976).

Chapman, G., *Why France Collapsed* (London: Cassell, 1968).

Choisy, M., 'Le Complexe de Phaeton', *Psyche*, 48 (1950).

Clément, R., and Jonah, B. A., 'Field Dependence, Sensation Seeking and Driving Behaviour', *Person. Indiv. Diff.*, 5 (1) (1984), pp. 87-93.

Cohen, D., 'My Fellow Americans This Is A Real Bomber', *Psychology News*, 39 (1984) pp. 10-110.

Cohen, J., and Hansel, M., *Risk and Gambling* (London: Longman, 1956).

Coleman, J. C., *Abnormal Psychology and Modern Life* (Glenview, Ill.:Scott, Foresman & Co., 1976).

Corballis, M. C., and Morgan, M. S., 'On the Biological Basis of Human Laterality', *Behaviour and Brain Sciences*, 1 (2) (1978), pp. 261-336.

Corso, J. F., *The Experimental Psychology of Sensory Behaviour* (London: Holt, Rinehart & Winston), 1970.

Cox, T., *Stress* (London: Macmillan, 1981).

Crook, T., and Eliot, J., 'Parental Death during Childhood and Adult Depression: a Critical Review of the Literature', *Psychol. Bull.*, 87, (2) (1980), pp. 352-9.

Dawkins, R., *The Selfish Gene* (London: Granada 1983).

De Mause, L., *Reagan's America* (New York: Creative Roots, 1984).

Dimond, S. J., 'Symmetry and Asymmetry in the Vertebrate Brain', in D. A. Oakley and H. C. Plotkin (eds.) *Brain, Behaviour and Evolution* (London: Methuen, 1979), pp. 189-218.

——, and Farrington, L., 'Emotional Response to Films Shown to the Right or Left Hemisphere of the Brain Measured by Heart Rates', *Acta Psychologica*, 41 (1977), pp. 255-60.

Diplock, W. J., *Report of the Commission to Consider Legal Procedures to Deal with Terrorist Activities in N. Ireland* (London: HMSO, 1972).

Dixon, N. F., 'Humor: A Cognitive Alternative to Stress', in I. G. Sarason and C. D. Spielberger (eds.), *Stress and Anxiety*, vol. 7 (Washington: Hemisphere, 1980), pp. 281-90.

——, *On the Psychology of Military Incompetence* (London: Jonathan Cape, 1976).

——, *Preconscious Processing* (Chichester: Wiley, 1981).

Dostoevsky, F., *Notes from the Underground*. In the *Short Novels* (New York: Dial Press, 1945).

Edwards, B., *Drawing on the Right Side of the Brain* (London: Souvenir Press, 1981).

Eysenck, H. J., *The Biological Basis of Personality* (Springfield, Ill.: Thomas, 1967).

Fenichel, O., 'On the Psychology of Boredom', in D. Rapaport (ed.), *Organisation and Pathology of Thought* (New York: Columbia University Press, 1951), pp. 349-61.

Ferriman, A., 'Health Correspondent', *Observer* (June 23rd, 1985), p. 3.

Fitzgerald., E., *The Rubaiyat of Omar Khayyam*, in *Oxford Dictionary of Quotations*, 1st edn. (Oxford: Oxford University Press, 1972), p. 206.

Flugel, J.C., *Man, Morals and Society* (London: Duckworth, 1945).

Fox, J., *White Mischief* (London: Jonathan Cape, 1982).

Freeman, D., 'Human Aggression in Anthropological Perspective', in J. D. Carthy and F. J. Ebliny (eds.), *The Natural History of Aggression* (London: Academic Press, 1964), pp. 109-19.

French, M., *Beyond Power: on Women, Men and Morals* (London: Jonathan Cape, 1985).

Freud, S., *New Introductory Lectures in Psychoanalysis,* vol. 2. (1933), in the standard edition of *The Complete Psychological Works of Sigmund Freud* (London: Hogarth Press, 1966).

Friedman, S. M., 'An Empirical Study of the Castration and Oedipus Complexes', *Genet. Psychol. Monogr.*, 46 (1952), pp. 61-130.

Fromm, E., *The Anatomy of Human Destructiveness* (Harmondsworth: Penguin, 1973).

Furnham, A., 'Extraversion, Sensation-seeking, Stimulus Screening – Type A Behaviour Pattern: the Relationship between Various Measures of Arousal', *Personal. Indiv. Diff.*

Galin, D., 'Implications for Psychiatry of Left and Right Cerebral Specialisation', *Arch. Gen. Psychiat.*, 31 (1979), pp. 572-83.

——, and Ornstein, R., 'Lateral Specialisation of Cognitive Mode: an EEG Study', *Psychophysiology*, 9 (1972), pp. 412-18.

Gazet, J., Rainsbury, R. M., Ford, H. T., Powles, T. J., and Combes, R. C., 'Survey of Treatment of Primary Breast Cancer in Great Britain', *Brit. Med. J.*, 290 (June 15th, 1985), pp.Gazzaniga, M. S., and Hillyard, S. A., 'Language and Speech Capacity of the Right Hemisphere', *Neuropsychol.*, 9 (1971), pp. 273-80.

Gooddy, W., 'Brain Failure in Private and Public Life', *Brit. Med. J.*, (March 3rd, 1979), pp. 391-3.

Haber, R. N., *Current Research in Motivation* (New York: Holt, Rinehart & Winston, 1967).

Hamachek, D. E., *Encounters with the Self* (New York: Holt, Rinehart & Winston, 1978).

Hamilton, V., with Warburton, D. M., *Human Stress and Cognition* (Winchester: Wiley, 1979).

Hammer, E. F., 'An Investigation of Sexual Symbolism: a Study of HTP's of Eugenically Sterilised Subjects', *J. Proj. Tech.*, 17 (1953), pp. 301-15.

Harlow, H. F., *Learning to Love* (San Francisco: Albion, 1973).

——, and Harlow, M. K., 'Social Deprivation in Monkeys', *Sci. Amer.*, 267 (1962), pp. 137-46.

Harvey, O.J., 'Cognitive Aspects of Affective Arousal', in S. S. Tomkins and C. E. Izard (eds.), *Affect, Cognition and Personality* (New York, Springer, 1965), pp. 242-62.

Hastorff, A. H., 'The "Reinforcement" of Individual Actions in a Group Situation', in D. Marlowe and K. J. Bergen (eds.), *Personality and Social Behaviour* (London: Addison-Wesley, 1970), pp. 105-20.

Hawkes, N., Lean, G., McKie, R., Pringle, P., and Wilson, A., *The Worst Accident in the World* (London: Pan, 1986).

Healy, S. D., *Boredom, Self and Culture* (London: Associated University Presses, 1984).

Hersh, S., *The Target is Destroyed: What Really Happened to Flight 007* (London: Faber & Faber, 1986).

Higgins, R., *The Seventh Enemy* (London: Pan, 1978).

Hilgard, E. R., *Divided Consciousness* (New York, Wiley, 1977).

Hill, P. and Young, M., with Sargant, T., *More Rough Justice* (Harmondsworth: Penguin, 1985).

Hoffer, E., *The True Believer* (London: Secker and Warburg, 1952).

Horne, A., *The Price of Glory* (London: Macmillan, 1969).

——, *To Lose a Battle: France, 1940* (London: Macmillan, 1969).

Hough, R., *Admirals in Collision* (London: Hamish Hamilton, 1959).

Hubel, D. H., *The Brain*, a *Scientific American* book (San Francisco: W. H. Freeman, 1979), ch. 10, pp. 2-11.

Hurst, R. (ed.), *Pilot Error: a Professional Study of Contributory Factors* (London: Crosby, Lockwood, Staples, 1974).

Ingvar, D. H., and Lassen, N. A. (eds.), *Brainwork: the Coupling of Function, Metabolism and Bloodflow in the Brain* (Copenhagen: Munksgaard, 1975).

Iremonger, L., *The Fiery Chariot* (London: Secker and Warburg, 1970).

Jacklins, H., *The Human Side of Human Beings* (Seattle: Rational Island Publishers, 1978).

Jamison, R., 'Personality, Anti-Social Behaviour and Risk Perception in Adolescents', unpub. Ph.D. thesis (University of London).

Janis, I. L., *Victims of Groupthink* (Boston: Houghton Mifflin, 1968).

Jaynes, J., *The Origin of Consciousness in the Breakdown of the Bicameral Mind* (Boston: Houghton Mifflin).

Jerome, J. K., *Three Men in a Boat* (Harmondsworth, Penguin, 1976).

Jesse, F. T., 'Rattenbury and Stoner', in J. Mortimer (ed.), *Famous Trials* (Harmondsworth: Penguin, 1984), pp. 15-51.

Katz, J. L., Weiner, H., Gallagher, T. F., and Hellman, L., 'Stress, Distress and Ego Defenses: Psychoendocrine Response to Impending Breast-tumour Biopsy', *Archive of General Psychiatry*, 23 (1970), pp. 131-42.

Kinsbourne, M., 'Eye and Head Turning Indicates Cerebral Lateralisation', *Science*, 176 (1972), pp. 539-45.

Kline, P., *Fact and Fantasy in Freudian Theory*, 2nd edn (London: Methuen, 1981).

Kohler, I., 'Experiments with Goggles', *Scientific American*, 206 (1962), pp. 62-86.

Kragh, U., 'Precognitive Defense Organisation with Threatening and Non-threatening Peripheral Stimuli', *Scand. J. Psychol.*, 3 (1962), pp. 65-8.

——, 'Predictions of Success of Danish Attack Divers by the Defence Mechanism Test', *Percept. Mot. Skills*, 15 (1962), pp. 103-6.

Kruglanski, A. W., 'The Human Subject in the Psychology Experiment: Fact and Artefact', in L. Berkowitz (ed.), *Advances in Experimental Social Psychology*, vol. 8 (New York: Academic Press, 1975), pp. 101-47.

Krystal, H. (ed.), *Massive Psychic Trauma* (New York: International University Press, 1968).

Kubie, L. S., 'Communication between Sane and Insane: Hypnosis', in *Cybernetics*, Josiah Macy Jr Symposium, IXth Conference (Caldwell, N. J.: Progress Associates, 1952).

Lashley, K. S., Chow, K. L., and Semmes, J., 'An Examination of the Electrical Field Theory of Cerebral Integration', *Psychol. Rev.*, 58 (1951), pp. 123-36.

Lasky, J. L. and Berger, L., 'Blacky Test Scores before and after Genito-urinary Surgery', *J. Proj. Tech.*, 23 (1959), pp. 57-8.

Lazarus, R. S., *Psychological Stress and the Coping Process* (New York: McGraw-Hill, 1966).

L'Etang, H., *The Pathology of Leadership* (London: Heinemann, 1969).

——, *Fit to Lead?* (London: Heinemann, 1980).

——, 'Official Secrets Syndrome', *The Physician*, 258 (1985).

Lewis, R., *Margaret Thatcher* (London: Routledge and Kegan Paul, 1975).

Lipowski, Z. J., 'Sensory Overloads, Information Overloads and Behaviour', *Psychother. Psychosom.* 23 (1974) pp. 204-71.

Longuet-Higgins, C., 'For Goodness' Sake', *Nature*, 312 (November 15th, 1984), p. 204.

Loo, R., 'Role of Primary Personality Factors in the Perception of Traffic Signs and Driver Violations and Accidents', *Accid. Analysis Prev.* 11 (1979), pp. 121-7.

Maccoby, M., *The Gamesman* (London: Secker & Warburg, 1977).

Malthus, T., *An Essay on Population* (London: Ward Lock, 1826).

Maslow, A. H., 'A Theory of Human Motivation', *Psychol. Rev.* 50 (1943), p.370.

——,*Motivation and Personality*, 2nd edn. (New York: Harper & Row, 1954).

Masters, B., *Killing For Company* (London: Jonathan Cape, 1985).

Maxwell, N., *From Knowledge to Wisdom* (Oxford: Basil Blackwell, 1984).

Milgram, S., *Obedience to Authority* (London: Tavistock, 1974).

Miller, A., *For Your Own Good* (New York: Farrar, Straus & Giroux, 1985).

Miller, M., *Plain Speaking: an Oral Biography of Harry S. Truman* (Berkeley, Cal.: Berkeley Publishing Co., 1974).

Montgomery, Viscount, *The Memoirs of Field-Marshal Montgomery* (London: Collins, 1958).

Moody, R. H., *Life After Death* (New York: Bantam, 1976).

Mortimer, J. (ed.), *Famous Trials* (Harmondsworth: Penguin, 1984).

Norris, W., *The Unsafe Sky* (London: Arrow, 1981).

Osgood, C. E., 'Towards International Behaviour Appropriate to a Nuclear Age', in G. S. Nielsen (ed.) *Psychology and International Affairs* (Copenhagen: Munksgaard, 196

Pollio, H. R., and Edgerly, J. W., 'Comedians and Comic Style', in T. Chapman and H. Foot (eds.) *Humour and Laughter: Theory, Research and Applications* (London: Wiley, 1976).

Pringle, P., and Spigelman, J., *The Nuclear Barons* (London: Michael Joseph, 1982).

Rangell, L., *The Mind of Watergate* (New York: Norton, 1980).

Reagan, R., *Where's the Rest of Me?* (New York: Karz, 1981).

Reason, J., and Mycielska, K., *Absent Minded? The Psychology of Mental Lapses and Everyday Errors* (Englewood Cliffs, N.J.: Prentice-Hall, 1982).

Rehman, R., *The Man in the Pulpit* (Munich and Vienna: 1979).

Rice, D., and Gavshon, A., *The Sinking of the Belgrano* (London: Secker and Warburg, 1984).

Richardson, L. F., *Statistics of Deadly Quarrels* (London: Stevens, 1960).

Roughead, W. N., *Classic Crimes*, II (London: Panther, 1966).

Rolt, L. T. C., *Red For Danger* (Newton Abbot: David & Charles, 1982).

Rutter, M., *Children of Sick Parents* (Oxford: Oxford University Press, 1966).

Ryan, C., *A Bridge Too Far* (London: Coronet, 1976).

Rycroft, R. W., and Szyliowicz, J. S., *Decision Making in a Technological Environment: the Case of the Aswan High Dam* (Boston: Intercollegiate Case Clearing House, 1980).

Ryle, M., *Towards the Nuclear Holocaust* (London: Maynard Press, 1981).

Sackett, G. P., Keith-Lee, P., and Treat, R., 'Food Versus Perceptual Complexity as Rewards for Rats Subjected to Sensory Deprivation', *Science*, 141 (May 17th, 1963), pp. 518-20.

Sackeim, H., Packer, I. K., and Gur, R. C., 'Hemisphericity, Cognitive Set and Susceptibility to Subliminal Perception', *J. Abnormal Psychology*, 86 (1977), pp. 624-30.

Sarnoff, I., and Corwin, S.M., 'Castration Anxiety and the Fear of Death', *J. Pers.*, 27 (1959), pp. 374-85.

Savage, W., *A Savage Enquiry*, (London: Virago Press, 1986).

Schell, J., *The Fate of the Earth* (London: Jonathan Cape, 1982).

Schreiber, F. R., *The Shoemaker: Anatomy of a Psychotic* (London: Allen Lane, 1983).

Schwartz, B., 'An Empirical Test of Two Freudian Hypotheses Concerning Castration Anxiety', *J. Personality*, 24 (1956), pp.318-27.

Schwartz, G. E., Davidson, R. J., Maer, F., and Bromfield, E., 'Patterns of Hemispheric Dominance in Musical, Emotional, Verbal and Spatial Tasks', paper presented at meeting of Society for Psychophysiological Research, October, 1972.

Seligman, M. E. P., *Helplessness – Depression, Development and Death* (San Francisco: W.H. Freeman, 1975).

Selye, H., 'Stress', *Psychology Today*, 3 (4) (1969), pp. 24-60.

——, *The Stress of Life*, rev. edn. (New York: McGraw Hill, 1976).

Shannon, C. E. and Weaver, W., *The Mathematical Theory of Communication*, (Urbana, Ill.: University of Illinois Press, 1949).

Sheridan, C. L., and King, R. G., 'Obedience to Authority with an Authentic Victim', *Proc. 80th Annual Convention, American Psychological Association* (1972), pp. 165-60.

Silverman, L. H., Martin, A., Ungaro, R., and Mendelsohn, E., 'Effects of Subliminal Stimulation of Symbiotic Fantasies on Behaviour Modification Treatment of Obesity', *J. Consult. Clin. Psychol.* 46 (3) (1978), pp. 432-41.

Solomon, P., and Mendelsohn, J., 'Hallucinations in Sensory Deprivation', in L. J. West (ed.), *Hallucinations* (New York: Grune & Stratton, 1962).

Spears, E., *Assignment to Catastrophe* (Reprint Society edn., 1956).

Spence, D. P., 'Lawfulness in Lexical Choice – A Natural Experiment', *J. Amer. Psychoanal. Ass.*, 28 (1980), pp. 115-32.

——, and Gordon, C. M., 'Activation and Measurement of an Early Oral Fantasy: an Exploratory Study', *J. Amer. Psychoanal. Ass.* 15, (1) (1967), pp. 99-129.

——, Scarborough, H. S., and Ginsberg, E. H., 'Lexical Correlates of Cervical Cancer', *Social Science and Medicine*, 12 (1978), pp. 141-50.

Spitz, R. A., 'Hospitalism: an Enquiry into the Genesis of Psychiatric Conditions in Early Childhood', *Psychoanal. Stud. Child.*, 1 (1945) pp. 53-74.

Stephens, W. N., 'A Cross-Cultural Study of Menstrual Taboos', *Genet. Psychol. Monogr.*, 64 (1961), pp. 385-416.

Stevenson, I., *Twenty Cases Suggestive of Reincarnation* (Charlotteville: University Press of Virginia, 1974).

——, *Xenoglossy: a Review and Report of a Case* (Bristol: Wright, 1974).

Stewart, C. H. M., and Hemsley, D. R., 'Personality Factors in the Taking of Criminal Risks', *Person. and Indiv. Diff.*, 5 (1) (1984), pp. 119-22.

Stokols, D., Rall, M., Pinner, B., and Schopler, J, 'Physical, Social and Personal Determinants of the Perception of Crowding', *Environment and Behaviour*, 5 (1973), pp. 87-115.

Stratton, G. M., 'Vision without Inversion of the Retinal Image', *Psychol. Rev.*, 4 (1897), pp. 341-60.

Taylor, G. R., *The Natural History of the Mind* (London: Granada, 1981).

Teresa, V., and Renner, T. C., *My Life in the Mafia* (St Albans: Panther, 1974).

Terizian, H., 'Behavioural and EEG effects of Intercarotid Sodium Amytal Injection', *Acta. Neuro. Chi.*, 12 (1964), pp. 230-40.

Tinbergen, N., 'Functional Ethology and the Human Sciences', Croonian Lecture to the Royal Society, 1972.

Totman, R., *Social Causes of Illness* (London: Souvenir Press, 1979).

Touhey, J. C., 'Penis Envy and Attitudes towards Castration-like Punishment of Sexual Aggression', *J. Research in Personality*, 11 (1977), pp. 1-9.

Travis, C., and Offir, C., *The Longest War: Sex Differences in Perspective* (New York: Harcourt Brace, 1977).

Tuchman, B. W., *The March of Folly* (London: Michael Joseph, 1984).

Turner, C. W., and Simons, L. S., 'The Weapons Effect Re-examined: Effects of Contingency Awareness and Evaluation Apprehension', unpub. MS (University of Utah, 1973).

Turner, G., 'What England Still Expects', *Observer* (August 2nd, 1983).

Tversky, A., and Kahneman, D., 'Judgement under Uncertainty: Heuristics and Biases', *Science*, 1885 (1974), pp. 1124-31.

Verdoorn, J. A., 'Doctors and Prevention of War', in B. W. Ike and W. J. E. Verheggen (eds.), *Medical Opinions on Nuclear War and its Prevention* (Nijmegen: Stichting Medische Polemulogre, 1983), pp. 13-29.

Waterbury, J., 'The Nile Stops at Aswan', Part III, 'Domestic Hydropolitics', *Amer. Univ. Field. Staff, N. African Services*, 22 (iii) (1977).

Whitton, J., *Disasters: the Anatomy of Environmental Hazards* (Harmondsworth: Penguin, 1980).

Wirsching, M., Stierlin, H., Hoffman, F., Gunthard, W., and Wirsching, B., 'Psychological Identification of Breast-cancer Patients before Biopsy', *J. Psychosomatic Research*, 26 (1982), pp. 1-10.

Wolff, S., *Children Under Stress* (London: Allen Lane, 1969).

Woodworth, R. S., *Experimental Psychology* (London: Methuen, 1950).

Wortman, C. B., and Brehm, J. W., 'Response to Uncontrolled Outcomes: an Integration of Reactance Theory and the Learned Helplessness Model', in L. Berkowitz (ed.), *Advances in Experimental Social Psychology*, vol. 8 (New York: Academic Press, 1975), pp. 278-332.

Yallop, D., *In God's Name* (London: Jonathan Cape, 1984).

Young, J. Z., 'Why Do We Have Two Brains?', in V. B. Mountcastle (ed.), *Interhemispheric Relations and Cerebral Dominance* (Baltimore: Johns Hopkins University Press, 1962).

Young, M., and Hill, P., *Rough Justice* (London: Ariel Books, BBC, 1983).

Zuckerman, M., *Sensation Seeking: Beyond the Optimum Level of Arousal* (Hillsdale, N.J.: Erlbaum, 1979).

Index

315